S

SHARING
THE WEALTH

SHARING
THE WEALTH
My Story

ALEX SPANOS

With Mark Seal and Natalia Kasparian

With a Foreword by Rush Limbaugh

Since 1947
**REGNERY
PUBLISHING, INC.**
An Eagle Publishing Company • Washington, DC

Cataloging-in-Publication Data on file with the Library of Congress
ISBN: 0-89526-158-8

Published in the United States by
Regnery Publishing, Inc.
An Eagle Publishing Company
One Massachusetts Avenue, NW
Washington, DC 20001

Visit us at www.regnery.com

Distributed to the trade by
National Book Network
4720-A Boston Way
Lanham, MD 20706

Printed on acid-free paper
Manufactured in the United States of America

10 9 8 7 6 5 4 3 2 1

Books are available in quantity for promotional or premium use. Write to Director of Special Sales, Regnery Publishing, Inc., One Massachusetts Avenue, NW, Washington, DC 20001, for information on discounts and terms or call (202) 216-0600.

To Faye
who has been my rock and inspiration

CONTENTS

FOREWORD

by Rush Limbaugh

Have you ever wondered why there are no books in the library on *How to Fail*? It is because everyone can do it. Most of us have, many times. And have you ever wondered why all the people involved in the *How to Be the Best You Can Be* business seem pretty well off? It is because success is hard—hard to achieve and really hard to maintain.

You are about to race through a marvelous and riveting account of a distinctly American life in which the concepts of "failure" and "can't" do not apply. You will discover how one man, who started his quest with but eight hundred dollars in his pocket, became one of the most successful people this country has produced, in every phase of his life, from career to family to friends.

One way in which Alex Spanos towers above many other successful people is his humility and character. The purpose of this book is not to detail his story so readers will marvel at him. It is, rather, to inspire people to reach deep within themselves to discover their true potential and capture it. Alex thinks—no, he *knows*—that most people are capable of achieving far more than they believe they can. He will inspire you to avail yourself of the glorious opportunities that abound in this great country. I have never met a more genuine, generous, and selfless man in my life. Rather than hoard the secrets of success and personal fulfillment, Alex Spanos shares all he has learned over the course of his life in an attempt to help as many people as possible reach their potential.

Why, you ask? Simple. Alex Spanos profoundly believes in this country and what it offers the human race. We have spoken many times about this. Two things separate America from the rest of the world. First is our freedom. Second is our Founding Fathers and their brilliance in constructing a Constitution that is itself founded on the notion of the yearning of the human spirit. Our Founding Fathers knew that this spirit is part of our creation. That spirit, that yearning for freedom, comes from God, not from other men granting it to some and not others, and they wrote a Constitution that limits not the freedom of the American people but rather the power of those we elect to govern us. This is the framework from which individual greatness grows, and to understand this is to understand the roots of this country's amazing success. You see, Alex Spanos loves this country and wants it to continue to be the greatest country in the world. And he believes that it is the American people, pursuing happiness and success, striving for excellence each day, who make America what it is. He wants you and everyone to understand what is possible, even today, in America, so that you will seek it and, in the process, contribute to the ongoing magnificence that is the United States.

So why should you take the advice of this man? Well, one reason is this: I have always believed that it makes much more sense to listen to people who have made a success of their lives than to those who haven't. Listening to someone tell you that you can't make it can be very seductive because it provides you an excuse not to try.

Listening to those who have made it, however, is inspiring and motivational, not defeatist and negative. You can trust Alex's views and thoughts on the subject of success. But you will also learn that success isn't easy.

Alex Spanos certainly hasn't had it easy. His father was a tough-talking disciplinarian who required him to get up at four o'clock every morning to work in the family restaurant before going to school. When World War II came along, Spanos served in the U.S. Air Force and after his tour returned home to join his father at the family business.

But he was unsatisfied. He longed to be on his own, to carve his own niche in life, and so, at age twenty-seven, he quit the security of the family restaurant and bakery and started his own business. He got no assistance from his father. It didn't matter. He was passionate and committed, and through sheer determination to succeed he made his first million at the age of thirty-three, in 1956.

Alex Spanos is not a phony or artificial man. He knows that his success is due primarily to his own efforts and commitment, just as he knows yours will be. Yet he makes massive donations to the community. The philosophy is simple: he believes in sharing the wealth (the title of this book). He doesn't donate money for phony PR reasons but rather to help those who need it most. And he targets his assistance so that it doesn't encourage dependence but instead helps people grab the innumerable opportunities for success that America offers.

Alex Spanos is such a self-starter that one of the most frustrating experiences in his life oddly accompanied the fulfillment of one of his lifelong dreams: to own a franchise in the National Football League (NFL). He bought the San Diego Chargers in 1984 and discovered that, unlike in his other businesses, his own personal involvement and hard work mattered little to the team's win-loss record. You see, he couldn't play the game each Sunday. All he could do was assemble the players and the coaching staff and try to instill in the organization all of his personal philosophies. But one of the reasons that Alex is so successful is that he learns from what doesn't work. In this case, he figured out exactly what he and the Chargers needed, and he turned the management of the team over to his son Dean. That enabled Alex to oversee the operation, advise his son now and then, and simply enjoy the fun aspects of owning his team—and the Chargers went to the Super Bowl that very season. He is now one of the most respected owners in the NFL and is routinely turned to for advice and guidance in league matters.

I will never forget the first time I spoke with Alex Spanos. He called me in the early 1990s and asked me to join him in a weekend fund-raising blitz throughout California for then-governor Pete Wilson and other Republican elected officials. I was speechless for a time, not believing Alex Spanos was actually on the phone seeking my assistance. The weekend he proposed was one I could not make, and I politely told him so.

Here is what he said: "Why, that is wonderful, that's great. I'll arrange for you to get out here and we'll have a heck of a good time. I'm so glad you can make it!"

"Uh, Mr. Spanos, I think you misunderstood me," I replied. "I just cannot do it that weekend. I am committed to other things at that time."

To which he responded, "I can't tell you how great it is that you will be joining us. So many people have asked for you and this will be great, just great that you can make it."

Alex Spanos simply does not know the word "no." It isn't in his vocabulary. Negative thoughts never enter his mind. I have never met anyone more positive in my life, and these traits are infectious when you are in his presence.

You are about to experience these characteristics yourself on the pages of this wonderful book. In reading *Sharing the Wealth*, you will discover things about yourself you may not be aware of. You will be moved to emulate the life of Alex Spanos—and you will finish knowing you can. The only thing standing in your way is you.

Be prepared to be dazzled, informed, entertained, and challenged. You will wish, as I do, that you had met Alex Spanos and his family much earlier. Remember, though, that it is never too late to encounter greatness, just as it is never too late to begin your quest for it. In *Sharing the Wealth*, you will discover that life is what you make of it, that you have much more potential than you ever knew, and that it is totally up to you to realize your dreams. Because you live in the greatest country on earth, the United States of America, you can accomplish anything to which you set your mind and heart. So be prepared. This is a book that will change your life forever and for the good.

Enjoy.

CHAPTER 1

The Secret of Success

Most of all, I remember the energy, the euphoric, heartbeat-in-your-throat adrenaline rush of being atop the Mount Olympus of American sports. Today, the experience recurs as an unforgettable dream. It's January 1995, and I'm riding in a police-escorted motorcade snaking toward Joe Robbie Stadium through the teeming streets of Miami. My team, the San Diego Chargers, the NFL's perpetual underdogs, shocked the sports world by beating the mighty Pittsburgh Steelers at the end of the 1994 season to face the San Francisco 49ers in Super Bowl XXIX. All week long I've been as excited as a little boy. Throat raw from screaming, hands cramped from shaking, face frozen in an ear-to-ear grin, I'm surrounded by everyone I've ever loved: my wife, my four kids, my entire extended family, and friends, all of us cruising through sunny streets lined with cheering fans, a mass of humanity melding into a single overwhelming scream.

The energy is a wave, and riding it is simultaneously exhilarating and exhausting. It propels me through a week of endless interviews, appearances, rallies, and parties, all lit by blinding TV cameras and played to a soundtrack of infinite voices of congratulations. The energy rises, ratcheting higher and higher until the Big Game, when 75,000 fans pack the stadium, singing the national anthem, cheering the kickoff, and . . . I won't bore you with the play-by-play. It took a while for the reality to sink in that we didn't win the Super Bowl. Our return to San Diego was anything but that of a defeated team: 200,000 ecstatic Charger fans clogged the streets to welcome us back in spite of our loss.

You can get hooked on this energy, this life force of victory. One taste and you long for it forever. When I finally crash back down to earth, I'm left with two questions: How did we get to the Super Bowl, and, of course, how can we get back again?

❖ ❖ ❖

To comprehend fully the significance of our 1995 Super Bowl appearance, you have to go back a decade to the morning of August 3, 1984, the day I purchased majority interest in the San Diego Chargers. Buying a team was the realization of a lifelong dream. It was supposed to be the crowning achievement of fifty years of hard work. Little did I know that, at sixty, I was going to have to prove myself all over again.

The newspaper sports sections all asked the same question: *Who is Alex Spanos?*

As my family and I flew to a press conference in San Diego from our home in the small farm town of Stockton, California, the media painted me as a phantom, an unknown, an enigma covered in question marks. Being thrust into the sports headlines was new to me. Yes, I was well known in the business world as the number one builder of apartments in America. But I was absolutely unprepared for the frenzy that awaited me in San Diego. Both the fans and the media wanted to know who I was—but, I would soon discover, for one reason and one reason only. They wanted to know if I had the stuff of champions, the magic of miracles, the ability to make the down-and-out Chargers *win*.

I had built my reputation in the construction and development business. But there's little glamour, publicity, or fame in construction. Builders aren't typically nationally known, except amongst their peers. My construction business represents ten or twenty times what I'll ever invest in football. But from the moment I bought the Chargers, I would become forever known as the owner of that NFL franchise.

A winner or a loser.

In my mind, I was, of course, a winner. But lately, I'd been missing the battle. Maybe things had become too easy, too normal, too safe. Maybe I yearned for a long-shot challenge, instead of the steady but sure work that my construction and development business had become. Maybe I longed once again to tap into that capacity that we all have within us for a come-from-behind victory when everyone has counted us out. I'd been there many times in my life. Maybe I *needed* to return there now. I've always said that the day when I'm satisfied with myself is the day they can bury me. And I certainly wasn't ready for that.

So as the jet took off toward San Diego for my first press conference, I was returning to the big game hunt that has occupied my entire life: the hunt for victory. The sportswriters wanted to reduce me to sound bites, something quick and easy for the public to digest. More than anything, they wanted to know the secret of my success and to assure the fans that I could transfer that success to the San Diego Chargers, who, in that summer of 1984, were sunk into the basement with six wins and ten losses.

Who is Alex Spanos?

What could I tell them? I had exceeded my wildest dreams in my business, raised four happy and healthy children, and been blessed with a long-lasting, soul-sustaining marriage with the love of my life, Faye.

We run a family business, a private company, reporting only to ourselves. We have no bureaucracy. Overhead is cut to the bone. In all my years in business I've never once worn a tie to the office. That independence has been a hallmark of our success. But now, flying out of the hometown where I was born and raised, surrounded by my wife, children, and grandchildren, I was leaving a world I knew and entering a world where I knew little. I was flying into an arena where I'd have to pass the ball to a team: managers, coaches, and players, none of whom I had ever met and all upon whom I'd have to rely. I was flying into a world where my performance would be gauged not by a balance sheet but by a scoreboard.

I've loved sports ever since I was a kid in Stockton, but my three brothers and I never got to play. We were too busy working at our father's lunch counter and bakery on Stockton's old Skid Row. Dad was a Greek from the old school, an immigrant named Constantinos "Gus" Spanos. From the time I was eight years old, I was expected to get up at four in the morning with my brothers and bake the day's supply of bread and pastry for four hours before going to school.

We were scared to death of Dad. He never once hugged us as boys or congratulated us as men. There was rarely a day that he didn't discipline us for some reason. Of course, in those days corporal punishment was not considered abuse. It was an accepted way of life in many families. "Spare the rod and spoil the child," they'd say. My dad was a big believer in the rod. He believed that a whipping could say more than any words he could speak. He'd take a small branch off a tree and strip the leaves and whack us right on the legs. To him, work was the only virtue, and time spent in sports was foolish.

When I made my fortune, I sponsored sports teams for kids across northern California, providing everything from new uniforms to new stadiums, so they wouldn't miss out on sports as I had. In the midsixties, I got my first taste of professional sports when, along with a group including the singer Pat Boone, I became involved with an Oakland branch of the fledgling American Basketball Association. The league didn't survive. But a path lit up before me, leading straight to the top of the professional sports world: the NFL.

I was too old to throw a football and much too manic to sit idly in the grandstands. I had but one option: I had to own a team. I started shopping around. Like everyone in Stockton, I was a San Francisco 49er fan. But the 49ers weren't for sale. So I made a bid for the Tampa Bay Buccaneers in 1974. I was too late. A Florida-based attorney snagged the team. Then, in 1977, Al Davis, the outspoken, maverick owner of the Oakland Raiders, called me. He had been commissioned by San Francisco's Morabito family to help sell the San Francisco 49ers. Was I interested?

Interested? Hell, yes! I offered $12 million. But the price quickly escalated to $18 million. Al gave me a 5 P.M. deadline on a Friday. I thought about it: Who's going to pay $18 million for a losing team that made a profit of only $100,000 that year? Thinking that no one would pay $18 million, I stuck to my original price. At 5:30 P.M. that Friday, thirty minutes after my deadline, the 49ers held a press conference: the DeBartolo family of Youngstown, Ohio, had bought the 49ers for $18 million. I'd lost out again.

I was like a fisherman who had briefly hooked a marlin only to have it spit the hook in my face. I became *obsessed*. Nothing could deter me from my dream. I could have bought the Oakland A's baseball team in 1978 for $8.2 million. But I wasn't interested in baseball. I had a chance to get into the newly formed U.S. Football League cheap, but, fixated on the NFL, I passed.

Then, through my friend Barron Hilton, I finally got a shot at the San Diego Chargers. The majority owner, Gene Klein, was having a rough year: the Chargers had been plagued by a fifty-seven-day player strike, widespread player drug problems, and several years of losing. After he'd suffered two heart attacks, Klein's doctors encouraged him to sell the team.

Friends and family tried to talk me out of buying the Chargers. Would I listen? Of course not. I wouldn't even be swayed by the members of my own executive board, who voted 10 to 2 against buying the ball club. I stood up in my boardroom, right in front of my four kids, my CPA of thirty-four years, and my attorney, and said, "I know I'm going against what I taught you about never investing a dollar unless you can get a good return. But I want this more than you can believe. I'm sorry. For the first time, I'm overruling all of you. When you get to be sixty, you'll know why I'm doing this."

I realized I was falling into the cliché of the successful businessman going crazy over the dream of running a sports team. But I hungered for one last challenge, one ultimate test. So, not believing in taking on debt, I paid $40 million cash. Then I flew south to San Diego. I was on yet another mission, a mission that, in many ways, I'd been on my entire life: to turn a loser into a winner.

I'd never once failed to accomplish exactly what I'd set out to do. How hard could this be?

❖ ❖ ❖

Touchdown in San Diego. Down went the landing gear, out came the stairs, and I stepped into a different world. The small crowd of fans at the airport and the members of the media at the team's training facility all looked at me for some word of wisdom, something that would raise their hopes of victory.

The first question from the media was something like, "Why do you want to own a sports franchise?"

I told them that I'd never had the opportunity to play sports when I was a kid, and it had been my lifelong desire to own an NFL team. I told them that I had vowed to own an NFL team by the age of sixty. I rambled on about my business and my background and my dreams. As I spoke, I watched the faces of my audience. *Absolute boredom.* It didn't take me long to discover that they cared about my background for one reason and one reason only. They wanted to know if I had the stuff to make us win.

"When will we win?" they soon seemed to be shouting in a chorus.

Or more specifically: "How long do you think it'll take to get to the Super Bowl?"

I got swept up in their enthusiasm. I knew a little bit about show business from my friend Bob Hope. We eventually appeared together in a song-and-dance routine at charity events everywhere from San Francisco to Las Vegas to Moscow. We even performed on stage together at a special charity event held at Carnegie Hall.

"When Alex was born," Hope would tell audiences, "the doctor slapped him, and Alex said, 'Would you like to rent an apartment?'"

"When Alex plays golf, if he loses the ball, he doesn't even bother to look for it," he would say on another stage. "He figures he'll just buy the property and find the ball while building apartments."

"Alex must be going to the moon," Bob said when he saw the A. G. Spanos Jet Center in Stockton. "He's bought all the real estate down here."

I learned more than dancing from Bob; I learned that when you're on stage, you *perform*.

So that's what I finally did in that first press conference. I performed.

"How long do you think it'll take us to get to the Super Bowl?" one sportswriter asked me.

I considered the question for a moment. I'd steered my entire life by five-year plans. Not once in thirty-five years of business had I ever failed to reach one of my five-year goals early. Granted, I didn't know anything about running an NFL team. But so what? I didn't know anything about construction when I started building apartments, but I became the number one builder of apartments in America. I didn't know anything about golf when I began playing the game, but I became a top-ranked amateur. I didn't know anything about dancing before Bob Hope taught me how to dance, but I ended up getting curtain calls at Carnegie Hall. How could getting to a Super Bowl be any different from achieving any of my other five-year goals? How can a Super Bowl be that big a thing? I didn't think. I *performed*. I made a statement that would immediately replace the *Who is Alex Spanos?* headlines.

"We'll spend whatever it takes for productive personnel," I said, "and, within *five years*, deliver a Super Bowl to Chargers fans."

Bam! That got 'em. My ears are still ringing. What enthusiasm! What energy! Oh, man, they were actually applauding. They figured I was going to come in and make things happen. I told 'em what they wanted to hear. I made a commitment, before I realized what professional football was all about. Maybe I was subconsciously trying to put myself and my team into that place where, I knew, victory lives—that place where the deadline clock is always ticking and where men and women rise to heights unimagined. I truly believed in my heart that we could build up the team and make it to the Super Bowl in five years.

But I was wrong. We wouldn't have even a winning season until 1987, and then we'd only scrape by with eight wins and seven losses. Then we began losing again . . . and losing, and losing. I couldn't cope with it; losing was a new and terrifying experience for me. Some Monday mornings, I'd shut the door to my office at the Chargers headquarters and actually cry. Other times, rage would overcome me. I'd come out of my office, charging. The coaches called me a "live volcano." They said they'd hear me coming into the office before they'd see me. But behind the bluster, I was suffering, becoming clinically depressed. I couldn't understand what I was doing wrong!

The press lambasted me almost daily. I didn't dare walk the streets of San Diego. Did they weigh my business success against my football losses? Not for a minute. Few fans even seemed to know I was in another business besides football. The San Diego Chargers became my image, my identification. And for eight years, all I did was lose.

Even Bob Hope began using me as a punch line.

"There goes Alex Spanos, owner of the San Diego Chargers," he'd say on stage. "The Chargers will win the Super Bowl next year—[pause to register audience disbelief]—and Joan Collins will become Mother Superior."

The worst day of my life came on the football field when the fans actually booed me. It was during a 1988 loss to the 49ers. We were down 48–10 and I was on the field praising quarterback Dan Fouts during a ceremony to retire his number. Boos began shaking the stadium. It was a moment of misery like I'd never experienced before. Afterwards, dejection hung over me for days.

My family encouraged me to sell the Chargers.

But I was stubborn in my refusals.

"I won't sell a losing ball club," I said.

Then it happened: we finally began winning. With our backs against the wall, with everybody counting us out, as the underdogs in a stadium packed with fans that despised us, we won. The road to redemption was tough, but on January 15, 1995, we achieved the impossible. We faced the 11–5 Pittsburgh Steelers on their home turf in the AFC Championship Game . . . and won. The media, the oddsmakers, and even most fans predicted that we wouldn't score a single point. But we bounced back from a halftime deficit of 10–3, and overcame a stadium full of frenzied Steelers fans, to win a slot in the 1995 Super Bowl.

For the first time in the history of the team, the Chargers were going to the Super Bowl. What a moment! The Chargers' lightning bolt logo electrified San Diego. Yes, it was five years beyond my prediction, and, yes, we would lose that Super Bowl. But suddenly people didn't just concentrate on our failures. Suddenly, I was hailed as a hero on the fields where I was once booed.

So who is Alex Spanos, and what is the secret of his success? As my first press conference after buying the Chargers illustrates, life can't be reduced to a headline and you can't sum up success in a sound bite. So let me explain it with a story…

❖ ❖ ❖

I stood on the border between mediocrity and success with only a thin wooden doorway dividing the two extremes.

Mediocrity ruled the side of the door where I was standing: the basement of my Greek immigrant father's tiny bakery, where I worked hard at the ovens for $40 a week, fifteen hours a day, seven days a week. It was a world where I was safe, secure—and slowly dying. The other side of the door, where I would eventually find success, did not offer a welcome mat. It was a dark, uncertain, forbidding place, which, for a dead-broke twenty-seven-year-old baker with a wife and child and a second baby on the way, seemed much scarier than staying chained to the basement where I stood.

I had no guarantee that walking out of that bakery would lead me anywhere. But I would quickly discover that that pivotal step would place me in a new world where success, through hard work, was at least a possibility. One thing was for certain: if I stayed in that basement, I would be sentencing myself and my family to an absolutely ordinary life: work, struggle, retire, die. Just another guy buried beneath an epitaph of excuses.

All I had to do to step from one world into the other was open the door and walk! But for a moment I stood frozen. I am the son of a family of hardworking Greek immigrants, the spiritual descendant of millions who abandoned meager existences around the world to sail off to America, leaving behind everything they knew for a shot at what they could become. But the passageway out of that flour-clouded basement seemed as wide as any ocean.

In writing this book, I kept returning to a singular question: *Why me?* Why did I become successful? I had nothing in the way of money, background, education, or connections. Eventually, I realized that the answer could be found in the place where I began my journey almost fifty years ago; the secret of my success stood squarely in that bakery's basement door. It was the type of door that I would walk through again and again and again in my life, each passage taking me one step closer to the place where I now stand. I knew nothing about the worlds on the other sides of these doors before I walked through them. I knew nothing about the fields that I would eventually enter—catering, construction, and, finally, football—before I walked through the passageways and began to learn what lay behind them.

So there I was, the lanky bakery boy in the flour-dusted apron, spending fifteen hours each and every day running an endless assembly line of doughnuts, cakes, pies, turnovers, and butter horns. I was sweating not only because of the heat of the ovens but also because of the even hotter temper of my dad.

The only thing that distinguished me from a million other dead-broke bakers was desire. I not only wanted more, I desperately needed more. Not much more—only $210 to be precise. That was the amount it would take to let my wife, Faye, check into the hospital for the delivery of our second child. Considering that the baby was due in six weeks, I figured a $35-a-week raise would get me by. I had every right to demand $75 a week from my dad. The union wage for a baker of my caliber was $125 a week, and that was for working six days a week, instead of seven.

In that basement bakery, I'd spent months rehearsing how I'd ask my father for a raise. I braced myself for a fight. Five-feet-seven-inches tall, Dad could be a kettle of screaming anger. His name was Constantinos Spanos, although he later had his name legally changed to Gus. Just like a million other immigrants, he'd left behind his family of sixteen siblings, and everything else he knew in his tiny Greek village of Naziri, to come to America. He was twenty when he first glimpsed the Statue of Liberty from a ship on the morning of September 17, 1912. He became a butcher in South San Francisco before finally accepting a job in a cousin's restaurant in a small farming town called Stockton in the heart of northern California's lush San Joaquin Valley.

Dad firmly believed that all of his sons should get a college degree. My three brothers followed the family plan. My brother George became a lawyer and could do no wrong in my father's eyes. I could do nothing right.

Things started out all right. I was sent to Cal Poly in San Luis Obispo, and later the College of the Pacific in Stockton, to become an engineer. I enjoyed life, lettered in swimming and diving, worked as a baker in the student cafeteria, and was on my way to earning that lofty engineering degree that my dad had preordained for me.

World War II interrupted my plans. I became a sergeant in the air force. I returned home to Stockton with my lovely wife, Faye, who would become the bedrock of my world. I did everything right— except returning to school to get my college degree after serving in the military. School just didn't interest me. So with no job prospects in sight, I accepted my dad's offer to become a partner in his lunch counter and bakery. Three years passed. The promised partnership never materialized. I was still working at the ovens for $40 a week. Dad never communicated with me; he only complained.

Once, I'd been his favorite son. Now, he considered me a bum. He had sent me to college to become an engineer, and I'd come back empty-handed. He thought I was no better than he was. In his mind, I *deserved* to be working alongside him for low wages.

Finally, one afternoon, fixated on the $210 I knew I needed to get my wife into the hospital to have our second child, I mustered the nerve to ask Dad for a raise. He didn't say a word, just waved me away as if swatting a pesky fly. The next morning, after discussing the situation with Faye, I gave my father my two weeks' notice. Two weeks after that, I walked out of the Roma Lunch and Bakery, and I never looked back.

Looking back on that incident now, recalling the scene without the veil of anger, I can see that my father planted the seed of my motivation, a seed that would rapidly grow. I literally *had* to succeed. I had to show my father, my family, my community that I was *more* than everyone expected me to be. I had to show them that I was capable of success in the only way success is measured: by achievement.

I placed a bet on the table with the only currency I had: I bet my life that I would succeed. I knew that the outside world beyond that basement door must be better than staying in that basement.

I shut the door on my past and vowed that I would rather pull out a gun and blow my brains out than go back to the place I was fleeing. I stood outside that bakery and tasted my first breath of freedom. I was technically an unemployed baker. But in my mind I was a king.

My first order of business? Sheer survival. You have to begin with what you have. But what did I have to begin with? What did I have to sell? Few people started with less than I did.

I began with the cheapest commodity available.

I began with bologna.

These days, when people who don't know me ask, "Who is Alex Spanos?" I answer that I am a man who has lived to see his dreams fulfilled. I am undoubtedly a lucky man—lucky to have a healthy and harmonious family, lucky to see a lifetime of work pay off in success beyond my wildest dreams.

For the past ten years, I have considered writing this book, but I didn't undertake it until, in the midst of the Chargers' losses, I experienced a form of mental depression during which I would reminisce with an overwhelming, unbearable sadness about the bittersweet years of growing up in a large and boisterous family of Greek immigrants. I would wake up every morning to begin a day of nonstop business activities, and all I could think about were those early years. I would think of my father and my mother, and I would think of my brothers and how hard life had been for us growing up. I would find myself trying to make sense of why everyone's life had turned out the way it did. Most of all, a single question would repeat itself endlessly in my mind: *Why did I succeed?* What did I do so differently from the others in my family, my neighborhood, my hometown?

I kept coming back to my father, who taught us to follow his fierce work ethic through a practical method: from childhood, all of us had to work in the family business. My brothers and I would rise at 4 A.M. and put in three or four hours of work before school, every single day of the week, all through elementary and high school. We worked away our childhood years under our father's watchful eye. He kept us bound by the old country traditions and his abiding belief that only hard work shapes character.

Since then and throughout my life, I have kept pretty much the same schedule. Old habits do indeed die hard! My day still starts at 5 A.M., only now I'm making deals, not baking doughnuts. But the work ethic is still the same.

Looking back, I have come to realize that hard work became an inseparable part of who I was and who I am today. In the beginning, I worked to escape my father's domination; later, when I got married, I worked to support my own growing family. What had started out as an unbearable yoke during my childhood eventually turned out to be a blessing, as the work ethic my father instilled led me to more and more profitable business ventures.

I owe what I am today to my father. He was my sole motivating force to become successful. If not for him, maybe I would not have expected and exacted such results from myself. When I left his bakery to make it on my own, I felt compelled to prove myself to Dad: that I was better than he believed me to be. Sadly, he never told me that he was proud of me, no matter my accomplishments. Until the day he died, in 1976, he never acknowledged my success to me. My father could never admit when he was wrong. He never forgave me for leaving his employ, and although I clearly understood that side of him, I could not help feeling hurt. As I grew older and wiser, that sharp, nagging need for his approval lost its edge, but it remains with me today. Whenever I think about him, which is often these days, a sense of loss and regret steals over my heart.

After I disappointed my dad by dropping out of college, he transferred all his affection to my brother George, who had done everything Dad had ever asked of him. George had always been the dutiful son. When he married and had his own family, he was a true family man, ever ready to make compromises for the sake of the family unit. When I think about the hardships we went through as kids, I always think of George and how well he bore it. He doesn't like to talk about the past, and every time I bring it up I see how he winces, as if to tell me, "Please, let's not talk about it, Alex." George has made his peace with the past; it's his way of being loyal to Mom and Dad. But unlike him, I want to remember. Because I can never forget.

I made my fortune in the small farming town where I was born. Stockton, California, in the heart of the lush San Joaquin Valley, served for most people as a stopover on the way to somewhere else. Back in 1955, Stockton had a population of 75,000. Today, it has grown to more than 250,000. I still maintain my corporate headquarters in Stockton. Living in Stockton makes me remember who I am and where I came from. A day does not pass when I don't reflect on my beginnings.

Until recently, when people sought my advice on achieving success, I replied intellectually. "Success has three key elements: vision, desire, and instinct," I would say. "The vision to know what one wants; the desire to see it accomplished; and the instinct that serves as a compass for making the right decisions at the right time."

But in writing this book, I learned there is more to success than that seemingly simple formula. Opportunities are as abundant today as they were when I was growing up. Dreams can still come true; the impossible can still occur. But complacency and a hundred other demons of distraction can blind you to the opportunities that stand ever ready to propel you forward.

In writing this book, I learned that the secrets of success can be shown only by sharing: openly, honestly, and analytically. Sharing the strategies, the knowledge, the insights, the wisdom, and the *stories* of success. Throughout my life I have tried to give back to my community and my world, but these were mostly financial contributions to noble and needy causes, charities, and individuals. In sharing the stories of my success, I hope to pass on an intellectual legacy for others to follow in creating their own success story.

This is what I mean by the title, *Sharing the Wealth*.

Because while success cannot be summed up in a sound bite, it can be explained in a story. Every success has its own story, and my story started when my father left his family home in Greece and landed on the shores of Ellis Island.

That was the beginning.

CHAPTER 2

Growing Up Greek

The same drive that brought me out of my father's basement bakery—the desire for more!—was the essential drive that brought my dad to America. Like me, he opened a door and walked through it. Like me, he sought success away from home.

He was one of sixteen sons and one daughter born to a dirt-poor family in the Greek village of Naziri, nestled in the hills of the Peloponnese. Dad's father ran a coffeehouse, and, just like me, he would have been expected to work for his father. But his dad died at thirty-nine, gored by a bull, leaving his sons with neither a father nor a future.

I recently returned to my family home in Greece. I had received a request from the local priest for help in rebuilding the 140-year-old church. I promptly sent money, as requested. Then, not having returned to the village in forty-one years, I decided to fly over for a visit. Today, the village of Naziri is called Eva. There is electricity and paved roads. My father's family house is still there, although, remodeled, it bears little resemblance to the home where he grew up. But there were enough memories—and relatives—to allow me to imagine my dad as a young man, walking down the dirt roads, saying good-bye to his village and family, and sailing off to America. He had nothing keeping him at home, where times were tough and living conditions marginal. So he joined the tide of European immigrants who flooded into the United States between 1900 and 1920, 60 percent of them from southern and eastern Europe. Like all of them, he came seeking the endless opportunities of America. *America!* Where the streets were paved with gold. Where a hardworking young man like Constantinos "Gus" Spanos could make his dreams come true.

He left his village with everything he owned—which amounted to $20, probably borrowed, along with the ship's fare—and sailed off alone aboard the SS *Macedonia* for the new land. His destination was Haverhill, Massachusetts, where he would stay with his older brother, George, who had preceded him in leaving Naziri to seek his fortune. Dad first glimpsed the Statue of Liberty on the morning of September 17, 1912. I can imagine his thrill when he saw the great lady's torch held high in welcome. Its inscription—"Send these, the homeless, tempest-tossed to me. I lift my lamp beside the golden door"—could have been written especially for him.

But no brass bands awaited Dad. His stay in Haverhill was brief, maybe a month. Then he traveled west to California to join others from his village in the San Francisco Bay Area. Again, no brass bands. But there was a job as a butcher in South San Francisco's meatpacking center. The slaughterhouse was located between what is now San Francisco International Airport and Candlestick Park. My father never spoke of his time in the slaughterhouse, but based on his short stay I can only surmise that he did not enjoy the work. Judged by today's standards, slaughterhouse work of butchering meat amid blood, rats, and flies would be grim. Still, the life of a butcher was better than the other options that awaited many new immigrants: working in the Colorado and Utah coal mines or building the

California railroad lines, jobs that first broke a man's back and then destroyed his spirit.

After a few months in the slaughterhouse, Dad was rescued by a cousin, Aristides Petropoulos, who invited him to work in his restaurant. So Dad traveled ninety miles southeast of San Francisco into the heart of the San Joaquin Valley and the town of Stockton. Once home to six different Indian tribes, as well as Spaniards, trappers, Mexicans, and European settlers, the area known as Stockton had boomed with the treasure hunters of the California Gold Rush mining in the nearby Sierra Nevada Mountains. Today, Stockton is a growing agricultural community with an inland port facility, a railroad hub, and the University of the Pacific. But when Dad arrived, it was a small farming town.

In 1914, about a year after his arrival, Dad sent word to Greece for his youngest brother, my Uncle Chris, to join him in Stockton. Uncle Chris's first job was as a farmhand. But Chris didn't come to America to work on a farm. He had done enough of that work in Greece. So he quit to work in the restaurant with my father. When Dad's restaurateur cousin decided to return to Greece, Dad and Uncle Chris bought the place, which was called the Roma Lunch. In retrospect, Dad's time as a butcher served him well in his life as a restaurant owner. He bought his meat whole and butchered it himself to save money.

Dad and Uncle Chris worked in the restaurant side by side until my father enlisted in the army. I don't know what prompted him to enlist, but I suspect he may have heard that enlistment was the surest and quickest way of becoming an American citizen. He served for one year, from 1918 to 1919. At the end of his service, he was granted his citizenship papers.

Seven years after arriving in America, Constantinos Spanos, twenty-seven, was an American citizen. He owned his own small restaurant. He didn't make much money, but enough to send some home to Greece each month.

He was ready to find a wife.

As was customary among immigrants in those days, he traveled back to Greece, where he planned to stay for six months to find a bride. Although he was nearly broke, he put on one hell of a show. He wore a brand-new tailored suit and walked with a ceremonial cane. I have a faded picture of him from that bride-seeking journey. With his immaculate dark suit, his crown of thick dark hair, and his imperial expression, he looked impressive—and rich. Regaling his compatriots with tales of his success as an American restaurateur, he seemed to be a man of means.

Evanthia Tsopelas Koumentakou, then nineteen, came from the village of Spitali, not far from Naziri. She was a beauty with black hair, olive skin, and blue eyes, a rare color for a Greek girl. She also had a rich stepfather. Evanthia's father had died when she was a little girl, and her mother had married Aristides Koumentakou, the village merchant, with whom she had two more daughters. Aristides was an extremely prosperous gentleman. He provided his family with a comfortable life and eventually adopted little Evanthia. Raised with maids, she was waited on and spoiled.

She had a line of salivating suitors and had even been promised to one of them, but Evanthia was immediately smitten with the seemingly rich restaurateur from California. Her Greek admirers must have seemed provincial compared to the handsome, immaculately dressed, silver-tongued Greek-American asking for her hand. Her entire family opposed the match. I can't imagine how Dad persuaded them to agree to a marriage that would take their daughter so far away. He must have done some pretty fast and fancy talking. Evanthia felt that she had found the man of her dreams. Eventually, her parents relented.

One or two months after Dad's arrival in Greece, he and Evanthia were married in Kalamata, the biggest nearby town, in a big wedding paid for by his new father-in-law. Although Dad was running short on the traveling money he'd borrowed from Uncle Chris, his ego was still firmly intact. When his father-in-law mentioned the dowry arrangements for his daughter, Dad once again put on a big show and said he didn't need the dowry, which would have been a sizable cash amount. Instead, he asked that the funds be deposited in a local bank to draw interest.

When my mother married my father and waved good-bye to her parents, she would never see them again. She never returned to Greece in her parents' lifetime. As for the dowry, the Greek banks failed during the Depression, and the funds were gone forever.

Dad's tales of the opportunities he'd discovered in his new land were so alluring that he returned to America not only with a bride but with six other people, including his cousin Charlie; his sister, Panayota; and relatives Angelo Georgopoulos and Evangelia Sims.

Perhaps foreshadowing the future, Evanthia became violently ill on her honeymoon voyage to America. She spent most of the journey bedridden in her steerage stateroom. Her new husband did little to console his new bride. He chose to spend his time with his friends and relatives on the upper deck. Their marriage, however, was not without passion. Mom was pregnant by the time she arrived in Stockton. Only then did she realize that my father was not a man of means and that she would be relegated to a life of menial tasks of the kind her servants had once performed.

They moved into a house right across from a vacant lot that would soon be home to St. Basil's Greek Orthodox Church. In their house, everyone spoke Greek, not English. Although my mother couldn't speak a word of English, my father was determined to learn. He kept a Greek-American dictionary with him at home and at the restaurant. Every day he read the local newspapers, and each time he'd run across a word he didn't know he'd look it up in the dictionary and write it in a notebook, until he had created his own dictionary with translations of the new words he'd learned. But Greek remained the first language of his new family.

Dad resumed his work at the restaurant, and Mom went about the business of adjusting to her new life. It couldn't have been easy for her. She had a new husband, new friends, a new country, and a new language to learn. But there wasn't any time for brooding. The month she arrived in Stockton, August 1921, she gave birth to a baby girl who died four months later of a childhood disease.

The following year, she bore her first son, my oldest brother, Danny. I came next on September 28, 1923. My birth certificate lists my name as Leonidas. But at my christening, when, as per tradition, the priest asked my godfather to announce my name, he stood before friends and family and exclaimed "Alexander!" after his hero, Alexander the Great. From that point forward I was Alexander. My brother George was born twelve months after I was. Within thirty-three months, my mother had given birth to four children. Raising the surviving three sons, while my father worked dawn to dusk at the restaurant, was tough. Perhaps washing dirty diapers on a washboard until her knuckles were bloody gave rise to the discontent that seemed to follow my mother throughout her life. In any case, she was never truly happy.

I was born into conflict. From the time I was two years old, my brothers, sisters, and I were witnesses to our parents' constant fighting. Although they would remain married for fifty-six years, they were two entirely different personalities, each unwilling to compromise. Mom had been pampered and privileged, accustomed to having her own way. Dad had grown up in a family of seventeen children, where nothing was ever handed to him easily. He had either to grab for things or fight for them.

My parents clashed daily. Anything could spark a screaming match filled with language like you wouldn't believe. Dad was a little guy, pigeon-toed, and walked with a shuffle. My mother was even smaller at five foot two, but she was as tough as Dad. She gave as good as she got and never backed down to avoid an argument, which may have been the root of their problems.

Like most Greeks of that period, Dad treated his wife as generations of tough, old-time Greeks had treated women in the old country. Which can be roughly translated as: "Hey, you! I'm the boss, and don't you forget it." It's wrong, but that's the way it was in our home and in many Greek immigrant homes of that period. All of our relatives sided with my father in my parents' arguments, except for Panayota, whom we called "Thia" Panayota, Greek for "aunt." Perhaps because she was a woman, my aunt could empathize with my mother's plight. Most relatives believed my parents' problems to be my mother's fault. She was expected to be submissive and subservient, but she had been educated and spoiled by her parents. Everyone thought she provoked Dad. Perhaps she did. She'd curse, she'd scream, she'd call him names. I loved my mother, but she never did anything to help the situation. I always thought that she shouldn't have fueled whatever internal fire was feeding his anger. She could have looked the other way, but never did.

We children received unconditional love from our parents, albeit in radically different forms. Mom was affectionate with us, always hugging us, drawing us to her lap, and kissing us. Dad, on the other hand, was cool and stern. He demanded proper behavior and considered it his responsibility to raise us to become men. But there was never a doubt in any of our minds that he loved us. He just showed it in different ways. He was totally dedicated to his children and intent upon our getting the best possible education and enjoying the best possible future.

We were a very close-knit family. We never went anywhere unless we all went together. Every night, after my father came home from the restaurant, we would all sit down to dinner as a family. Growing up, Mom had had family servants to take care of household duties. But she made up for lost time. My mother became one hell of a cook, learning most of her skills from Dad and Thia Panayota. Her *stifado*, a stew of onions and meat, was wonderful. Our house was always open to friends and relatives. Our closest friends called my parents Mama and Papa Spanos.

Dad was tireless. If he worked hard when he was single, he worked even harder now that he had a family to support. But it soon became apparent that the small restaurant he shared with Uncle Chris could not support two families. So they decided to go their separate ways.

Always the overachiever, Dad opened up an even bigger Roma Lunch restaurant, with cooks and waiters and way too much space, on East Main Street in downtown Stockton. He worked seven days a week, arriving at 3 A.M. to begin the baking and the day's menu, staying until late at night for cleanup. Mom, who now had four children, having given birth to my sister Stella in 1928, stayed home to take care of the house and kids. Their only outing together was Sunday morning church.

In that little house in that little farming town, we three sons would sleep in one bed until high school and had to take off our shoes when we entered the house so we wouldn't wear them out. As soon as we could walk, Dad put us to work sweeping floors and peeling potatoes at the restaurant. He felt if he kept us busy we'd stay out of mischief. By the time I was eight, I was baking doughnuts, washing dishes, waiting tables, cleaning up, and doing anything else that needed to be done. My older brother, Danny, had started before me, and soon younger brother George joined our crew. By the time we got to school, we had already put in half a day's work. Sometimes, unable to keep my eyes open, I would fall asleep on my desk. But that was just the beginning of our education.

My father gave us the keys to our destiny, although I didn't realize the value in these things at the time.

First and foremost, he taught us to take pride in our Greek heritage. We were taught that we were heirs to the long and illustrious history of ancient Greece, sons and daughters of the cradle of democracy and the birthplace of Western philosophy. We learned the minute details of the long and valiant struggle of our homeland's independence from the Ottoman Empire during the 1800s and, later, its heroic stand against the Italian and German invasions. We were taught to wear our historical and cultural heritage as a badge of honor, and that heritage gave us an everlasting sense of identity, even though, as children, we had never been to Greece. "Be proud of your heritage!" my dad would endlessly insist.

He taught us to take pride in our religion, the link that has held Greek-Americans together as both a community and an ethnic minority. Whether practicing believers or not, the members of the Greek Orthodox Church are devout defenders of their church and religion. Throughout the modern history of Greece, the church and its clergy have played a leading role in the course of political and social events. In America, Greek immigrants relied on the church as the center of community and social life. Large social halls adjacent to churches served as gathering places for community events, social functions, and holiday festivities. My parents were faithful Orthodox, diligently following the cherished traditions of their religion and culture. They made sure that their children were reared within the fold of those traditions. As kids, we were required to attend church weekly. We learned about the history of ancient and modern Greece and served our church faithfully as altar boys. When we had our own families, we upheld the same traditions and beliefs.

At the same time, we were devoutly American, striving to learn the language and the ways of life of our homeland. Dad taught us, mostly through example, the immigrant's chief article of faith: the abiding belief in a better life. For him, life boiled down to the basics: hard work, self-improvement, education, and self-knowledge. Greek immigrants were tenacious and resourceful. Greek restaurants and houses sprang up in every city where there were Greek-American communities, paving the way for succeeding generations to pursue careers in medicine, law, engineering, education, and other fields. But no matter how far an immigrant traveled professionally, you were taught never to abandon the roots of your identity. Being Greek-American meant having the best of two worlds, enjoying the benefits of dual heritage: American, abundant in civil liberties and individual rights, and Greek, rich in tradition and history.

So there we were, straddling two cultures like thousands of other immigrant families. It was crucial to my father that we observe many of the old ways in which he grew up. But he also considered it critical that we take advantage of his adopted country's endless opportunities, the opportunities he never had. So when he finished working at the restaurant, he came home to spend the rest of his day with us, determined to shape us into everything he believed we could become.

To this end, he constructed a daunting schedule. After school, we would head straight to the Greek Orthodox church for Greek language school. I am convinced that there hasn't been a Greek child born who enjoyed Greek school. Yet reading and writing Greek was and still is considered a requirement for all children of Greek parentage. Our school was located across the street from our house on Lafayette Street. We were shoehorned into small crowded rooms, where we hunched over rickety desks to read aloud haltingly from hand-me-down reading books.

For my father, there were no excuses good enough to allow missing Greek school or Sunday school. Danny, George, and I served as altar boys for Sunday service, along with my cousins Pete and Harry. Since we lived across the street from the church we were perpetually on call for service. When we weren't at the altar helping the priest, we were in the back of the school playing cards or shooting craps in the baptismal fountains. When we were caught doing something unacceptable—as we often were—the church elders grabbed our ears and twisted them for punishment.

My siblings and I had no time to participate in anything Dad considered frivolous, like sports. But performing in public was something else, something important. Dad enrolled us in endless after-school activities: tumbling, tap dancing, ballroom dancing, ballet, baton twirling, piano training, and more.

He was our coach, mentor, and cheerleader.

I can still see him sitting in the front row of infinite audiences, beaming with pride. For some reason, baton twirling was his favorite. Few poor Greek families had store-bought batons. So Dad fashioned our batons out of aluminum pipes. He taught us how to twirl in the backyard. Hearing about a talented tap-dancing instructor in San Francisco, he took us to the city every Saturday for lessons. I remember Danny, George, and me practicing our tap-dance steps on the kitchen floor, streaking the linoleum with our shoes. Mom would have to mop the floor after each of our dancing sessions, but she never complained about that, at least not to us. I have a picture of the three of us dressed identically, hats in hand and toes pointed in a classic vaudevillian pose. We got so good at tap that we won an audition at San Francisco's Golden Gate Theater. We did everything as a trio. We played the piano, the three of us at the keys. Being the youngest, George would be in the middle. I played bass keys on the left and Danny would be on the right. George was in charge of melody. Any mistakes brought two elbows jabbing George on both sides.

Thinking ballet might be beneficial, Dad drove us to watch a ballet troupe perform at the College of the Pacific (now the University of the Pacific). He liked it enough to sign us up for lessons with one of the dancers. But when the instructor pranced out in his ballet tights, my father shouted, "No more of that!" And that was the end of our ballet career.

With the Depression, Dad's Roma Lunch was crippled by its excessive overhead, while Uncle Chris's Roma Lunch, a little hole in the wall with a lunch counter and three tables, survived. Dad had to shut down in 1932, and this proud and defiant man was reduced to odd jobs, peddling aprons sewn by my mother to barbers, butchers, and grocery store clerks. We kids sold magazines on street corners and had a Sunday morning newspaper route. Afternoons, we sold the *Stockton Record* in front of Johnny's Waffle Shop.

But by 1935, the Depression had lifted, and life was looking up for Gus Spanos & Family. My youngest brother, Leo, was born that year, and Dad opened a new restaurant, with financial backing from Uncle Chris. Smaller than his original, it was on El Dorado Street. Because Uncle Chris's Roma Lunch was still in operation, right around the corner from Dad's, the new place was named the Roma Lunch #2.

Stockton had once been a port city for gold miners. They'd travel from San Francisco to Stockton's deep channel port by boat, then take a wagon or mule to the Sierra Nevadas. When the gold rush ended, Stockton replaced gold with farming, becoming the center of the San Joaquin Valley agricultural community. The city boasted the biggest Filipino population outside of the Philippines. A half dozen Chinese gambling joints stayed open all night, and more than twenty houses of prostitution kept the farm workers happy.

Right between the whorehouses and gambling dens, eight blocks from our home, sat the Roma Lunch #2. The café served a cross section of Stockton's population. The Depression had brought a large influx of people in search of jobs. The area west of El Dorado Street, including Chinatown, became known as Skid Row. At first, the area was populated primarily with the Filipino farm workers who had migrated from the Philippines and Hawaii when their farm contracts expired. As farmers in the Midwest were driven from the dust bowl, they began to settle in Stockton as well. Skid Row became a street of potential work opportunities—and hungry laborers.

Dad's customers included the strippers at the Pelican Club down the way and the "ladies of the evening," who worked out of the nearby Lincoln Hotel. They stopped at the Roma Lunch #2 for coffee fixes between tricks. While my father was tough at home, he was kind and cordial to employees who weren't family and to all of his customers.

At first, the Roma Lunch #2 was just an all-night restaurant where you could eat three meals a day and have a glass of beer or wine. But then, recognizing the potential of the early-morning farm worker breakfast business, Dad transformed a cramped, basement dishwashing area into a rudimentary bakery. When I was old enough to work, with assistance from my two brothers, I became chief baker in charge. Morning came before the sunrise. The Roma Lunch #2 never closed. It was open seven days a week, twenty-four hours a day.

Like my father, I learned that work, not leisure, was life's driving force. But I sought diversion wherever I could. I became the instigator, always leading my brothers into trouble. One opportunity for fun came each Fourth of July when we would earn extra money by selling firecrackers under the Roma Lunch's awning. We didn't just sell any fireworks, we sold what we called "The Rocket." There was no way to predict which direction the Rocket would go. One day, Danny was fiddling with the lighter and accidentally lit one of the Rockets. It took off and got stuck in the awning, popping wildly. The ensuing sparks ignited the rest of the firecrackers, which flew into the Roma Lunch. Customers screamed and scattered amid the explosions and shattering glass. Fortunately, no one was hurt, but we thought we were in big trouble. Surprisingly, Mount Constantinos didn't erupt. Dad actually laughed about it. Maybe he chalked it up to the hazards of selling firecrackers, but I think the reason was that he liked firecrackers, which he had made in Greece during the Easter celebration. Like him, they were explosive—and unpredictable.

Although Stockton had a sizable Greek population, there was still widespread anti-immigrant sentiment against Greeks as well as other nationalities. It didn't seem to matter that I was born in America. I was constantly harassed with chants of "Greasy Greek" and "Dirty Greek" at school. My dad felt the hatred, too. The Ku Klux Klan had made its way to Stockton and tangled with Dad (unsuccessfully) on more than one occasion. The discrimination suffered by the Greeks across America gave birth to the American Hellenic Education Progressive Association (AHEPA) in 1926. AHEPA brought unity, support, recognition, and strength to the Greek ethnic minority both nationally and locally.

But the center of the Greek community was the church. Our church had two factions whose members rarely saw eye-to-eye. But both factions belonged to a group called Adelphotita, which means "brotherhood." This group raised the money to build the church during the Depression. Every family in Stockton's Greek community could get medical insurance coverage through Adelphotita.

Dad and his kin belonged to one faction. A big, tough farmer named Bill Poullos headed the opposite faction. Dad had a personal feud with Poullos, who had ridiculed him or made some snide comment. The Poullos group had managed to ace Dad's group out of the management of the Adelphotita, and my father and his friends were furious about it. Dad demanded that Poullos apologize, but Poullos refused. Dad and his cronies made plans to crash a church management meeting and seize the books.

But on the day that Dad, my uncles, and a dozen of their friends were to storm the Adelphotita meeting at the church hall, most of the men in his group got cold feet. Everyone dropped out except for Dad, his friend Papaspeliou, and my godfather, Steve Chiarchanis. The three of them decided to go it alone. Steve was going to drive the getaway car, waiting outside while Dad and Papaspeliou stormed the meeting.

There were about forty people in the meeting when Dad and Papaspeliou rushed in. Their entrance was greeted by a shocked silence. Dad headed straight to Bill Poullos, carrying a brick in a paper bag.

"*Pare to logo sou piso*," he demanded of Poullos, Greek for "Take back your words."

At six foot two, Poullos towered over Dad. But according to witnesses, Poullos seemed petrified. He thought Dad had a gun in the bag. Dad demanded three times that he apologize. When Poullos finally refused, Dad bashed him on the head with the brick in the bag, opening a gash that would require stitches. Making a quick getaway, Dad and his buddies forgot to grab the books.

Dad raced through the church's back door. His friend Papaspeliou wasn't fast enough to escape. He was caught and beaten. Dad escaped into Steve's getaway car and they drove to his sister's house to hide.

We watched everything with my mother from the window of our home. We saw Dad walk into the church but never saw him leave because he had made his escape from the back door. We saw people rushing out the front entrance of the church hall, yelling and pointing at our house because they thought Dad was hiding there. The police arrived and eventually found my father and took him to jail. We hired an attorney who bailed him out. The case was eventually settled out of court; Dad had to pay a fine and the medical expenses for Bill Poullos, which he did with help from Uncle Chris and Thia Panayota's husband, Uncle Pete.

I don't remember having any close friends outside of my family until high school. My brothers and our cousins were my friends. The hours I spent playing with my brothers and cousins were the only time I felt free, without my father monitoring my every move. They followed me without question.

But no matter what scrapes I got us into, I'd never get the blame. The blame always went to Danny, the oldest. "You're the oldest, Danny, you should have known better!" became my father's endless refrain, as he'd line us up and spank us for our (or my) latest infraction. We'd all get spanked, but Danny would get blamed.

When Danny was nine and I was eight, something happened that would alter our lives forever. We were playing a game of tag at Uncle Chris's house with our cousins Pete and Harry. It was a beautiful summer day. The city had dug up the street for streetcar tracks, creating ditches four feet deep with dirt piled up alongside. We had been running and jumping the ditch. Danny started chasing Harry, who took a sharp right to avoid being tagged "It." Danny ran straight on. I don't think he had time to react to the car barreling straight at him. It all happened so fast. The car ran over Danny and never even stopped. We rushed inside the house and called Dad. Danny was still sprawled in the street, his head and leg seriously injured. An ambulance raced him to St. Joseph's Hospital. The attending physician, Dr. Vichy, was not hopeful.

Danny stayed in the hospital for eleven months. In the next two years, Danny had eight operations to reset his leg, which wouldn't heal properly. Every time it would begin to heal, the bone would slip and the doctors would have to rebreak it and start all over again. One day, Dr. Vichy told Dad that they'd have to amputate Danny's leg because gangrene might set in.

Dad's face turned purpled and he exploded with rage.

"I'll see him *dead* before you'll amputate his leg!" Dad roared.

Dr. Vichy said there was nothing else he could do.

"Then I'll find someone who can!" Dad said. He picked up Danny and carried him out of the hospital. The nurses followed behind, urging, "You have to sign out! You can't do this!"

"Does anyone want to try to stop me?" Dad asked.

They were lucky he didn't have a brick.

Luckily for Danny, a nurse in Dr. Vichy's office told Dad of a doctor in San Francisco who had come up with a new procedure, using pins to set broken bones. Dad drove Danny to the doctor, and the procedure eventually saved Danny's leg.

Dad dedicated the next two years of his life to Danny's rehabilitation, becoming my brother's physical therapist. He loved him so much and was determined to help him to walk again. But Danny felt the pain perhaps more than my father's love. The entire neighborhood could hear Danny's pained screams while Dad massaged the leg and forced him to exercise. Night and day, Dad worked diligently on Danny's leg. He was Dad's new mission, and Constantinos Spanos never failed at his job.

Seven years later, when Danny was sixteen, he was participating in high school track and gymnastics. Later, he enlisted in the navy during World War II and passed the physical with flying colors. Dad made it happen.

But Danny was never really the same. He had a big scar on the side of his head. He had always been bright, especially with numbers and figures, but after the accident everything got twisted. His personality changed. The years of pain and misery soured him. He became belligerent, especially with Dad, who did not accept belligerence passively. I could sweet-talk the old man; Danny *demanded* things, which was the wrong tactic to use with Dad.

Danny's accident affected us all. Because of the terrible experience Dad had with Danny's doctors, he lost respect for doctors in general. After the accident, Dad hired Lafayette Smallpage, a local attorney who handled cases for most of Stockton's Greek-American community, to sue the driver of the car that hit Danny. Smallpage was able to secure a judgment against the driver, a great stroke of luck since it was Danny who had darted into the street. After the trial, Dad came home, looked at George, and said, "You are going to become a lawyer."

He chose George because he was the most studious of the kids, always reading and carrying books. Later, during his teen years, George developed an interest in medicine, but Dad was adamant that he become an attorney.

As for me, I continued in my role as the family's rebel. I ran away from home when I was eleven after getting into another major scrape. I can't remember the specifics, but I decided it would be better to run away than face my father's wrath. We lived by the railroad tracks, so I hopped a boxcar to escape. But the damned train never moved! After three hours of waiting to be whisked away, I realized I wasn't going anywhere. Finally, I walked three miles to my godfather's house. That's where I often went when I was in trouble—either there or to Uncle Chris's. Both would talk to me, empathize, and send me back home. Uncle Chris and I had an extraordinarily close relationship. Unlike my dad, who could never compliment his sons, Uncle Chris recognized possibilities in me and prodded me along. Years later, after I had started my own business in my late twenties, Uncle Chris would tell me, "My only regret is that I will not live long enough to see how far you will go."

CHAPTER 3

Finding Home
by Leaving

W hen I think of my mother, Evanthia, I remember her hugs, kisses, and ever present generosity. Her door was always open to friends and relatives. Her refrigerator was always packed with food. And her heart was filled with love. Everyone called her "Mama Spanos." She was a survivor in the new land that had been misrepresented to her by my father. It must have been extraordinarily difficult for her to leave her life of wealth and privilege in Greece and suddenly become saddled with a difficult and demanding husband, four children (a brood that would eventually grow to six), and endless housework. Since she didn't know how to drive, she had no opportunity to go anywhere alone, even to a friend's or a relative's house, for temporary relief from her constant household pressures. But she never complained, at least not to her children, and, eventually, the pressure of her unhappy marriage became too much for her to bear.

The war between my parents escalated until one day in 1936, when my mother escaped. There were no warning signs. Her move came as a complete surprise, although her reasons were obvious. Life with Dad had become unbearable.

One morning, the moment Dad left for work, she grabbed her prepacked black battered suitcase, scooped up my sister, Stella, my baby brother, Leo, and me, and told us we were "going somewhere," although she wouldn't give specifics.

She told my brothers George and Danny they'd have to stay behind, a decision that George finds painful to this day. Danny, however, didn't even want to come. His accident had caused enough upheaval in his life and he could not endure another change. I'm sure that Mom wanted to take all her kids with her, but she could not afford the additional fare. I had a life savings of $45, which she used to purchase the train tickets. It must have been difficult for her to ask for the money.

To this day, I have never been able to understand fully how my mother could have left two of her children behind, no matter the circumstances. She had to take her two youngest, Stella and Leo, because they needed her most. I'm convinced that she took me with her for two reasons. First, because she needed one of her older children to help her, and at that age I was the most mature and responsible of my brothers. She also knew I had "street sense." But most importantly, Mom took me because I was then my father's favorite son. Taking me with her was her way of getting back at Dad, whom she had grown to hate.

We left without saying good-bye to anyone, slipping out of the house like thieves. One of our neighbors gave us a ride to the train station five blocks from our home.

Before we could board the train, Dad, with police in tow, caught up with us. We were standing on the platform waiting for our turn to board the train. Mom spotted him before he saw us. She panicked. Quickly, she pulled Stella, Leo, and me close and hid us until it was time to board the train.

I don't remember how long we were hiding, but soon I heard a wild commotion. I peeked out of our hiding place and could see my father consumed by rage. Just in case the police couldn't take care of the situation, he had brought a pistol—a silver Tom Mix six-shooter that was normally hidden on one of the top shelves in a closet at home. My brothers and I had often sneaked a look at the gun and even held it, always putting it back exactly the way our father had left it. I still don't know whether he meant to use the gun or he just wanted to scare my mother so badly that she would go back home. But I've always felt that had he found her in the station that day, it would have been bloody. While waving the gun, he repeatedly screamed out our names. I can only imagine Dad's anguish at the idea of my mother taking his children away. I assume Dad had enlisted the police to get his kids back, but when they saw him brandishing the gun, his plan backfired.

My next glance came just in time to see the police haul my father away. As they struggled to contain him, he continued to wave the gun over his head, shouting out our names and screaming, "Where are you?" Finally, the cops hauled Dad out of the station. The image of my father being hauled away by the police haunted me for the rest of the journey.

I had always suspected that Danny and George told him that we were leaving, but to this day they swear that they didn't. Today, I understand that Mom's escape was meant to be her liberation from an unhappy marriage. But I wanted to stay with my brothers. We were inseparable. We did everything together. Wherever we were going, and Mom never told us for sure, it meant I wouldn't be able to see them for a long time, if ever. I was only twelve and had no choice but to do what my mother said. Like most children who take far too much responsibility for their parents' problems, I also believed that Mom needed my help and that maybe I could help solve her problems.

It took us four days to get to our destination, which turned out to be New York City. It was bitter cold and snowing when our train pulled into Penn Station. No one was there to greet us. Being from the sunny San Joaquin Valley, where the winters were mild, did little to prepare us for the misery of constant snow and piercing cold. We took a cab to the Brooklyn home of my maternal grandmother's brother, Bill Babalis. His wife, Mary, a big, husky, hardworking German woman, showered us with attention. My mother immediately started working at a factory, and Stella and I enrolled at P.S. 72.

On one particularly bitter cold day, I returned from school and no one was home to let me inside. I didn't have a key, so I was forced to wait out in the cold for two hours. Two hours is an eternity in a freezing New York winter. I felt completely alone, and that single day outside convinced me that New York was not the place for me. I longed to go home to be with my brothers and cousins in sunny Stockton. I begged my mother to let me rejoin Danny and George, but she wouldn't let me go.

However, it soon became obvious that she had no choice but to send me home if she didn't want an emotionally sick child on her hands. After six months in New York, she allowed me to call Dad.

"Dad, I want to come home," I immediately said.

He sent a one-way ticket.

I boarded the train for the long ride home to Stockton. Mom, Stella, and Leo stayed behind. The moment I got on that train, I made a promise to myself never to leave Stockton again. I have often wondered whether that young boy's pledge so many years ago had any bearing on my decision to continue living in this small community even when my business began to expand and I was building residential and commercial projects across the U.S. "Why Stockton?" my business associates endlessly ask. "Why not San Francisco, L.A., New York?" I can never give them an answer that makes sense from a business perspective, except that Stockton is home and where I belong.

I traveled alone on the crowded train for four days. I don't remember the route, but I do remember changing trains in Chicago. Not many twelve-year-old boys were taking cross-country train trips by themselves in those days. My seat was next to a peddler. He kept me company and watched over me. When we pulled into Stockton, my dad and my brothers were waiting for me in the train station. The knot in my stomach that had been my constant companion for six months instantly disappeared. I was home and I felt whole again.

With the absence of half of his family, my father had eased up on George and Danny. He was much calmer and more solicitous of their feelings. When my mother took us away, he bought bicycles for Danny and George, a luxury he could ill afford. As soon as I returned I got a bike, too. My father did not discuss his feelings with his children. The bike was his way of telling me he missed me. I rode that bike for one whole week before it was stolen in front of the movie theater. I never got another bike.

For two-and-a-half years, it was just us boys.

Then Mom returned home. I don't know for sure what convinced her to come home, but most likely it was Stella, who was medically sick, and Leo, who was homesick. But although Dad accepted her back, he would never forgive her for taking his children away. Their conflicts continued until the day Dad died, although Mom never left her home and children again. After Mom's return, my youngest sister, Madeline, was born in 1940. Her birth didn't seem to bring my parents any closer. But separation and divorce, especially among immigrant families, was very rare in those days.

Mom's return brought a sense of normalcy back into our lives. We put the incident behind us and never spoke about it again. It was as if it had never happened. To the outside world all seemed well, and we felt content because once again we were together as a family. But it was never the same again for my parents. They lived the rest of their lives as unhappy with each other as they had been when Mom had tried her great escape—and failed.

By the 1930s, our financial situation had improved. Things had been looking up ever since Dad opened the second Roma Lunch around 1935. By 1938, Dad had bought a brand-new Buick. In 1940, he bought a house on Willow and Hunter Streets for $8,000, which he remodeled, little by little, by himself. Finally, in 1943, we moved into the house—and up in the world. Throughout this time, business at the Roma Lunch had picked up considerably. Stockton had become an important site for the war effort. Its shipyards were working around the clock. The increased activity brought increased prosperity for my family, and we became members of the middle class. There was money for tailor-made tuxedos and dance and piano lessons. In his spare time, Dad began cultivating an impressive garden, which became his pride and joy. Children were allowed to smell the flowers, but picking even one was a cardinal sin.

By our high school years, Dad had turned us into local stars; we performed at county fairs, schools, churches, *anywhere*. At halftime during Stockton High School football games, the crowed cheered for the Spanos Show. Our performance was frequently the highlight of the game. George and Stella became so skilled that they entered and won individual competitions with routines that pushed the envelope of baton-twirling mastery. As a group, we won both the regional and state baton-twirling championships.

We became master baton twirlers, bakers, and dutiful sons, working to win our dad's attention, respect, and love. Dad had specific dreams and exact plans for each one of us:

Danny and I would become engineers.

George was going to be an attorney.

Stella would get married to a industrious husband and have a brood of healthy children.

My father guided us through his grand scheme with an almost ruthless discipline and determination, never allowing any hardship or handicap to stand in his way.

I was my father's favorite, but I never lived up to his expectations. To him being somebody meant a profession—specifically Alex Spanos, Engineer, a role I never achieved. I would forsake his design for me, eventually entering a realm of even greater achievement. But there was no plan, not even a semblance of a direction. I drifted wherever the winds sent me.

In time, my years in the bakery made me one of Stockton's best bakers. I made everything: sourdough bread, apple turnovers, pastries, wedding cakes. For my sister Stella's marriage to local farmer Tom Graham, I spent three days creating a five-tier masterpiece with a scallop border; each scallop was made of dolls the exact color of her bridesmaids' dresses. But my specialty was doughnuts. I'd make three hundred dozen doughnuts a day and sell them to the farms surrounding Stockton. Dad bought a rickety truck in which I'd go forth, peddling two doughnuts for a nickel to farm workers in the fields within a twenty-mile radius of Stockton.

I was always exhausted. I couldn't concentrate on my studies; I'd fall asleep in class. My life had no balance. But I found time and energy to do what I loved most, palling around with buddies like Ben Pores, Skip Hewlett, Bert Mauer, Fred Chinchiolo, and Armando Minneto. We would go to the drive-in or the Stockton Ballroom, or skip school and drive to San Francisco for the day.

Dutiful George, who got his law degree, would fulfill Dad's dream for him.

I would boomerang back on Dad's doorstep, a failure in his eyes.

❖ ❖ ❖

While I was never a good student, barely passing my classes, I found ways to advance academically. I hatched one scheme with my best friend, Ben Pores, also a poor student. His father owned the local ice cream factory. In the evenings, we'd set out, Ben in his father's ice cream truck, I in my dad's bakery truck, delivering ice cream and cake to our teachers' houses, appealing to their sweet tooth for passing grades.

But my chief academic ally was Kay Ladas. I met Kay when I was fourteen. Bright and attractive, she came from a Greek-American family in our neighborhood. I met her through my older brother, Danny: he had taken Kay to a dance give by DeMolay, the Shriners' youth organization. Dad insisted that my brothers and I join DeMolay and that my sister become a Rainbow Girl. I met Kay at a black-tie DeMolay party.

She was both a beautiful and brilliant straight-A student. Pretty soon, we were a pair. Kay would spoil me, applying her A-plus knowledge to my C-minus homework and book reports. She coaxed me to study and made sure I was prepared for tests. She helped me to get through high school.

By the time I was sixteen, I was quite popular with the girls. I was never really handsome but I had something that girls seemed to like. Maybe it was my personality or my talent on the dance floor; the years of tap and tumbling mandated by my father had paid off. Whatever it was, girls were attracted to me. My brothers and cousins would follow me wherever I went. I was the pied piper; just as I'd once led them into trouble, now I led them to girls. "Let's go with Alex, because we'll always meet a girl," they'd say.

But my main girl was Kay. We attended all of the Greek-American events together: church socials, community picnics, AHEPA dinners, and any place where Greek music and food took center stage. In those days, Greek teens did not go on dates with each other, because the unspoken rule was that you could not "fool around" with your own kind. So Kay and I would meet at these functions. The common belief in Stockton's Greek community was that Kay and I would marry after high school. We graduated at the same time, thanks to her willingness to do my schoolwork for me. After graduation, Kay was accepted at the University of California at Berkeley, where she was elected a member of Phi Beta Kappa.

As for me, my high school counselor and English teacher, Mrs. Humbarger, advised me to enroll for an engineering degree at Cal Poly in San Luis Obispo, which was a good nearby school for engineers. I discussed it with Dad, who decided to send me and my older brother, Danny, to Cal Poly. Because Danny had lost a year of school due to his accident, we graduated in the same high school class. I decided to enroll in aeronautical engineering. My dream was to become a pilot. I had dreamed about piloting ever since I was seven, when Dad, awestruck by technology and wanting us to experience what it felt like to be on an airplane, took us up on a short flight in a two-passenger biplane at the nearby Orange Brothers Airport.

Dad had also once dreamed of becoming a pilot. When he had enlisted during World War I, he tried to sign up for pilot training, but he was not accepted. Every pilot was required to have mechanical knowledge and experience in airplanes, which Dad lacked. So he approved of my goal to become a pilot, as long as that goal included a college degree in engineering.

Kay and I continued to be close during college. I was in love with her, and I believed that she was in love with me. Whenever we were back in Stockton, mostly holidays and summer vacation, we'd see each other. But I never touched her. I didn't think I should—or could—out of respect for Greek traditions. She was the girl I was going to marry!

In college, all I wanted to do was have a good time. At first I pursued an engineering degree as decreed by my father. But I wasn't excited by my studies. Some of my friends had enlisted in the military. Bored and aimless, I followed the pack. The Japanese had attacked Pearl Harbor on December 7, 1941, and World War II was raging. I was eager to serve my country.

On February 9, 1942, at eighteen, I left college and signed up for three years and three months in the U.S. Air Force. I had taken my examination for cadet training, and I intended to become a pilot. I was thrilled and somewhat shocked when I learned that I'd passed the examination, although I later learned that I barely passed, scoring 116 when the passing grade was 110.

At least I was going somewhere. Alex Spanos, Pilot. I loved the sound of those words. My parents, brothers, and sisters all gave me a grand farewell at Stockton's Santa Fe train station. The train took me to Oakland, where I transferred to a train bound for Lincoln, Nebraska. The train was full of kids going to summer camp, but they had a set of berths set aside for the cadets. I was settling in on the lower berth when I heard somebody yell, "Hey, Greek!" I stuck my head out of my berth, and Jim Kourafas from Fresno stuck his head out of the berth right across from me, both of us thinking that someone was calling us. We both immediately knew we'd found a fellow Greek-American. We spent the rest of the trip talking and discovered we had everything in common. By the time we arrived in Lincoln, we were friends. Years later, Jim would introduce me to the businessman who would launch my career in construction.

It was snowing when we pulled into Lincoln, Nebraska. Even my six freezing months in New York had not prepared me for this kind of cold. We stayed in Lincoln, taking examinations, for thirty days.

From Lincoln, we were sent to Wayne State Teachers College, about forty miles from Sioux City, Iowa. It's a very small community, but the college had about 1,200 students—all women. I had landed in a dream: 250 cadets to 1,200 women. Our bunks were arranged in five flights, forty cadets per flight. I was made a flight lieutenant.

What a mistake that was! My flight was probably the wildest in the whole school. As the leader of the flight, I was always pursuing forbidden activities, especially interacting with the girls on campus. Jim Kourafas, who lacked the nerve to go up to a girl, would ask, "Where are you going, Alex?" I always took him with me. Although I dated a lot, I never fell in love. I felt that Kay was still my girl.

Our training was supposed to last six months. Every Saturday morning, there was a review of all the flights before the commanding officers. During one review, I heard my name being called over the loudspeaker: "Cadet Alex Spanos, report to the office." *My God, what have I done this time?* I thought. As I entered the captain's office, I saw a girl I knew sitting with a woman who was obviously her mother.

"Well, Cadet Spanos, you have a real big problem on your hands," the captain said.

"What's that, Captain?" I asked.

"You see that young lady out there?" he said, pointing through the glass window to the girl waiting in the adjoining office. "She claims she's pregnant with your child."

I felt the earth move under my feet. We had dated, but nothing more. I was not the father of her child, and why she had fingered me was a complete mystery. I explained the situation to Captain Starr. My words must have struck a chord with him, because after I finished he said, "I believe you. Unfortunately, I've only two choices. Either I have to wash you out and send you back to Santa Ana, or you can stay here and face the consequences."

I wasn't willing to take responsibility for something I hadn't done. I asked him to wash me out. My dreams of becoming an air force pilot would always remain dreams. My friend Jim Kourafas stayed on and became a pilot.

I guess I was never meant to be a pilot. Had I been one, how different would my life have been? Where would I be now, and what would I be doing? Once I arrived in Santa Ana, I begged the review board to send me again for cadet training somewhere else. It didn't matter where; all I wanted to do was fly. But the board turned me down. Instead, they sent me to the B29s, where I became a gunner.

I heard once that fate is the hand that life deals you, while destiny is what you do with that hand. I have been dealt some serious reverses. Being forced to leave cadet training was one of them. I regularly thank the air force brass for packing me off to Florida. Because of them I eventually met my future wife, the woman who brought to my life the light and direction I needed and instilled in me the strength to pursue and achieve my goals.

I am not an easy man to live with. I am convinced that there was only one woman in the world who could live with me and still love me. I had the good fortune to find her through an unexpected turn of events, which proved to me the existence of destiny and the opportunities that await each of us if we stay alert, open, and interested.

CHAPTER 4

Faye

"**W**here do you want to go to dinner?" I asked Kay Ladas one weekend when I was home from the service on furlough.

She was a junior at UC Berkeley. I had traveled three thousand miles with the express purpose of seeing her, calling her before I left base to say I was on my way. The moment I arrived in Berkeley, I rushed to her dormitory, swept her into my arms, and felt relief and release to be with her again.

But when I asked her where she wanted to go for dinner, Kay said she couldn't go anywhere. She had a date.

Her words stung. "Break it," I said.

She refused, attempting to pacify me with a flimsy excuse.

In that moment, everything changed. I had traveled three thousand miles to see the woman I had long believed I was going to marry, and she was standing me up for someone else.

It was *Tihi*, Greek for "Fate."

Although we had discussed marriage, I had never formally asked Kay to marry me. I believed it was understood. I didn't mind that she dated, as long as I was her first priority. But Kay apparently didn't want to commit her life to a lowly sergeant with an unsure future. Her image of a knight in shining armor apparently didn't include the apron of a baker. I felt that the excitement of Kay's new college life had made her look for more than what I had to offer.

I walked away, and that was the end of our relationship as far as I was concerned.

The air force sent me first to Colorado, then to Shreveport, Louisiana. From Shreveport, I was transferred to Drew Field in Tampa, Florida. You never know where you'll find your destiny, but I found mine a half hour from Tampa, in the sunny, seaside community of Tarpon Springs.

In those days, Tarpon Springs was predominantly populated by Greeks, most of whom had immigrated from a cluster of islands known as the Dodecanese. They had settled in Tarpon Springs to pursue what they knew best: fishing and diving. Tarpon Springs was famous for its Greek sponge divers and its sponge trade.

One day, I stood on a Tarpon Springs street corner in my uniform and watched my future walk by. She was gorgeous, with olive skin and curly coal-black hair, wearing a scarf around her neck. She was crossing the intersection of Tarpon and Pinellas Avenues. I immediately knew that she was Greek. Watching her cross the street, I put her on a pedestal—ethereal and untouchable. She never even glanced in my direction, but from that moment forward I had but one goal: to meet the black-haired girl.

One midnight, the Greek Orthodox church in Tarpon Springs delivered her to me.

It was the Saturday night of Easter weekend. My air force buddy Nick Mahleres and I had gone to the midnight Resurrection service at St. Nicholas Cathedral. Sitting in the pew in front of me was the black-haired girl. Once again, I couldn't take my eyes off of her. After the service, the Pappas family invited all of the soldiers to dine in their restaurant. It's a Greek tradition: when newcomers show up at church, the community will welcome them and invite them to dinner and other events. We were a group of young Greek-American soldiers, far away from home during the Easter season. We didn't know the Pappases, but that didn't matter to them. We were fellow Greek-Americans.

We all squeezed into Luke Pappas's car and headed for the restaurant. The black-haired girl, whose name I learned was Faye Papafaklis, had already gone home. I asked the Pappas brothers to invite Faye to dinner and to introduce me to her. They stopped and called her, and Faye accepted. When we arrived at Faye's house, the car was already packed. Luke Pappas and two of his friends occupied the front seat. The back was taken by me and my service buddies. When Faye came to the car, there wasn't a place for her to sit. "You can sit on my lap," I suggested to Faye.

She crawled in and sat right on the edge of my knees. I put my arms around her and pulled her back. "I won't bite," I said. "Sit back more comfortably." She did. Naturally, I was thrilled, but Faye looked embarrassed. She and I didn't speak much that night. She was surrounded by friends and relatives. She had known the Pappases her entire life, so we didn't have a second alone. After the night in the restaurant, I called her occasionally and would see her at church. Faye's family didn't believe in dating. Greek or not, I was off-limits for her.

The next time I saw Faye, I was on furlough with my buddies Nick Mahleres, John Mirageas, and Nick Pappas, soaking up the sun at Clearwater Beach, which was fantastic in those days. Lots of sand and a great boardwalk. There was a beach pavilion called Everinham, where everyone would dance to a jukebox. That Sunday, the beach was crowded with afternoon bathers. Suddenly, I saw Faye walking down the beach with her cousins, Mary, Pauline, Connie, Minnie, and Popi. Wasting no time, we rushed over to Faye and her cousins. "Oh, there's those boys we met in church," one of them said.

The whole group of us spent the rest of the day together. I was an accomplished swimmer and diver, having lettered in both in college. I always believed that if you have a talent, you should show it. So I began diving off the pier, trying to impress Faye. I picked her up and dove into the water with her in my arms. I asked Faye and her cousins when they would return to the beach, and they told me after church on Sunday afternoons and after the stores closed on Wednesday afternoons.

We all spent the afternoon together until six o'clock, dancing, swimming, and having water fights. Before she left, Faye asked all of us, "Don't you have girlfriends back home?"

Hoping to impress her, I pulled out my wallet and showed her two faded pictures: one of Kay from Stockton, the other of Vula Xeorogianis, an old girlfriend from San Francisco. But by the end of the afternoon, I knew I had room in my wallet for only one picture: Faye Papafaklis's.

I went home on leave the following week. But I found I couldn't get Faye out of my mind. I decided to send her a telegram, saying that I would return to Tarpon Springs soon and hoped to see her again. When I returned to Tarpon Springs, I saw Faye every chance I could. I couldn't take her out because her family wouldn't allow her to go out on dates. But we would meet on weekends at Clearwater Beach with her cousins, and a couple of times I convinced her and her brother, Michael, to meet me at the movies. By 9 P.M., she had to be home.

That was the extent of my relationship with Faye. I never made a pass at her, which was entirely out of character for me. I just felt great tenderness for her. I kept thinking how gorgeous she was. She was completely unspoiled. She had a luminous beauty and radiated a sense of calm and sweetness. I felt good just being around her. If I ever get married, I thought, I'll marry someone like Faye.

We came from similar Greek-American worlds. Faye's parents, Nikitas and Despina Papafaklis, had both emigrated from Simi, a small island in the Dodecanese, and had met and married in Tarpon Springs in 1924. Her dad was a cobbler. When Faye was two and her brother, Michael, was six months old, their mother died of cancer. Her dad, one of the kindest and gentlest souls I have ever met, was prompted by his parents to remarry for the sake of his young children. About a year after his wife's death, Nikitas Papafaklis married Elizabeth Milioratou, who was also from Simi and lived in his neighborhood. She loved his children as if they were her own and raised them with a lot of care and affection. Just like Faye's mother, her stepmother didn't live long. She died twelve years later, and her father never remarried. From then on, it was up to Faye, who had lost two mothers, to keep house for her dad and younger brother. Her family didn't have much.

I regularly returned home to my family during furloughs. But I still couldn't get Faye out of my mind. I would send her telegrams, telling her I'd like to see her again during my next furlough. I took weeks off at a time, spending most of it in Tarpon Springs seeing Faye. The more time we spent together, the more I thought I'd found my destiny, my future wife, the woman who would bring light and direction to my life, giving me the strength to pursue and achieve my goals.

At the end of 1945, I was transferred to Albany, Georgia. From there, I was sent back to Santa Ana, California, where I was discharged in February 1946 with the rank of staff sergeant. My dreams of becoming a pilot, born the moment Dad took my brothers and me to see our first airplane, had not materialized. But back in Stockton I began to take flying lessons. At twenty-three, thanks to my godfather's cosigning an $800 note at More Thrift Finance, I bought my first airplane, a BT13. Shortly afterwards, I received my pilot's license. I painted my name across the plane's nose and felt proud of my accomplishment, maybe too proud for my own good.

One day, I decided to fly to visit my cousin Gus, who was in a military hospital in Vallejo, California. My cousin Pete and I met at the Stockton airport, boarded my plane, and took off without incident. Once in the air, we flew over the Port of Stockton. I decided it would be a good idea to dive-bomb the port. I changed the pitch of the propeller and swooped down, getting close to the buildings. I must have been distracted, because I got lost. We had to land in Napa and ask for directions. We finally reached our destination, had a short visit with our cousin, and took off again for Stockton. I got lost again and wound up in the nearby town of Tracy. Cousin Pete had been in the air force before he went into the infantry. With twelve hours of flying time, he took over the plane, following Highway 99 back home. He let me land the plane once the runway was in sight.

My fledgling career as a pilot didn't last long. Flying to Santa Cruz one day with my buddy Freddy Chinchiolo, I had to make a crash landing, which terrified me. The landing gear cracked, and when I heard how expensive it would be to fix, I balked. I had the mechanic rig the gear so I could get home. After I landed the plane in Stockton, I never piloted an airplane again.

Soon after my crash landing, I called Faye and asked her if she would visit me in Stockton. I wanted her to meet my family. It was unheard-of in the Greek-American community for a young girl of eighteen to visit her boyfriend's house. But Faye consented to come, if my parents would write to her father and extend the invitation themselves. Dad surprised me by agreeing to write the letter. I still don't know how Faye overcame her father's objections to the trip. But she arrived in Stockton by train in June of 1946, and she fell in love with my family and relatives, all of whom immediately adored her. She stayed with us throughout that summer.

Throughout Faye's visit, I was leaning toward making a commitment to her, but I wasn't quite sure I was ready. When my cousin Gus Fotinos asked me to join him on a week's vacation to Catalina Island, I left Faye at home with my family and took off with Gus. It was not a wise move. The trip angered Faye. A few days later, when I took her to the train station to return home to Tarpon Springs, I could tell that she was holding back from me. I chose to ignore her mood and hoped that it would pass.

I didn't see her again until the following summer, June 1947, when I went to visit her in Tarpon Springs. I stayed at her house. Her father and I bonded over rods and reels and tales of fish that got away. Despite his chosen profession of cobbler, Faye's father loved to fish. On one of our fishing trips, we stayed out on the boat all day. Not thinking that I could get sunburned through an overcast sky, I took off my shirt and got sunburned so badly that my whole back blistered. For the next few days, I suffered excruciating pain. Faye nursed me with total devotion. I thought I'd be crazy not to get down on my hands and knees and beg her to marry me. *What was I waiting for? What other proof did I need that this girl was perfect for me?*

I bought a ring. For the next few days I carried it in my pocket, afraid to make the commitment, both to Faye and to myself. One early afternoon, still trying to recover from my sunburn, I took the ring out of my pocket and showed it to Faye.

"Look, Faye, I'm really not good enough for you, and you'd be crazy if you accepted this ring," I said.

It wasn't the most romantic of proposals, but it was the only way I knew. I was commitment-phobic, and I really didn't think I was good enough for sweet, kind, faithful Faye Papafaklis. My parents' long-running war had not made marriage appealing. Because I was more like my father than any of my siblings, I feared that I would repeat his pattern of marital neglect. But Faye was undaunted by my lack of sentimentality. Without a word, she took the ring and put it on her finger. I could tell that she was excited. She immediately ran to tell her father of our engagement.

I returned to Stockton; Faye remained in Tarpon Springs. I enrolled in the College of the Pacific, known today as the University of the Pacific, where I attended classes for the next two years. I eventually dropped out, and never received my college diploma. Of my parents' older kids, I was the only one still around. My older brother, Danny, had just reenlisted in the army. My younger brother George, discharged from the service in the same year as I, enrolled in the Hastings School of Law in San Francisco, which made Dad tremendously proud. The only thing I knew how to do well was work at a restaurant.

When Dad decided to remodel the Roma Lunch and Bakery, we agreed that I would go in the business with him as a partner. I soon had a tough eye-opener. The partnership turned out to be all promises. For three years, every time I brought it up, he would ignore me.

After our engagement, Faye and I discussed getting married soon, but once again, I began having second thoughts. My Uncle Chris urged me on. "This is not a girl you find every day," he said. "She is one in a million, one in a hundred million." But being home again with Mom and Dad brought back all my reservations about marriage. I hadn't counted on Faye's subtle way of persuasion.

In December of 1947, I sent a plane ticket to Faye to spend Christmas with my family and me. It didn't turn out to be much of a Christmas, because on the day of Faye's arrival, my sister Stella became seriously ill with ulcerated colitis and was sent to Stockton's St. Joseph's Hospital. The doctors wanted to perform a colostomy, removing her intestines and sentencing her to a colostomy bag for the rest of her life.

"No!" my father bellowed. "I'd rather see her *dead* than have her wear a bag!"

It was the scene from Danny's accident all over again. Dad picked up Stella and carried her out of the hospital, with all of the nurses following him, insisting that he couldn't take her without following proper procedure.

"Does anybody want to try to stop me?" Dad asked.

They didn't. However, they refused to send an ambulance to transfer Stella to the University of California Hospital at San Francisco; they didn't think she would survive the trip. So Dad called an ambulance and followed in his car. Stella stayed in the UC hospital for the next two months. Her condition was not improving. After a week, the doctors said her problems were stress-related, caused by the constant conflict in our home.

For the first week of her hospital stay in San Francisco, my mother remained with Stella, while Faye took care of my brother Leo, then twelve, and my sister Madeline, then seven. Then Faye took my mother's place in San Francisco to be with my sister for the remaining two months. Even though Faye was only two years older than Stella, she became like a mother to her. Because Faye was essentially raised without a mother, she was accustomed to being the head of the household. Stella had been coddled and sheltered by my parents. They wouldn't even allow her to go to her senior prom unless my brother George chaperoned. Stella grew to depend on Faye. It was through Faye's devotion to Stella that I realized the depths of Faye's devotion to me.

Stella eventually returned home, but her condition was still critical. She couldn't take care of herself and was bedridden most of the time. My parents hired a night nurse. When the nurse would leave at 7 A.M., Faye would take over her care. Faye and I didn't get to see much of each other. I was working night and day at the restaurant, and she was busy with my sister every day. I knew it was a tough burden for Faye to carry, but I didn't know *how* tough it was until one morning, the first week of July of 1948, she announced she was going home. I couldn't talk her out of it. She said she missed her father and brother, but I felt that she was only telling half the truth. She had stayed with us for seven months and had worked hard to help my family during an incredibly tough time. "And if there is going to be a wedding, it will be in Florida, not Stockton," she told me ominously as she was leaving. I felt that Faye's farewell statement insinuated that I might lose her, something I was not at all prepared to do.

After Faye returned to Tarpon Springs, my old girlfriend Kay Ladas and her mother came to our house. It was the night before Kay's wedding to another young man, who ran a restaurant with his father in Los Angeles. Shockingly, the purpose of their visit was to talk to me and to my parents about Kay. Would I reconsider and make up with Kay? they wanted to know. I had been in love with Kay since I was fourteen, but there was nothing she could say that would change my mind. I had met Faye, who accepted and loved me unconditionally, something that Kay had never been able to do. "I'm sorry, but I can't forget the day I traveled three thousand miles to see you and you refused to have dinner with me," I said. "For me, that was the end of our relationship, and I would like to leave it at that."

The following day my parents and I went to Kay's wedding. "This could have been for us," she whispered to me during our one dance.

The last time I saw Kay was years ago at our fortieth high school reunion. I attended the reunion with Faye, and although seeing Kay brought back a flood of memories, I didn't have much to talk about with her. All night long, she kept reminding me that I would never have graduated from high school without her help. She was absolutely right about that. But as I sat among my classmates, I silently thanked Kay for opening my life to Faye.

Once Faye had gone, I knew that if I didn't visit her soon, I might lose her.

So within a month, I was on my way to Tarpon Springs, resolved to marry Faye while I was there. But as soon as I arrived, I got cold feet again. I avoided the subject entirely, as did Faye. She was proper in every way. The days stretched on without a word about a wedding, until one day when we were driving to Clearwater Beach with Faye's cousin Fran, her newlywed husband, Tony Tulumaris, and our friend Nick Cladakis. The conversation turned to Faye's cousin Pauline, who had just gotten married that week. I knew I was on dangerous ground with this kind of talk, but I also knew that Faye would never mention our plans unless I brought up the subject first. However, I hadn't considered cousin Fran, who was very protective of Faye and quite outspoken. In the middle of our drive to the beach, Fran directed her gaze at me and asked bluntly, "Well, when are you two getting married?"

"Unfortunately, there isn't enough time on this trip," I told Fran. "I have to leave by Monday to get back to work at the restaurant. Otherwise," I added, "this would have been a good time."

"When did you say you are leaving?" Fran persisted.

"Monday," I said.

We were having this conversation on Wednesday, so I thought I was pretty safe. There would be no way that anyone could arrange a Greek wedding, with all its elaborate preparations, in just four days.

"Don't worry," Fran said. "We'll take care of everything. We'll have the wedding on Sunday."

For the next three days, Fran did the planning. Faye's relatives arranged for her cousin Pauline's bridesmaids to be in our wedding. Instead of invitations, they published a notice in the local paper that we were getting married on Sunday, August 22, at 3 P.M., adding, "All friends are invited." Fran arranged for the reception at the Stratford Hotel. "All you have to do, Alex, is be at the church with your best man on Sunday afternoon," Fran told me.

I had come to Tarpon Springs to get married, and there was no way to back out now. On Sunday, August 22, we got married at St. Nicholas Cathedral in Tarpon Springs, with my best man, Nick Cladakis, at my side. Everything was in place and nothing was lacking—except that not one single member of my family was in attendance. The wedding had been arranged so hastily that neither my parents nor any of my siblings or relatives had time to fly from Stockton to be at my side. But everything else looked as if the wedding had been planned for months.

Faye's father, normally a very quiet man, danced at the reception. I was told that was the first time he had ever done that. While dancing, my new father-in-law pulled all of the coins and cash from his pockets and threw it over our heads, a traditional Greek gesture. It was a portent of good things to come.

Immediately after the reception, we left Tarpon Springs by car for California as Mr. and Mrs. Alex Spanos. On our way home, we stopped in Tampa, then drove up to Price, Utah, to visit my army buddy Nick Mahleres and his wife, Helen, who had married the year before. Then we made our way back home to Stockton.

We moved in with my parents for financial reasons. Things had gotten tough back home. Our restaurant had primarily served the agricultural workers and the community on Skid Row. Stockton had been a wide-open town. But by the late forties, the city had cracked down and closed the gambling joints and the houses of prostitution, leaving behind an empty downtown where a boomtown had once raged. The impact on the family business was immediate and severe.

Faye helped at the house and the restaurant, and we began saving for our own place. During that time, my sister Stella had a relapse of her colitis. Once again, Faye nursed her back to health. Faye never complained about the increasing demands my family made on her, but I could see how hard she worked at pleasing everybody. I knew in my heart she wanted to move out of my parents' house as much as

I did. We were both ready to be on our own. After seven months, we finally moved into our first apartment at Eden Square on El Dorado Street. It had one room and a wall bed. We barely fit within its walls, but I'll never forget our relief and pride over having our own place. Our rent was $40 a month.

CHAPTER 5

The Power of Family

I didn't start out to fulfill a "get-rich" fantasy. All I sought was security and peace of mind for my family. That was the goal; the rest occurred because of hard work. But I couldn't have accomplished much without my wife, Faye, and our children, Dean, Dea, Alexis, and Michael. My greatest assets are my family members. My private office is a virtual gallery of hundreds of family photos, and I look at them constantly with love, pride, and gratitude.

I owe everything to Faye and her unconditional love and support. Faye gave me something I didn't have, something I could never have found on my own: peace of mind. There is nothing I prize more than the knowledge that everything is well at home with my family. No matter how badly things go in business and the outside world, I have always been sustained by knowing I could return to someone who truly loves me. I have traveled almost every week of my business life, sometimes two or three days, sometimes longer. And I breathe an audible sigh every time I return home to my own private sanctuary where the rest of the world rarely intrudes.

Faye and I have now been married for over fifty years and I don't recall one real argument. Sure, there were times when I would try to pick a fight over the smallest excuse: the food didn't have enough salt, the air conditioning wasn't cold enough…just to see whether she would take the bait. Faye never did. She'd brush off my attempts in her own inimitable way, letting me know that she'd read me loud and clear. She is a woman of strong values and principles, and she has distinct opinions of her own. Her approach to life and life's hardships is to accept them with a sense of serenity. Whenever I disappointed her with something I did or said, Faye never said a word. Instead, she would give me the silent treatment. She would simply refuse to acknowledge me. It was as if I had fallen out of favor in the eyes of this graceful, gentle, and generous woman, which was a state that I couldn't bear too long.

A few years ago, my oldest daughter, Dea, was going through a very painful divorce. During one of our many heart-to-heart talks, Dea told me, "Dad, you and Mom were unfair to us. I grew up in a home where there were no fights and no arguments. I've never heard you once yell at each other. I had no idea that marriages could be like the one I had." I realized that maybe Dea was right. Although Faye and I have not sheltered our children, perhaps we hadn't prepared them for the rigors of the outside world. They grew up in a large, decidedly ethnic and boisterous family, with many cousins, aunts, and uncles always around. They attended public schools and lived a generally normal small-town life. They grew up in a house of unconditional love, and I credit Faye not only for that but also for everything that sprang from it: our strong marriage, our close family, and the business success I have enjoyed.

For me, family is everything, and everything good in my life began with family.

❖ ❖ ❖

For some people, maturity comes with age. For me, it developed with responsibility. I never realized that I was fully accountable for my actions until 1950, when my oldest son, Dean, was born. The responsibility I felt for him was powerful. For the first time, I began to realize that I had my own family, separate and apart from my father's, and that I alone was responsible for making a good life for them.

I was twenty-six years old when Dean was born. Up until that point, my life had been simply a succession of events taken for granted. I was flighty, doing this, doing that. Life didn't mean much beyond my own needs and desires. By contrast, even though Faye is two-and-a-half years younger than I, she was mature. She had lost two mothers. She took care of her brother and her father. Dean's birth enriched my life with a sense of meaning and purpose that I had never experienced before. I had a son to look after, and with his birth came the realization that my future had become inextricably tied to his. The surge of pride and joy I felt looking at my son infused me with renewed energy. I worked harder and longer.

When Faye became pregnant with our second child, our already cramped home became intolerable. We moved to a duplex that my father owned on Vine and Sutter Streets. I worked hard at the bakery, but without ambition. I felt that the bakery wasn't truly my own. When Faye and I married, my father had raised my salary to $40 a week. With one baby at home and another on the way, I knew I needed more.

My father was the patriarch in every sense of the word. He felt it was his duty to provide everything he thought we needed. We, in turn, had to abide by his wishes unquestioningly. The relationship worked as long as none of us challenged it. It seemed to me that, in Dad's eyes, I was no better than or different from any other employee. I had ideas for streamlining production and making the restaurant more efficient, but he wouldn't listen. His response was always the same: "Call your brother George and see what he thinks." My brother

George was, of course, the young lawyer. Never mind that law had nothing to do with doughnuts. To my father, I was just a lowly baker, a college dropout. I couldn't possibly know anything. In the three years I worked for him without a single day off, he mostly ignored and disregarded me. Once, I had been his favorite, but I lost that position the moment I dropped out of college. I had failed him and there was nothing I could ever do to make it up to him.

On the morning of July 1, 1951, after a night's work, I summoned my courage and told Dad I needed an extra $35 a week to support my family. I didn't even have time to finish the request before he turned me down. "*Afise me,*" he said in Greek, which means "Leave me alone." Then he waved his hand in dismissal. Without another word, he went back to work.

Today, my siblings insist that it wasn't that Dad didn't want to give me a raise; he just didn't have the money. The loss of restaurant clientele, coupled with the estimated $35,000 he'd spent on Stella's illness, had just tapped my father out, they insist. But because Dad never even suggested that this might be the cause of his refusal, I felt he just didn't believe I deserved the raise.

That night, I went home and told Faye what had happened and that I was ready to quit the bakery. We had nothing. Nothing in the bank. Not even a real house to live in. At twenty-five, Faye was eight months pregnant with Dea, our first daughter. With one child at home and another on the way, there are a lot of things she could have said. She could have asked me how I expected to support her and the children. She could have infused me with fear about the uncertainty of unemployment. But she didn't. You have to meet my wife to really know the inspiration that woman has given me. She looked at me— with one baby to feed and another on the way, living in a one-room apartment, with no guarantee of anything—and she said, "Alex, you do what you think is best for all of us." Faye's confidence gave me the strength I needed to stand up to my father.

At eight o'clock the next morning, after working all night in the bakery, I walked through the bakery's basement door, climbed the stairs, and found my father in the restaurant kitchen. I took off my apron, looked Dad in the eye, and said, "Dad, if you don't give me a raise, I'm quitting in two weeks."

No response. Absolutely nothing. Two weeks later, I once again walked upstairs from the bakery into the restaurant kitchen. I took my apron off and I hung it on the meat cleaver for the last time.

I loved Dad and dreaded confronting him, but I had made up my mind. He had left me no choice. Backing down meant that I had to be content with $40 a week. My conflict with my father was not merely about money; it was about asserting my own identity. This was something I had to do for myself and my family.

"Dad," I said in Greek, "I hope you found somebody else. This is my last day."

He was the patriarch and couldn't believe that I would leave him. He looked at me, pointed a finger, and screamed, "You!" His voice was filled with derision. Dad was worse than a Doberman when he bared his teeth. I was a married man with one child and another on the way, but he still treated me like an errant child. He gritted his teeth and screamed through a snarl.

"You're going to quit? You? You're going to crawl back here on your hands and knees and beg for this job!"

Now I couldn't back down even if I wanted to.

"Dad," I replied, "if I have to come back here on my hands and knees for this job, I'd just as soon blow my brains out."

And I walked out the door. Dad didn't speak to me for almost two years. I had challenged his authority and then defied him. He would neither forgive nor forget. Was I hurt? You bet. I realized that in my father's eyes I was a good-for-nothing. He gave me one more reason to go out and do something with my life.

One day, I promised myself, I would show him.

❖ ❖ ❖

I had no idea what to do next. For the next two weeks, I agonized over my prospects.

Faye's due date came and with it our beautiful daughter. We named her Despina Elizabeth—Despina after Faye's mother, Elizabeth after her stepmother—and called her Dea for short. I still had no job and no money, much less the $210 to pay my wife and baby's hospital bill. As the hour approached for their release, I hurriedly tried to borrow the cash. First I went to my Uncle Chris. It never occurred to me that he would say no, but he did. I asked my other relatives. They all said no. No one would cross Dad by lending me money.

Finally, I went to a high school friend, Ray Kossich, who owned Tiny's, a downtown restaurant and café. When I asked him for the loan, Ray said, "Come on, Alex, let's go to the bank." He cosigned a $200 note, and I was able to pay the bill to bring Faye and Dea home from the hospital.

The loan alleviated one problem, but I still had no income to sustain my family. I'd left the bakery on July 15. Dea was born on July 31. A month later, I was still unemployed, with no ideas except that I wouldn't take a conventional 9-to-5 job. After working for my father for so many years, I was determined never to work for anyone else again. But what skills did I have? Only baking and delivering doughnuts to farm workers. Buying or opening a restaurant of my own was out of the question. If I had to borrow money from the bank to get my wife and baby out of the hospital, I clearly did not have the capital to undertake a business venture.

But then I saw an opportunity right in my own backyard. Farms encircled Stockton. I knew a lot of the farmers from my days peddling doughnuts for Dad. The farmers employed workers, mostly Filipinos and Mexicans, to plant and harvest their crops. Close to half a million Mexican farm workers circulated through the central valleys of California every harvest season during those years. I suddenly realized that if the farm workers needed doughnuts for breakfast, wouldn't they need sandwiches for lunch? Immediately, a path seemed to stretch out before me: I launched my career as a sandwich peddler.

The first question was simple: what kind of sandwiches to sell? I chose bologna for one reason: it was the cheapest meat. I could buy bologna and bread from the grocery. Faye and I could make the sandwiches at home. All I needed was a truck.

I told Faye about my idea. "We're going to make and deliver sandwiches to the labor camps!" I said.

"That's a great idea, Alex!" she said, as supportive as ever.

I figured I needed $1,500 to launch my sandwich catering business. I asked all my relatives for a loan, and, once again, fearing my father's wrath, they turned me down. So I went to see Ernie Segale, branch manager of the local Bank of America. I knew Ernie through my father and figured that he'd at least give me a chance. Dressed in my customary khakis, T-shirt, and boots, I laid out my plan to the banker.

The Bank of America had been founded on the principle of supporting "the little guy." Its founder, Amadeo Peter Giannini, began his banking career in the early 1900s, when banks mainly served the wealthy. Giannini was a pioneer: he gave hardworking immigrants and the working class home mortgages, auto loans, and installment credit. He was also a visionary, making loans to up-and-coming industries like the early California wine industry and bankrolling Hollywood studios before the motion picture industry had been proven viable. I was one of the multitudes who received Giannini's financial assistance.

I can still see the Bank of America branch manager looking me straight in the eye. "Alex, I know you to be a hard worker," Ernie Segale said. "But I'm not allowed to give you $1,500. I'll tell you what I can do. I can give you $800. That's the maximum I'm allowed, because I need authorization for anything above that. I know that you can make this work out."

I stretched the $800 as far as I could, buying a cheaper-than-planned panel truck, a slicing machine, a meat cleaver, bologna, bread, and sandwich condiments. Bologna became the bedrock of the A. G. Spanos Agricultural Catering Service. Faye and I spent our nights making the sandwiches in our kitchen, and then I'd get up early to drive to the farms. The farmers liked me and welcomed my truck on their ranches. They knew I worked hard and I always made friendly conversation during my rounds. The farmers would buy the sandwiches and deduct the cost from the workers' wages. Before I began my catering business, the farmers fed their own workers—and the meals were meager at best. By the end of each day, my truckload of 250 sandwiches would be sold. The first few weeks, from about August 1 to August 20, went smoothly.

Then I saw another opportunity within the original one. Time and time again, the farmers would ask me the same thing: "Alex, we need more workers to harvest our crops. Do you know where we can get some braceros?" Braceros was the term used back then for Mexican laborers.

Every night I'd go home and tell Faye, "Dammit, these guys keep asking me for Mexican laborers."

I've always believed in supply and demand. It was a natural progression: the more laborers, the more sandwiches I could sell. The farmers on my sandwich route couldn't afford to leave their farms in search of labor. They needed my help. A bell went off deep in my brain, in the lobe that senses opportunity if you stay open to it.

I got excited. "If I can deliver sandwiches to the farms, why can't I deliver laborers?" I told Faye.

Asking around, I discovered that the Mexican border town of El Centro was a main point where Mexican farm laborers had migrated across the border in the past. Because of an agricultural labor shortage during World War II, Congress enacted the Mexican Bracero Program, encouraging temporary importation of farm workers from

Mexico. From 1942 to 1964, four million Mexican farm workers were employed by the U.S. agricultural industry. At its peak in 1956, about 445,000 Mexican workers were admitted to the U.S. annually for employment. Supported by both the U.S. and Mexican governments, the program stipulated that the laborers return back to Mexico after each year's harvest was completed. The cash they'd bring back to their country would be a sorely needed infusion into the Mexican economy. (However, I didn't know about the bracero program when I heard about El Centro.) "I'm going down to El Centro and find out how can I get some laborers and bring them back here," I told Faye. Always supportive, Faye encouraged me to move forward. I sensed that this might be another case where I had stumbled into precisely the right place at the right time.

One morning, with twenty dollars in my pocket, the same amount my father had when he first left Greece for America, I began the journey that would radically change my life. I boarded a bus from Stockton to El Centro. It's hard to describe how bad buses to Mexico were in those days. It was August, 106 degrees, with no air conditioning, and I was embarking upon a long and miserable eighteen-hour trip. We arrived in a tiny town without even a bus terminal. The bus just dropped us off in the middle of the street. El Centro's population of three hundred lived in sweltering, dusty squalor. There was one cheap little hotel, probably built in the late 1800s. Again, no air conditioning. But for two dollars a night, it was within my budget.

I had no plan, no contacts, and absolutely no idea how to recruit farm labor. But in that border town I instituted the strategy that has served me exceedingly well throughout my business career: I played it by ear. I had no other choice. I had taken the trip on faith, and that faith immediately paid off.

After checking into the hotel, I began asking around about farm labor. A meeting was being held in one of the hotel's meeting rooms for farmers seeking braceros. At first, I thought maybe someone else had the same idea I had. I decided to go to the meeting uninvited. I entered the room, which was packed with people. Right in the middle, there was a group of men wearing cowboy hats listening to this one man. I walked up to them and listened to what was being said.

Certain moments in my life reaffirm my belief in the power of fate. This is one of the big ones. Staying alert to opportunities is like fine-tuning the reception on a radio. Unless you keep your mind clear and open, you'll never hear the music. On this day, I was dialed in perfectly to the station of fate and good fortune. I stood right next to the speaker, who was holding the attention of the other men. I was a twenty-seven-year-old kid, completely in the dark about what was going on. I knew only a little Spanish, but I knew enough to understand that the man was talking to the farmers about the bracero program.

Suddenly, he stopped talking to the men and turned to me.

"And who are you?" he asked.

"I'm Alex Spanos," I replied.

"Where you from?"

"Stockton, California."

"How about that! I'm from Stockton, too!" he exclaimed extending his hand. "My name is Bill Duarte."

He was a tall Portuguese farmer and I liked him immediately.

"What are you doing down here?" Bill Duarte asked me.

"I'm here to find laborers for farmers in Stockton," I said.

"What do you know about that!" he said. "I just formed the San Joaquin Farm Production Association, and I'm here to bring back 350 braceros to the San Joaquin Valley."

He told me the names of the farmers he represented. His list included all of the farmers on my sandwich route.

"Do you speak Spanish?" he asked me.

I spoke only a little Spanish. But not wanting to give Bill Duarte any reason to doubt me or my abilities, I relied on what would become another hallmark in my business career: I bluffed.

"Yes, of course I speak Spanish," I said.

Bill Duarte smiled.

"Tomorrow morning, six o'clock, I'll pick you up," he said. Then he turned his attention back to the men in the cowboy hats.

I went to bed that night feeling as if I had made some progress.

The next morning, Bill introduced me around El Centro. I met everyone from local farmers to Javier Escobar, the general consul of Mexico for the United States.

"You know," Bill Duarte said as we drove around El Centro, "I'm going to need housing for the 350 braceros I'm bringing back to Stockton. Do you know where I can house them?"

I had no earthly idea where to house 30 men, much less 350. But once again, I acted reflexively.

"Yes," I said. "I've got just the spot."

"Where's that?" Bill asked.

"Don't worry about it," I replied. "You'll like it when you see it."

"You mentioned you were in the restaurant business," Bill Duarte continued.

"Yes, I am," I said, not knowing where he was leading.

"Well, I have to find somebody to feed all these people," he said. "Can you handle it?"

Once again my voice spoke up before any logic could stop it. I figured I could worry about the details, including what Bill Duarte and the farmers might pay me for my work, later; the important thing was not to let opportunity slip away.

"Sure, I'll take care of that, too," I said. "No problem."

"Great," said Bill. "I'll be back in Stockton in four days. When are you going home?"

It was a Friday. I had until Tuesday to get things arranged for him.

"Immediately," I said. "I'll have everything ready for you when you get back on Tuesday."

I knew I was in way over my head, but there was no way I could pass up this unbelievable stroke of luck and opportunity. On the eighteen-hour ride back to Stockton, I kept thinking how the farmers back home would be impressed when they heard about the 350 workers that were on their way to their fields. Only twenty-four hours before, I had nothing. Now I was returning home with a verbal contract for a business bigger than anything I had ever imagined. By sheer luck I had met Bill Duarte, and he had put his trust in me.

But where would I find housing for 350 men?

Back home, I excitedly told Faye the good news. Not only was she typically encouraging and optimistic, but she led me straight to the place where I would find housing for the workers. Faye wanted to visit the San Joaquin County Fair, which had just opened for the season. A great annual attraction for the area residents, the fair consisted mostly of displays by local farmers showing off products and livestock. As Faye and I walked around the fair that night, we soon arrived at the vegetable exhibit, which was housed in a massive building about 300 feet long and 150 feet wide.

Once again, opportunity practically stood up and slapped me in the face.

I turned to Faye and said, "I could put three hundred beds in here!"

The fair's director, Ed Vollman, was a family friend. He lived right across the street from my parents. The next day, I went to Ed's house and told him that I wanted to rent the building, although I didn't have any money to pay him—not yet, anyway. "Alex, whatever you want, don't worry about it," Ed said. He said I could pay the rent whenever I got the money. And just like that, I'd found housing for 350 workers. When Bill Duarte arrived, he liked what he saw.

Having arranged for the housing accommodations, I next had to find 350 beds, mattresses, and blankets. I went to the Phillips Forwarding surplus store, which was owned by our old family friend John Phillips. I told John that I needed 350 beds, 350 mattresses,

350 blankets and pillows, and enough kitchen equipment to feed 350 men. "I don't have the money to pay you yet," I told John, "but I will soon."

John trusted me, advanced me the equipment, and even helped me build a crude kitchen. We piped in gas and built a platform on which we could make sandwiches, boil beans, and serve the meals. It was almost magical how smoothly everything fell in place. The whole thing came together in less than thirty days, and the A. G. Spanos Agricultural Catering Service was headed into the big leagues.

The 350 Mexican nationals arrived in an armada of buses on September 15, 1951. Beds, kitchen, and tables for meals were all in place. The farmers paid me $1.75 per day per man. My cost was 75 cents per man. After making breakfast, lunch, and dinner, I still pocketed $1 profit per man per day.

I didn't take the responsibility of housing and feeding 350 men lightly. These were the days long before today's mass illegal immigration along the U.S.-Mexico border. The workers were coming to Stockton, where they had no place to sleep and nothing to eat. If I hadn't made provisions, they would have slept in the fields instead of the beds I provided, and they would have eaten whatever the farmers could scrounge instead of the three meals that I served them each day. These days, many immigrants who come to America, sometimes legally, sometimes not, are horrendously exploited. But during the 1950s bracero program, the exodus of laborers from Mexico was well organized, and their stay, at least in the accommodations that I provided, was both suitable and nourishing.

For ninety days, I housed and fed the farm workers. By December, when the harvest was over and I paid all my bills, I had $35,000 in the bank. Four months after walking out of my father's bakery, I had made more money than I had made in twenty years of baking. I owe enormous thanks to Bill Duarte for opening the door for me, to Ed Vollman and John Phillips for having faith in me, and to the local farmers and ranchers, like Frank Pellegri and the Marchini family, who opened their farms and ranches to me. They had all trusted a twenty-seven-year-old to do a good and honest job.

With the $35,000, I told Faye to pay cash for our first house. She found one on Leesburg Place. I told her to take $6,000 and furnish our new home. We paid cash for our very first car, a brand-new navy blue 1952 Lincoln Continental. I had one last thing to do. Dad was still deep in debt as a result of my sister Stella's illness. He owed $3,500 to the bank and $7,000 to one of my uncles. I paid off all of his debts.

Finally, I turned my attention to my mother. I had promised her that someday, somehow, I would give her the things she had never had. I bought her the first full-length dress she ever owned, a fur coat, and much more. It brought me tremendous joy to give something back to the woman who had shown me so much love and care.

The following year, I moved my catering operation to the Stockton Metropolitan Airport, which had old army barracks and a large and roomy mess hall with tables and chairs already in place to house and feed the braceros. This was a far better setup than the hasty accommodations I had originally arranged. It soon became clear that what I had first fed the braceros—boiled beans and bologna sandwiches—was not an appropriate menu for their diet. They were accustomed to rice and beans, tortillas, and beef or pork. So the next year I bought a tortilla machine, hired Mexican cooks, and served the laborers their favorites dishes. Within a year, I was feeding and housing 1,500 braceros each harvest season.

My success story had begun, based on faith, fueled by the grace and good deeds of others, and fed by the ability to recognize and seize opportunity. I gained some much needed confidence for the journey ahead.

CHAPTER 6

By the Grace of Golf

I continued to house and feed farm workers for the next nine years. Since the bulk of my business was with Mexican nationals, Faye and I regularly entertained the Mexican consulate and other Mexican government officials at our home. We traveled to San Francisco, Los Angeles, and Mexico City to meet with the officials. It was all part of basic public relations, and as a result my business grew rapidly.

By 1956, five years after I quit the bakery, I was preparing seven thousand meals a day. I was still making almost 60 percent profit on the fee I charged the farmers to feed their workers. By the end of that year's harvest, I had cleared almost $700,000, which was an unbelievable amount of cash for those days. One day, my accountant, Herb Bowman, whom I had retained in 1951, called me to say that I was paying too much in taxes. "I suggest you find some real estate investments and take advantage of some tax shelters," he told me.

His suggestion put me in the perfect place at the perfect time, specifically in Stockton and in California at large.

During World War II, everything from aerial bombs and airplane parts to the reconditioning of army trucks and motors made the civilian work force swell in Stockton. The city's military installations, the Stockton Naval Base and Stockton Field, transformed our town. Stockton became the supply base for the American Pacific forces. The city's growth mirrored what was happening across California, where federal defense spending was revolutionizing what had been a primarily farm-based economy. Stockton's population swelled. Emergency housing and military barracks were thrown up hastily in and around the city to keep pace with demand. The city was bursting at the seams.

After World War II, Stockton's metropolitan area had extended its boundaries as the county planning commission allowed a new development of a virgin area north of town. During the fifties, housing complexes sprang up north of the river on the fertile soil that had been used for farming, changing Stockton's complexion from a settled farm community to a rapidly sprawling town. Because of this growth, Stockton needed housing.

As in my experience in feeding and housing migrant workers, I knew absolutely nothing about real estate. But I kept my mind clear and open to whatever opportunities might come my way. I followed my accountant's advice. I called some local realtors and began buying real estate. By 1956, I had bought three buildings: a $110,000 building in Stockton, a $220,000 five-story San Francisco apartment building, and a $200,000 San Jose office building. The real estate investments gave me some needed tax shelter. I was able to write off the buildings' expenses plus depreciation, or operating expenses. At the same time, I began dabbling in land deals. I bought land in San Jose for $5,000 an acre, and six months later I doubled my money by selling it for $10,000 an acre, which I immediately reinvested in more real estate.

Soon, I had the opportunity to buy my first parcel of raw land outside of the northern California town of Gilroy. The price was approximately $300,000, but I had only $150,000 in the bank. I took my brother George with me to ask Ernie Segale, still at the Bank of America, for a loan.

Ernie looked at my financial statement and shook his head. "I can't do it, Alex," he said. "You're overextending. You have a loan here, a loan there, and this one would put you too close to the edge."

As we walked out of the bank, my brother George said, "If I were you, I wouldn't do business with them anymore."

I was upset, but not as angry as George. Ernie Segale had given me a chance when no one else would. I turned to George and said, "That bank will never say no to me again. From this day forward, I'll make sure I'm never turned down for a loan."

And that was the last time it happened. I vowed never to overextend myself and never to have to depend on a lender to make or break a deal. I decided to ensure that I always had enough cash to cover anything I ventured into, whether it was a new project, a new business, or a new investment opportunity.

By 1956, I was on top of the world. My catering business had low overhead and a staff of thirty that I trusted to run the business for me. Everything I had touched since walking out of my father's bakery had turned to gold. For the first time in my life, I realized what it felt like to be respected. I felt there wasn't anything I couldn't make happen. But I soon found myself at another crossroads. *What next?* I thought. *Where am I going next?*

I found direction at a seemingly unlikely place, where I was presented with new avenues to build upon my success.

I began to play golf, and golf changed my life.

My old air force buddy Jim Kourafas had begun playing golf long before I did. He lived in Fresno, and one day in the fifties he invited me up for a game.

"I don't know how to play golf!" I told Jim.

"Come on, Alex," he said. "I'll teach you."

The first time I played with Jim at Fresno's Fort Washington golf course, he and his brother Nick beat me soundly, even though they spotted me two strokes a hole. I couldn't stand being beaten by anything or anybody. I swore that I'd get good at the game.

Ego, the great motivator that drives most successful businessmen and women, propelled me on the golf course, just as it had in business. With a goal of becoming as good as or better than my opponents, I hired Jim Faltus, a Stockton driving range pro, to teach me everything about the game. He worked with me day and night. My insistence on instruction became another vital aspect of my success story. Whenever I embarked on something new, I always met and teamed up with the best experts in the field. These professionals became instrumental in helping me find success in areas in which I knew nothing.

Golf became an all-day ritual. I played eighteen, thirty-six, and sometimes fifty-four holes a day. I became completely obsessed. Within eleven months, I had gone from a thirty-six handicap to a fifteen. In the next four months, I lowered my handicap to five. Jim Kourafas and I played again. I spotted him two strokes a hole, just what he had given me a year before, and beat him soundly. It was a joy to give him two strokes and leave him wanting more.

I became addicted to golf, and the game led me into even more lucrative fields of success. On the golf course, I met fellow golfers who would dramatically alter my business destiny.

First I met Art Berberian. He was one of Stockton's wealthiest men and a fellow member of the Woodbridge Golf and Country Club. Low-key, but extremely cheerful, Art had been a food distributor in the 1920s, and went into liquor distribution with his brother after Prohibition. Their company, Berberian Brothers, Inc., distributed liquor in northern California and Nevada. An Armenian born in Syria, he'd immigrated to the U.S. as a child with his parents. Although he was ten years older than I, our ethnic backgrounds gave us a common ground.

Art was just passing his time with golf; his real game was gambling. He was a high-stakes gambler, a familiar face in the casinos of Reno, Lake Tahoe, and Las Vegas. He invited me on a gambling trip. Figuring gambling would be a nice diversion, I flew with Art to Reno.

Art was friends with all of the casino owners. Every weekend, they would fly him up and treat him royally. Free rooms, free food, free shows, free *everything*. Art was one of the first recipients of Harrah's Gold Card, which meant, "Whatever Art Berberian wants, he gets." Back then, in the early to midfifties, he would sometimes win—or lose—upwards of $50,000 a night. Art taught me the difference between a gambler and a player. "A player just likes to play, he's not there to beat the house," Art told me. "A player tries to make a big show of winning, but he usually loses because he hasn't taken the time to learn the game. Casinos love those guys. But a gambler is there to win. A gambler knows what the odds are, he studies them, and then he bets. He's there to beat the house."

Art was a gambler. "You don't take $10,000 to make $100,000," he would say. "You take $100,000 to make $10,000." He saw gambling as an investment, and Art Berberian's investment of time and money almost always paid off. He would remain at the tables for twelve to fifteen hours at a stretch, showing absolutely no emotion, never drinking alcohol, always in deep concentration, ever alert to the game.

I was just the opposite: I was a player, shooting from the hip, too impulsive and impatient to learn, much less heed, the science of odds. I went to the casinos to have fun, not to make money. Roulette was my game. Pretty soon, I was a high roller, too; the casinos catered to me. I'd bring up friends and relatives, and everything would be on the house. And though Art tried to teach me how to play, I never quite grasped the intricacies. Compared to Art, I was considered small-time, even though I won, and usually lost, thousands of dollars a night.

Pretty soon I became as obsessed with gambling as I was with golf.

Before I knew it, I was losing $15,000 to $20,000 a night, and, as I said, I hate losing. But until I quit in 1983, I never once won big.

The same risk-it-all strategy that worked for me in business left me busted at the gambling tables. I was losing big-time cash, but it really didn't matter. As long as I kept gambling in business, I would continue to win.

My air force buddy Jim Kourafas did two great things for me. First, he introduced me to golf. Then, on a golf course in 1956, he intro-duced me to his longtime Fresno friend Leo Michaelides. After becoming successful in the jewelry business, Leo began building apartment buildings on the side for the tax write-offs, which enabled him to deduct expenses and depreciation from his tax returns. Leo and I frequently played golf together and became friends. I really liked Leo. I began to trust and value his knowledge and advice.

During one golf game, Leo suggested that we become partners in an apartment project. I didn't need much convincing. He had already earned my trust and respect. He suggested the following deal: I would put up the money for the apartment building; he would con-tribute his knowledge. Once again, I was entering a field where I knew absolutely nothing. But I could hear that music on the radio station where the songs of success are always playing, I didn't tune it out. "You've got a deal!" I said to Leo.

I was eager to learn everything Leo knew about apartments. Like Art Berberian, he was a gambler, not a player. He always found ways of reducing risk in his ventures. Reducing his risk was, of course, the main reason he asked me to become partners with him in a project. The project turned out well. Leo took me under his wing and we continued to partner in projects.

Next, we went into motel ventures together, making money on each of them. We became partners in two Fresno motels, the Smuggler's Inn and the Water Tree Inn, both of which we still own. At the same time, I began to do more and more real estate deals on my own, buying three hundred or four hundred acres of land at $5,000 per acre, holding on to it for six months to a year, and eventually selling it at up to $10,000 per acre. I always made a profit. It would have been nice to keep some of that property, which today sells at astronomical prices. But I never look back on what I *could* have done, and I never knock profit, no matter how small.

From 1956 through 1960, I invested in real estate with Leo and on my own, while playing golf and tending to my catering business. Thanks to what I learned from Leo Michaelides, I made more money from real estate investments than I ever did in catering. Investing in real estate instead of keeping my money in the bank paid handsomely. By 1956, I had made my first $1 million. That same year, my catering business was incorporated under the name A. G. Spanos Catering, Inc. Averaging seven thousand meals a day, I became the largest caterer of braceros in the United States.

With my newfound financial security, I decided to semiretire. I was thirty-three years old. For the next four years, I worked only during the peak seasons of my catering business, dabbled in real estate, and devoted the rest of my time and energies to golf.

I began to play in Pro-Am tournaments. My first was the Phoenix Open. I played with the great John Brodie, the retired San Francisco 49er quarterback who was also a great golfer. Although we didn't win the tournament, we won the betting round against other pros and their amateurs. That first tournament was a great experience for me, mainly because Brodie was such a good player, so good that he eventually became a golf pro. By the time the tournament was over, I was determined to become a top-ranked amateur golfer. I had begun playing late in life, but I hadn't embarrassed the pros, and John Brodie accepted me as an amateur. I was proud of that.

From then on, John and I played together frequently. After my first Pro-Am in Phoenix, I played in more than sixty tournaments. I began to play golf all over the world. Trophies soon crowded my shelves back home in Stockton. One of my favorite tournaments was the San Francisco Amateur, one of the most prestigious tournaments in California, sponsored by the City of San Francisco and the *San Francisco Examiner*, which attracted galleries of ten thousand fans.

Soon I was playing more golf than anyone outside of the pros. Six years after I started, I became one of the top-ranked amateur golfers in the country. At my peak, I was a three handicap. I had switched teaching pros to Swenson Park's Mike De Massey, and by 1960 I was with Art Bell, the respected pro from the California Club in San Francisco. Art Bell had instructed many of the top professional players of the day. He taught me the mechanics and the finesse of the game. Victory finally arrived when I was on the winning team at the first Bob Hope British Classic, which was then held in England. When I later won the Bob Hope Desert Classic in Palm Springs, I became the first person ever to win both of Bob Hope's tournaments.

I always tried to play with a different pro. This way, I figured I'd receive a multifaceted perspective on the game. For some golfers, too much friendly advice can ruin their game, but I thrived on the varied viewpoints. The game had already introduced me to Art Berberian, who taught me much about gambling both in the casinos and in life at large, and Leo Michaelides, who got me into real estate. But they were just the beginning of the gifts that I would receive from the glorious game of golf.

Golf gave me my first opportunity to visit Greece. Although I had been raised in a decidedly ethnic environment, I never even thought of going to Greece as a young man. My parents' homeland had no attraction for me.

Then, in 1960, I received an invitation to be one of the golfers to represent the United States in the British Amateur Championship, which was going to be held at the Royal Portrush Golf Club in Northern Ireland, just outside of Belfast. Just holding the invitation letter in my hand made me dizzy with pride. It came on a letterhead bearing the seal of the Royal and Ancient Golf Club of St. Andrews, Fife, Scotland.

I had an idea: since I'd be taking my first trip to Europe, perhaps I could extend the trip to visit Greece and take my parents with me to see their relatives, whom they hadn't seen for forty years. I went to my parents' house and told them about my idea. "When are we leaving?" my father exclaimed. He was sixty-eight; Mom was fifty-nine. Faye could not join us on what would be a six-week trip because our youngest son, Michael, was just about a year old and she didn't want to leave him.

In May of 1960, Mom, Dad, and I arrived in London. After leaving my parents with friends from Stockton, I traveled to Belfast for the golf tournament. We were proclaimed the worst American team since World War II, but I was nonetheless elated to be among the 183 international competitors.

The first round was played in the worst possible weather. Ten of the fourteen Americans playing in Round One lost. I was paired against Alan Thirwell of England for the second round, teeing off at 11:36 A.M. I never realized how different it would be to play in Ireland; playing in the heather took some adjustments. In match play, the lowest score wins the hole and goes "one-up." If a player is up by more holes than holes remaining, he wins the match. Thirwell ended the match by sinking a twenty-foot put on the twelfth green. I missed a five-footer and was defeated 7 and 6. I had lost to the best, however; after beating me, Alan Thirwell went on to win the tournament.

I returned to London, where my parents had been thoroughly enjoying themselves. For the first time in their lives, they had been pampered, and they loved every minute. From London, we went to Paris for a few days, then from Paris to Nice. I hadn't spent so much time alone with my parents since I had gotten married. I wish I could remember the trip fondly. But my folks were driving me crazy. I have always been a fast mover. Especially back then, I moved at a rapid clip, taking off and landing quickly to get wherever I was going. Mom and Dad, being older, were physically slow and would take a long time to accomplish what a younger person could achieve in minutes. Of course, none of this was their fault. But being extremely impatient, I was soon climbing the walls. Finally, in Nice, I made a desperate call to Faye.

"Faye, I can't take it anymore!" I said. "Mom and Dad are driving me crazy. Please, meet me in Greece right away!"

Hearing the desperation in my voice, Faye arranged to leave the kids with Emma Mathews, who always helped take care of them, and booked the next flight to Athens. Emma, a tough Nebraska native, has been part of our family for the past fifty years. Without her, Faye would not have been able to accompany me in my travels. When I saw Faye get off the airplane, I breathed a big sigh of relief.

In Athens, we met relatives and toured the Parthenon and the Agora with one of my father's first cousins. I played golf on a brand-new course in Athens and, once again, the game's power for social interaction was proven to me. The pro introduced me to another golfer, with whom I played a round. He was Constantinos Kara-manlis, who was then prime minister of Greece.

Next stop: my parents' villages on the Peloponnesian peninsula on the southernmost point of Greece. First we went to my mother's village of Spitali. Her arrival sparked a celebration; younger sisters with families she had never seen swarmed around her. Next, it was on to Kalamata, which served as the capital of the county government. Our plan was to stay at a Kalamata hotel and visit Dad's nearby village of Naziri, which was no more than twenty minutes away by car.

As he had done on his last visit forty years earlier, Dad played the big shot. He rode into Naziri in a brand-new suit and with a regal bearing, arriving like a titan, a conqueror, a king, which, in comparison to the other men in his village, he had become. Naziri had no running water and no electricity. There was a well in the square where people drew water for cooking, cleaning, and drinking. The *kafeneion*, or local coffee shop and gathering place for the male villagers, was directly across from the well. Dad joined the men, sipping coffee and playing cards throughout the day, while the women and children struggled to draw water from the well, which never worked right. I don't know how long it had been since the well had not worked properly, but for as long as we were there no one took the time to get it fixed. Their lackadaisical attitude amazed me.

I never knew what the word *ekmetalefsis* meant until I traveled to Greece. I found out within the first few days. *Ekmetalefsis* means to knowingly take advantage of someone. "Why did you come?" one relative finally asked me. "You should have sent us the money you spent for the trip instead."

Watching my Greek relatives suffer under such primitive conditions was difficult. I did what I could for them financially, yet it was never enough. Someday, I hoped I could do more for them.

Finally, after thirty days in Greece, I returned home, frazzled, to Stockton. It was May 1960. I was thirty-seven and sensed it was time for a change, mainly because I was bored to death. I had played golf all over the world, and as much as I loved golf I had no desire to spend the rest of my life on the greens. I was on the verge of great changes in my catering business. The character of California's farm labor program had changed dramatically. The unions had become vocal opponents of the bracero program, claiming it was taking jobs away from American union workers. At the same time, farmers were relying more and more on mechanization and needing fewer braceros. I could see that the catering business was coming to an end, and I had to prepare accordingly. Eventually, I closed the business.

My biggest problem with catering was taxes. I was making a lot of profit but also paying a lot of taxes. I called my accountant, Herb Bowman, and he told me that my taxes were still inordinately high, despite the shelters I already had. The way to offset the situation, he said, was something he called "first ownership of property."

"What's that?" I asked.

"You have to go out and build your own buildings," he said.

"You mean go into the construction business?"

"That's it," Herb replied. "But wait a minute. I'm not recommending you go out and start building. I've seen more people go broke in that business than you'd care to hear about. Stay out of construction, Alex. You don't know anything about it."

"I'll learn," I said.

At my insistence, Herb told me how "first ownership of property" worked. He used a property with $100,000 in rental income and $40,000 in expenses as an example. It would appear that I would be making an annual profit of $60,000. But depreciation lessens the tax liability considerably. Since the property has a life beyond the current tax year, I could depreciate it, or spread the operating cost over a number of years and deduct a part of that cost each year. The depreciation for first ownership property was approximately 80 percent, which meant that on a property with $100,000 in annual income I could deduct an additional $80,000 above the original $40,000 in expenses. Subtracting this amount from the rental income of $100,000, I would have a loss of $20,000 on my tax return.

Once again, I decided to take advantage of this new opportunity. I had nothing stopping me from getting into construction, none of the top-heavy, action-reticent, risk-averse management plaguing corporate America. The luxury of being able to make a decision without being accountable to anyone else has been one of the keys to my success. Even now, when I face a decision about moving forward in a new venture, I ask myself two questions. First: *Can I do it?* Am I mentally and financially able to undertake and carry out the full scope of the new project? Second: *Does it make sense for me to do it?* If the answer to both questions is a resounding yes, I don't waste any time. And I say a resounding yes, because I don't believe in doubt or misgivings. Believing in yourself is half the battle of any success story.

Everything comes down to believing in yourself. This is the force that gives you the power to persevere and try new things. If I hadn't believed in myself, I would never have left my father's bakery and found my way in the catering business. If I hadn't believed in myself, I would have never had the self-confidence to venture into construction, where I ended up making my fortune. Believing in yourself, having the self-confidence to say "I'll try" and "I'll learn," instead of the more commonly expressed "I can't," is essential to any success story.

Another essential component is using simple common sense.

I knew nothing about the construction business, but I wasn't afraid to pursue the opportunity to learn. From that point forward, all I had to do was to follow the steps that suddenly seemed to stretch before me. First, I had learned about buying real estate from Leo Michaelides. Then Herb Bowman opened my eyes to the opportunities of building my own buildings, steering me into the construction business. I didn't even know the definition of a 2 x 4. But I knew something more important: I needed to hire the best to teach me. I hired Al Toccoli, a respected Stockton building contractor who knew the construction business inside and out. A. G. Spanos Catering, Inc., became A. G. Spanos Construction, Inc. With a four-person staff, I was on to the next phase of my career, one more link in the chain of events that led me from one venture to the next in a natural, seemingly preordained progression.

When I went into the construction business, I asked Faye to become my business manager, just as she had helped me with catering. She was the one person I trusted completely, and I knew she would do an incredible job. But Faye turned me down. We had our small children to raise, she said, and home was her priority. Faye was as successful at running our home as I would be in running my business, if not more so. She made our home a haven, a source of strength and pride, for me and our children. I can only imagine how great she would have been as a businesswoman if she'd gone into business with me—but I now appreciate her wise decision to turn down my offer.

So I embarked on my new venture alone. I was committed to learning everything about building apartments, from the simplest to the most complicated facet. It was a business I intended to master as quickly as humanly possible. I asked Al Toccoli how much my first project, a twenty-four-unit apartment complex, would cost to build. He came back with an estimate of $210,000. I couldn't afford it. We made a deal. He said he'd do it for $200,000. Although $10,000 doesn't seem like a lot of money today, it seemed considerable to me back then. I appreciated Al's discount, and borrowed $200,000 for the cost of construction from San Joaquin First Federal. Once I got the loan, I gave Al one stipulation: I wanted to watch every step of the building process. He tried to get me off his back by scheduling meetings at 4 A.M. But my childhood at Dad's bakery had taken the sting out of early mornings a long time ago.

I named the apartment complex the Bali Hai. The theme was South Pacific. Located on Pershing Avenue in Stockton, the Bali Hai had a stone god guarding its entrance, a luau pit, and a canopy of palm trees. Designed by A. G. Schofield of Fresno, all of the apartments in the two-story project would have two bedrooms with 840 square feet of living space. The ground-floor units would have private patios. Each apartment would have central heating and air conditioning, built-in appliances, carpeting, draperies, grass-cloth wallpaper, and walnut paneling. The white stucco and brown wood on the building's exterior and the unusual roofline borrowed from the architectural style of the South Pacific islands would give the Bali Hai a refreshingly new and modern look. Newspaper advertisements read, "Bali Hai is Calling—Stockton's newest, most delightful garden court apartments are calling YOU!"

Covered extensively by the newspapers and local television, the theme struck a chord with area residents. The Bali Hai was a hit. Even today, four decades later, it still looks as beautiful as ever. As the project progressed, I learned every step of the mechanics of contracting. For the nine months it took Al Toccoli to complete the project, I never left his side. When the job was completed, my first apartment complex was up and leasing. It was one of the most beautiful sights I'd ever seen in my life.

Having learned the mechanics of construction from Al Toccoli, I was ready to begin building on my own. I took complete charge of construction of my second apartment complex, which I called the Outrigger. Sister property to the Bali Hai, but a bigger investment at $350,000, it also had a South Pacific theme. Once again I partnered with A. G. Schofield to design a complex, this one inspired by the outrigger boats that sailed the South Pacific. The Outrigger was also an immediate hit and also still stands today.

Next, I built my first office building with my brother George on the corner of Park and Center Streets in downtown Stockton. We demolished a cluster of aging structures and replaced them with a contemporary office center. The Park Center was a gorgeous two-story, 15,000-square-foot building with a large L-shaped parking area. A travertine marble front, a floating stairway, a trio of light pendulums, and a variety of trees and shrubs enhanced the intrinsically interesting lines of the building. When we completed the building, George moved in on the lower floor to set up his law practice, and I moved my office to the top floor.

By the early sixties, my new business was well under way and, most importantly, my family was complete. We lived in a small house on Leesburg Place that kept growing in square footage with each child that Faye and I had. All of our relatives' kids as well as kids from the neighborhood would congregate at our house, which Faye welcomed because she preferred that our children stay at home. Like my dad did with us, I insisted that my kids take Greek language lessons, although I spared them the daily trip to the Greek Orthodox church by hiring a tutor three times a week.

After dinner, we'd gather at the piano, I at the keys and my kids—Dean, Dea, Alexis, and Michael—sitting at barstools behind me. I'd lead them in admittedly rough renditions of standards like "I'm Looking Over a Four-Leaf Clover," "These Foolish Things," and "Clair de Lune." Some nights, to give Faye a break and time to organize the house without four rampaging kids underfoot, I'd take the three oldest children to the driving range down the street. I'd buy buckets of balls for each of them, give them each a club, line them up, and show them how to swing. We'd spend hours hitting balls and having a great time.

We did everything as a family. In summers we'd rent a house in Clearwater Beach, Florida, where Faye's relatives were nearby, and Faye took the kids and my mother (whom our kids called "Yiayia," Greek for "grandmother") to Lake Tahoe for two weeks each summer. I'd meet them there after work every weekend. In the winter, we'd take a twenty-four-hour trip on the Southern Pacific train to Aspen.

We were the typical American family, and the time I spent with my wife and children were the most wonderful moments of my life. Unfortunately, once my construction business grew nationally, I had to travel every week. But I always made it home on weekends.

When I was away, I'd phone Faye and our children at dinnertime every night, no matter where I was. I'd phone again before the kids went to bed.

I had a lot of ground to cover. By 1962, California was the most populous state in the nation. The state's sand, sun, and allure brought new residents in droves. All across California, housing was in short supply. Suburban communities sprang up and spread prodigiously, based on the advent of mass-produced housing. My apartments were something new. At the time, I called them the "biggest, jazziest apartment houses north of the Calaveras." By 1977, I would be saying, "People are turning to apartments because there just aren't that many people who can afford to pay $55,000 to $100,000 for a new home. Apartment builders are constructing more units suitable for family living—a lot more three-bedroom units. We are also setting aside whole sections of some projects for families."

After the Outrigger was completed, I decided to branch out into shopping centers. I purchased a fifteen-acre tract in nearby Tracy, California, for $12,500 an acre and had it rezoned for commercial use. Along the north side of the property was an irrigation canal that I had committed to covering. A local rancher took his best shot at undermining the project by claiming that the additional acreage of the canal was more than allowed by my permit. I learned that the rancher had requested rezoning for a site for a shopping center of his own only a block and a half east of my site. His request had been denied by the city planning commission. We got into a bit of a battle. Before it was over, he would apply for rezoning three different times, each request denied by the city planning commission on the grounds that two shopping centers in such close proximity would not be self-sustaining.

The entire shopping center project, which I called McKinley Village Center, was fraught with difficulty. My goal was to make McKinley Village a proud asset for the community of Tracy and a profitable investment for everyone concerned. I envisioned an entire multiuse development around the shopping center. I was so confident of its success that I got my friend Frank Pellegri, the local farmer who'd supported my catering business, my brother-in-law Tom Graham, who lived and farmed in Tracy, and my cousins Pete and Harry Spanos to invest $25,000 each in the deal.

McKinley Village Center was way ahead of its time. Today, Tracy is considered a San Francisco Bay Area bedroom community. It's growing at a much faster rate than Stockton and its real estate prices are considerably higher—but considerably lower than San Francisco's, making it attractive to commuters. But when I built the McKinley Village Center, Tracy was still a sleepy farming town. My development sat half empty, and the surrounding land never supported development. I sold the center at a loss in 1973. Feeling awful about getting my friend Frank Pellegri, my brother-in-law, and my cousins into the deal, I personally paid them back their original $25,000 investment.

Although I went into construction for financial reasons, I was also determined to build high-quality projects. I dedicated myself to constructing buildings that would stand long after I had moved on. Regardless of their future owners, I would always be the builder of record, and I wanted my record to be spotless. The manner in which I conducted my business, what my peers thought of me, and what my name meant as both an individual and a businessman have always been of paramount importance to me. A reputation is an intangible commodity that no self-respecting businessman should ever consider trading for a quick buck. An honorable reputation takes a very long time to build, but it can be destroyed with one bad move.

Whatever I built, I wanted it to be the best. I hired the best architects to design buildings that would afford privacy and the quality of an individual residence for people who could not afford to buy a house. We targeted the top 10 percent of the market, who could pay higher-than-average rents. Our company trademark was a design that was simple and elegant, reflecting the casual California lifestyle: maximum use of living area, open-spaced corridors, recreational amenities, and landscaping that added color and enhanced privacy between the buildings. I used this apartment design style first in Stockton, then in Modesto, then in the surrounding areas of Fresno, Sacramento, Antioch, San Jose, and points beyond. Except for, curiously, my hometown of Stockton, our projects have won environmental and design awards in every city where we have built.

My apartment complexes were unique and became popular quickly. We couldn't build them fast enough to fill the demand. *Build, build, build*—this became my mantra. Then in 1963, I made one of the largest land acquisitions of my burgeoning real estate career. The state of California had put out for bid about sixty-nine acres of state hospital farmland in north Stockton on what is now Robinhood Drive. I was convinced that Stockton's future growth lay in this northerly direction and had a hunch that this property that had so unexpectedly become available for purchase was another opportunity being laid at my feet. My instinct told me that this could be the deal of a lifetime.

I had about $350,000 cash in the bank, not nearly enough for the price of the land, which was valued between $500,000 and $600,000. Though I was short the necessary funds to bid for the land, I was undaunted. I decided not to take a loan but instead to seek a partner to put up the rest of the cash. Even if I had to split the profit, I figured I could still make an enormous amount of money from this property. I approached one of my closest friends and asked him to become a partner.

I laid out my plans for shopping centers, apartments, office buildings. All he had to do was partner with me on a dollar-for-dollar basis. "Alex, you got a deal!" he said, and we shook on it. For the next eight months, I went to work with the engineers and confirmed my initial assumption: if developed properly, the Robinhood Drive property would make us millions.

Ten days before the bid deadline, my friend came to my office and told me that he had just made $800,000 from a business transaction and didn't need our deal anymore. He wanted out. I couldn't believe he would leave me in the lurch, but he did exactly that. The deadline was only days away, and I was back to square one. Once again, I went to Ernie Segale at the Bank of America and told him of my predicament. Ernie promised to help but said he needed time to think it over.

Two days before the deadline, Ernie called me to his office and introduced me to Max and Merrill Stone, two brothers who were involved in real estate in Stockton. Ernie suggested that I take them as my new partners in the deal. Because of the respect I had for Ernie's judgment, I agreed to take them on as full partners even though the Stone brothers couldn't come up with the balance of the required funds. Had I had more business experience at that time, I would have known that with my credit and available cash I didn't need a partner. I could have taken on the deal by myself. Instead I felt compelled to seek a partner because this land purchase was bigger than any I had ever made and I wasn't sure I could handle it on my own.

On the official day of bidding, the Stone brothers and I drove to Sacramento, prepared to offer $560,000 for the land. There were six other bidders, which worried me. At the very last minute, I suggested to the Stone brothers that we raise our bid to $570,000.

That extra $10,000 gave us the winning offer. Success comes from following your hunches.

Almost immediately, we went to work on the land. We leased two-and-a-half acres to Firestone, Goodyear, and the Bank of California for $600,000. In less than a year, we had made back all of our investment, leaving the rest of the land free and clear. The Stone brothers divided their half up between themselves, and we parted ways. I developed the rest of the land on my own. Today, the headquarters of my company is still located in the Robinhood Drive office buildings I built in 1964.

Although my brief business relationship with the Stone brothers was not unpleasant, and the deal worked out fine, the experience of having to rely on a partnership to make a deal in the first place soured me on partnerships forever. From that point forward, I decided never to take partners on a fifty-fifty basis. Over the years, I have had limited partners and percentage partners but never equal or full partners. If I don't control a deal, I will not participate; if I need full partners in order to make a deal work, I won't go in on it. I don't believe in venturing into new and uncharted territory from any position other than strength. The fundamental fault in full partnerships is that they are inherently restrictive and conceived out of weakness. I've always believed that if I am to control my own future, I must be in charge of making all the decisions that affect it.

After Robinhood, I became involved in the Stockton Redevelopment Agency's plans for a street near and dear to my heart, El Dorado, former home of the Roma Lunch and Bakery. As suburbs developed under county control in Stockton, decay set into the hundred-year-old inner city. I owned a building on the corner of El Dorado and Weber Avenue, which was among the first of six parcels to be acquired by the agency in a nine-block West End redevelopment project. A picture ran in the *Stockton Record* of me giving a key to the building to Redevelopment Agency chairman Dean DeCarli. I would have priority to make a bid to repurchase the property. If I won the bid, I planned to erect a three- or four-story commercial building. A few months later, I was invited to make a bid. Joining me were the other former owners of the property, including M. Tabuchi Co., neighbor of the Roma Lunch and Bakery. My bid to buy back my property was successful. Construction was soon under way.

By 1963, I had projects across northern California, but fate once again brought me home, where I met someone special. His name was George Filios and he was a friend of my first cousin Tasia Kavalas and her newlywed husband, Jim. Tasia and Jim found a piece of property in the Bay Area town of Antioch and proposed that we build an apartment complex on it as partners. George, a painter by trade, worked on our new apartment project day and night. At eighteen, George had immigrated to San Francisco from the Greek village of Meligala, Messinia, a stone's throw from my father's village. He was in his late twenties when I hired him to work on the Antioch project. He spoke broken English but immediately showed great talent for the construction business. As I watched him paint those apartments, I was certain that I had never seen a man work so hard in my life. I'd go to the job at nine at night, and he was working. I'd go back at five the next morning, and he was still working. Soon, George Filios would become an integral part of my business family, in ways I couldn't imagine at the time.

CHAPTER 7

Cash Is King!

I recently became reacquainted with a buddy of mine whom I hadn't seen for thirty years. He walked into my office and, before he shook my hand or uttered a greeting, he asked me, "Have you ever made any mistakes?" He didn't say, "How are you, Alex?" or, "Great to see you, Alex!" No. The first words out of his mouth were, "Have you ever made any mistakes?"

"Sure," I said, "lots of them."

Curiously, people don't usually look at my mistakes. They look at all the positive accomplishments, never knowing that out of every ten projects I have built, two were far from being perfect. Because those two were overshadowed by the eight successful projects, the two failures are swept away and forgotten. But I've learned that failure precedes success, and the right decisions are an extension of the wrong ones. Without the mistakes you make, how can you really appreciate how well you do when you make the right choices?

I made a big mistake in my early days in the construction business when I fell in love with all of my buildings. That mistake took its toll in 1968, when I faced my biggest crisis ever as a businessman.

In my early years in the construction business, my buildings became my mistresses. Each building was my masterpiece, beautiful and spectacular. My first building, the Bali Hai Apartments, still looks as beautiful to me as the day of its completion. Many times I have driven by and thought of buying it back for sentimental reasons, but my business sense gets the better of me, and I remember the lesson I learned a long time ago.

When you build a building, any kind of building, it is a visible embodiment of you, your work, and your business ethics. It is literally a dream come true. In the early stages of my career, I wanted to shout from the rooftops, "Look at what I built!" I loved everything about building: acquiring the land, planning and design, and, best of all, construction, when I would prowl the site in my hard hat, ensuring that everything was done exactly right. I always wanted to be sure that if I ever had to sell a building, I would personally know that every word I might say to a prospective buyer would be true. But, of course, I wouldn't sell, not back then.

Not until I almost went broke.

For years, I spent my life building, building, building, but rarely selling. Then the 1968 recession hit. I looked at my buildings and looked at my books and realized that I had nothing in the bank. Even though I was rich in real estate holdings, I had no cash reserves. Essentially, I was building up the equity in the projects and servicing the debt, but that doesn't generate cash flow. My real estate holdings couldn't feed my family or run my business, and I couldn't buy more land or build new projects. "You better sell some buildings before you go broke," my accountant warned me.

It was a defining moment. I put all my projects together, which constituted about a thousand apartment units built for the top 10 percent of the market, and I immediately put out the word that I was seeking buyers. I got a call from a group out of San Francisco that was interested in buying all one thousand units. When we concluded our deal, I walked away with $10 million cash.

The morning after the closing, once I had deposited the check in the bank, my manager Dick Crane said, "Well, Alex, you've got enough money now to retire and never work another day in your life."

He was absolutely right; $10 million in 1968 was a fortune. I could have retired and lived comfortably for the rest of my life. Instead, I looked at Dick and said, "Are you kidding? I just figured out how to make money in the construction business!"

The lesson I learned?

Cash is king.

From then on, I made a vow: never to fall in love with my buildings again. From that point forward, everything I ever built was for sale. I realized that selling, not building, creates value in apartment construction. I started building and selling as fast as I could. This is still the basic method by which I run the company. I soon had buyers banging on my door.

The other directional change I made in 1968 concerned the type of renter for whom we were building apartments. Before, I built for only the top 10 percent of the market. But after my 1968 epiphany, I began building for the masses. The quality of our projects remained the same; what changed was the size of each unit. We began to build smaller apartments per unit, but these were within much larger apartment projects.

In 1971, I bought twenty acres in Stockton near El Dorado and Hammer Lane and built a complex for 90 percent of the population instead of the top 10 percent. The space per unit was not downsized, but the complex's landscaping became less important and the interior of the units became less elaborate. I was able to save money and build affordable housing for renters who could not pay top-dollar rent.

This change in strategy created such a turnaround in demand that I would sell my projects to investors before I had even broken ground.

With projects across the west, and only twenty-four hours in a day, I needed a way to maximize my time. Ever since my time in the military, I had been fascinated by airplanes. I enlisted with the intent of becoming a pilot, but my dream fizzled. If I couldn't pilot a plane, I would do the next best thing: I could own one. So in 1968, I purchased my first passenger plane, a twin-engine, seven-passenger 421 Cessna.

I hired Ron Weidman, former president of Aeronaut Aircraft of Phoenix, as my pilot. The plane allowed me to make the entire state of California my company territory. I could start my day with breakfast in Stockton, fly to Modesto to inspect an office building, have lunch with real estate agents in San Diego, zip to Concord to check out an office building and apartment project in midafternoon, then hit Sacramento and be back at my Stockton headquarters by 6 P.M. Not bad for a day's work. I kept that plane for almost three years and then traded it for a larger one. In 1971, I bought a brand-new Citation—my first jet. The jet prompted me to expand into Reno and Las Vegas. I opened our Reno division in 1971, and two years later we moved into the Las Vegas market.

In 1969, with $10 million in the bank, I returned to my favorite pastime: golf. One weekend I went to play in Palm Springs, and, once again, golf delivered magnificently. I told the pro at the El Dorado Country Club that I wanted to play with whatever threesome needed a fourth.

"I'll let you know as soon as a good threesome comes along," the pro replied.

I went out and hit some balls. Before long, the pro came rushing over.

"Alex, I got a great threesome for you," he said.

He led me into the pro shop, where I met the men with whom I'd be playing. I couldn't believe my eyes. There stood Bob Hope, Bing Crosby, and one of Bing's friends. Never in my wildest dreams would I have guessed that I would be playing with not just one but two of the top entertainers in Hollywood. I had admired both of these men ever since I could remember. Their talent and accomplishments were phenomenal. I tried to contain my excitement. I didn't want them to see that I was absolutely star-struck.

The pro made the introductions. We shook hands and moved on to the tee. Before we teed off, Bob told me that he and I would be partners against Bing and his friend.

"We're going to play for a hundred a hole," Bob said.

"No problem," I said, and we began the game.

Bob was a nine handicap, Bing was a six, his friend was a ten, and I was a three. I'm still shocked that I played as well as I did, given my excitement. Bob and I won the game, and he was absolutely thrilled. Bob loved to win at golf, especially against Bing, who was a much better golfer.

After the game, we went into the club for a bite to eat. Bob let Bing and his buddy have it, showing his delight over the victory in every way he could. I wished I had a camera to take a picture. Nobody would believe that I'd played golf with these two guys. At the end of the lunch, Bob asked for my card. After that we shook hands and I left, figuring I'd never see them again.

Little did I know that I was embarking upon one of the longest and best friendships of my life.

The next time I played with Bing was five or six years later. I don't think he even remembered me. Bing was not a very warm man— almost the exact opposite of Bob. But two weeks after our victory at El Dorado, Bob called to invite me to play at his hometown golf course in the Los Angeles suburb of Toluca Lake. In time, we'd play hundreds of golf games together and partner in dozens of tournaments. One of the first tournaments we played was the Houston Open, an annual charity event. We didn't win, but we made a great showing. From then on, we played golf whenever we could.

Bob and I had similar backgrounds. We were both sons of immigrants who started out with little in life. Bob was the fifth of seven sons born to a stonemason from Eltham, England, who brought his family to Cleveland, Ohio, in search of a better life. They were so poor they had to take in boarders, and Bob worked as a meat market delivery boy, a soda jerk, a shoe salesman, and a pool hustler. As adults, Bob and I share multiple passions—including politics, golf, and football—and, of course, I laughed at all his jokes.

Bob also liked me because I had airplanes. He was doing shows across the U.S., and we'd play golf on his days off. He'd ask me to meet him wherever he was performing, and I would jump in my plane and fly to play golf with him between shows. A week didn't go by that we didn't talk to each other or play golf. Pretty soon, we had played every major golf course in the country.

Sometimes we paired up with some of Bob's buddies, like Jackie Gleason. Jackie loved golf as much as Bob and I did, and he played with passion, betting heavily on his golf games. Sometimes he won; more often, he lost. I remember one dinner when Jackie was in rare form. He began telling stories about Bob, teasing him about his golf game, his golf clothes, and anything he could think of, which was quite a bit. Always good-natured, Bob responded to each of Jackie's barbs with his best Gleason material, of which there was a lot. One example: "They thought they'd found a beached whale in Florida. Then they found out it was Jackie Gleason getting some sun."

Bob and I are opposite personality types. He's the easygoing, fun-loving, joke-cracking superstar the world has come to know and love. But beneath the veneer of fame is one of the most decent men I've ever met. On the other hand, I have always been extremely intense, quick-tempered, and sometimes quite difficult to get along with. If anything ever bothered Bob, he never showed it, preferring to spend every spare moment humming to himself and dancing. Never once did I hear him curse; never once did I see him angry.

In 1971, when I entered the Bob Hope Desert Classic charity golf tournament for the first time, I brought Faye down to Palm Springs with me. The tournament was a one-week affair surrounded by social events. Every night had its own schedule: Friday, arrival; Saturday and Sunday, tournament check-in; Monday, charity ball; Tuesday, free day; Wednesday, private party hosted by Bob and Dolores Hope's friends Katie and Bill Juvonen; Thursday, Italian night at the Hopes; and every day, the golf tournament.

When Faye and I attended our first Hope Classic, we stayed at a hotel. I was excited to be at the tournament, but I could tell that Faye was a little apprehensive because of the Hollywood crowd. Bob and Dolores made sure we met everyone, and they made us feel immediately at home. Faye and Dolores Hope soon bonded over their mutual love of gin rummy, as quickly as Bob and I had bonded over golf. Sometime later, Dolores insisted that we stay with her and Bob whenever we came to Palm Springs, which we did for the next twenty-one years of the Bob Hope Classic. Soon, we were inseparable: Bob and Dolores, Faye and Alex, four spokes in the same wheel, rolling toward endless games of golf, gin rummy, and, eventually, professional football.

Not long after meeting Bob, I met another legend through golf. I had gone to Vegas for a golf tournament. One night, I went gambling with Faye. Losing at my normal game of roulette, I decided to try my luck at baccarat.

Faye and I had barely sat down at the table when a striking tall gentleman sat down and began playing. We recognized him at once: the bald head, the full lips, the big nose, the furtive eyes. It was Telly Savalas, then famous for starring in *The Dirty Dozen* as Maggot, the sex-obsessed religious fanatic, a character he once described as "the ugliest S.O.B. you ever saw." A Columbia University honors graduate with a bachelor's degree in psychology, Telly had been director of news and special events for ABC before he fell into acting. He starred in more than sixty feature films and was nominated for an Academy Award for *Bird Man of Alcatraz*. But back then, before he struck superstardom in the TV series *Kojak*, Telly wasn't that well known. He once told a reporter that when he walked by, everybody said, "There goes what's-his-name." But after three weeks on *Kojak*, he said, "Everybody knows me."

But even in the midsixties, Telly was known to every Greek-American because of his deep love of his heritage. He was a true "Grekaro," a true Greek, never missing an opportunity to proclaim his roots and display his pride. Whenever he attended Greek-American events, he would energize the crowds with fiery and passionate speeches, recounting anecdotes from his years growing up in New York City.

But on that night in Vegas, as he began losing hand after hand, he wasn't championing Greece; he was cursing in Greek. The rest of the crowd had no idea what he was saying, but I looked over at Faye and saw that she had flushed pink with embarrassment.

"Please be careful what you're saying," I told Telly. "We speak Greek."

He stared at me, a bit surprised, then turned to Faye and asked, "Do you understand Greek, too?"

"Yes, I do," said Faye.

He immediately apologized and we continued to play. During the course of the game, Telly asked me my name and what I did for a living. I told him about my business and he seemed to find it interesting. Pretty soon, we were in a long and deep conversation. By the time we got up from the game, we had agreed to meet for dinner in a private room.

That dinner marked the beginning of a close personal friendship that would last until the day Telly died. Before the dinner was over, Telly threw his arms around Faye and said what he always said to everyone, "Who loves ya, baby?" Then he wrapped his arms around me and said something that he would say, half-joking and half-serious, repeatedly through our long and loving friendship: "Alex Spanos," he bellowed, "make me rich!"

CHAPTER 8

Going National

"**M**r. Spanos, I understand you are looking for money to build a casino." The caller identified himself as "a member of the Teamsters Union."

"Whatever your needs, we can cover them," he continued. "We'd love to give you the money for your casino. How soon can we set up a meeting?"

The call was unexpected. I was shocked to hear that the Teamsters even knew of my plans to build a hotel/casino in Reno. Back then, it was rumored that the Teamsters had unsavory connections. Those rumors scared the hell out of me, and I cut the phone call short.

In 1971, with the tremendous success of my construction business, I was ready to venture into new arenas. I loved a challenge, and I was never afraid to undertake a new project if it made good business sense. Reno was a casino town, and although most of its citizens were antigrowth, the addition of a new casino was welcomed by the city. To me it was a logical next step, and I was excited about embarking on what was then my dream: to build my own hotel/casino, which I planned to call Alexander's.

Reno was the natural location, first because my building operations there were progressing well, and second because, back then, I was a regular in Reno's casinos. I was still a player, not a gambler like my friend Art Berberian. It was routine for me to lose thousands of dollars without batting an eye. I would jokingly tell my friends that I might as well lose my money to my own joint.

During the seventies, Reno was still a small town with a population of about forty thousand, not at all what it is today. It was more of a cowboy town than a gambling Mecca. Cattle and farming were the mainstay, and there were only five casinos: Harrah's, the Cal-Neva, the Primadonna, Mapes, and Fitzgerald's.

I bought seventy-eight acres on the corner of Kietzke and South Virginia Street, which was then the outskirts of Reno, from Joe Duffel, a developer from Contra Costa County. My plan was to build apartments on a portion of the land and the hotel/casino on the rest. I appointed George Filios, who had become my right-hand land man, as Reno division manager and asked him to begin working immediately on getting zoning on the property.

George Filios had blossomed in the years he had worked for me. From his humble beginnings as a painter, he had become a "back-pocket builder," meaning he could figure out how much a project would cost to build without estimates and plans, and then go out and make it work for the estimated amount. He was also an ace at spotting high-potential future development sites, which next to cost is the most critical component in the construction business. If the location is right, then the project is a sure money-maker. George had supervised our projects in Stockton and elsewhere in California.

My architects, Irby Iness and Warren Thompson, drew up plans for one of the most elaborate casinos in Reno. It was going to be the best. I'd directed the architects to design it in the style of ancient Greek architecture. Our plans called for a 50,000-square-foot casino, a 720-room hotel, and a 1,500-seat theater. I spent about $350,000 on the plans alone. All I could visualize was the big neon sign in front of this modern casino screaming "Alexander's." What an ego trip I was on!

I recruited Angel Naves, one of the top casino managers, to help me make my dream come true. Naves brought in his assistant, Mike Ensign, who today is one of the biggest and brightest in the Las Vegas gambling industry.

All we needed was the financing: $32 million.

I went first to the Bank of America, which had long been my main source of funding. To my surprise, the bank was not interested in participating. The same was true with every other lending institution I approached. Angel Naves and I went to Boston to meet with Cabot, Cabot, Forbes, which we heard would be interested in financing a venture like ours. But once we got to Boston, the story was the same: no legitimate lending institution was then interested in getting involved with the gambling industry, unlike today, when gaming attracts the biggest names in business and is considered a legitimate investment opportunity. I returned home empty-handed and frustrated.

Then I got the phone call from the Teamsters. For me, this was the kiss of death. I told George and Angel Naves that I had shelved the casino plan and would not change my mind on the subject. Getting involved with the Teamsters would have put me in a different category of business. In a sense, the phone call may have been a blessing in disguise. If I had gone ahead with my plans for Alexander's, my life might have changed dramatically.

It's all about knowing when to walk away. Moving forward with building the casino would have been foolhardy on my part. I didn't have the funds, no conventional lender would help me, and I would not even think of a partnership with the Teamsters.

Because of my Reno experience, I also walked away from an opportunity to do business with Vegas casino operator Bill Bennett. This turned out to be a huge mistake. Sometime in 1972, Bennett came to visit me in Stockton. He was seeking private financial backing for a new concept in casinos. He said that his casino would be family-oriented, with entertainment designed specifically for children. He asked me to invest $3.8 million in exchange for 30 percent of the project. I turned him down. My experience with Alexander's and the call from the Teamsters had scared me away from the gaming industry. If that was the only way to get business done in the gambling industry, then I wanted no part of it. Bill Bennett eventually put his deal together, and the stock for Circus Circus skyrocketed. Had I agreed to go in on the deal, my share would have been worth around $700 million.

I still had the forty-nine acres in Reno. My agreement with the city specified the construction of a casino, which meant that if I wanted to build anything else on the property I had to get it rezoned.

George Filios went to Reno City Hall to change the zoning and get approval for us to build the apartments we had planned on thirty-eight acres. On the remaining acreage, we planned to build the Kietzke Plaza Office Building. The plans called for a 120,000-square-foot commercial building, at the time the biggest single-story office building in all of Nevada. Getting approvals from the Reno City Council proved to be problematic, even for George.

Reno's mayor, Sam Tipitano, was a likeable local businessman. His family owned and operated a small hotel downtown. But Sam was the kind of politician who would tell you what you wanted to hear but never commit himself to doing anything about it. George got nowhere with Sam. His next step was to speak with each council member individually. Still, no progress.

George asked me to meet with Mayor Tipitano, which I did on more than one occasion. Sam and I hit it off. He would keep me in his office for two or three hours. It took a year and a half, but we finally succeeded in rezoning the back portion of the land for apartments and a shopping center. Although we couldn't rezone the entire parcel, at least they allowed us to build our first apartment building and the office complex. It wasn't until a year later, in 1972, that the property was partially rezoned and we began construction of the office complex.

There were more problems. Running through the middle of the property was an irrigation ditch that watered the farms down below. There were also three families renting some rundown houses on the site. According to our agreement with the city, we had to give these residents sixty days' notice plus financial compensation to move. We needed to clear the site and begin bulldozing immediately. Enter the magician, George Filios. He became friendly with the families and convinced them to vacate the premises. We compensated them generously. But before we broke ground, George faced another problem. One of the neighbors, who kept horses on his farm, did not want an apartment complex next to his field. Most of the time he was drunk, and during one of his drunken periods, he took a shot at George with a gun. George ran for his life. The farmer didn't bother him again, and George never told me about the incident until much later.

Our next problem was the irrigation ditch. We had to divert it if we were to build our project, and for that we needed a permit. George met with the water master, who turned out to be a prince. He worked with George and gave us his stamp of approval, along with that of the local farmers' board, to divert the irrigation ditch from the center of the plot of land to just outside the property line.

Finally, we started building, but problems still dogged us. As soon as we graded the site, George discovered that we were encroaching on a private easement by six feet, and we didn't have enough parking for the number of apartment units we were building. To comply with regulations, we had to shift the buildings, even though the ditches had already been dug. George called our architect, Irby Iness, and told him to move the buildings. He gave George a plot plan to fit in the additional parking. But this was not just a matter of changing plans; the new adjustment required a public hearing.

George dreaded going back to the city council, because it had taken such a long time to get initial approval for the project. Still, since George had never failed, I knew he could get the approvals. George could make things happen. He has a lot of personal charm and imparts a strong sense of sincerity and honesty that is genuine.

George went to the director of the Reno building department, with whom he had become quite friendly. In his broken English, George explained the problem and concluded by saying, "I don't want to go in front of a public hearing for this." The director looked at George and said, "I understand. Give me an hour to think about this."

The last thing George wanted to do was tell me about this additional problem. Fortunately, he didn't have to. The director called and told George to bring his plot plans to a coffee shop near the job site the next morning. The next morning, the building department director brought his city stamp and, over coffee, stamped approval on two sets of plans. He gave George one set and took the other back for filing at city hall. We hadn't broken any rules; we had just subverted the bureaucracy by going straight to the source.

Within two years, we had finished the office building, the largest single-story building in all of Nevada, and the adjacent Village of the Pines, a 318-unit apartment complex. Our other projects also progressed. Of course, there were always problems with inspectors who just didn't like us and would rather "red tag" the project for no apparent reason. Whenever this would happen, we would stop work, and George would meet with the building department director. They never failed to find common ground.

George had an office by the airport terminal in Reno. Next to his office was another office managed by a realtor, Bill Sylvester. One Friday morning, unbeknownst to me, Bill Sylvester bought a plane ticket for George to fly with him to Vegas to see some land. It was George's first trip to Las Vegas. After landing, he was shown fourteen acres on Wilbur Street and Tropicana Avenue. It was owned by Wilbur Clark Estates, which also owned the Desert Inn. An estate auction of the land was taking place that week, George learned, which prompted an urgent phone call to me.

He tracked me down on a Sunday afternoon in Stockton.

"What's up, George?" I asked. I was more than a little curious about the urgency of his call, as that usually meant problems.

George said he'd found this great piece of property in Las Vegas that I couldn't pass up. "It's a real bargain!" he exclaimed.

As George described the property, I could feel my face redden. *What was George doing?* I had not authorized him to seek out property in Las Vegas. I lost my temper. "Who told you to even go to Las Vegas, George?" I said, barely containing myself. "Let's mind our business in Reno and forget Vegas!"

I was angry with him for taking an initiative that seemed too impulsive. Our projects in Reno were always running into problems: inspectors were constantly red-tagging our buildings or reporting other inconsistencies to delay construction, which would send George back to the director of the building department. Not believing in launching new ventures when unsolved problems remained on existing ones, I didn't want George to go anywhere until we finished our Reno projects. Yes, I did look forward to moving on and expanding, but I also had a very conservative streak, always urging, "Let's take care of what we have and not worry about something new." Besides, moving into the Las Vegas market had never entered the picture at all. I told all of this to George—and more.

He patiently endured my tirade without interrupting, then finally said, "Are you finished?"

"Yes, I am," I said. "Let's mind our business at hand and forget Las Vegas."

"Well," he said, "I will buy the land whether you like it or not."

I was dumbfounded, but not dumb. If the magician George Filios was willing to defy me so brazenly, I thought, the property must be pretty good. Most people know enough to stay out of my way when I am right. I can be volatile when I see stupidity flying in the face of simple common sense. Our reputation in the building industry was made on the quality of our finished product and not on speculative land deals. I knew I was right to rail at George, but I also had enough trust in his judgment to hear him out and, if necessary, back down and let him have his way. In this instance, George taught me that some business decisions require the surrendering of ego and listening to common sense.

"Is the property that good?" I asked George.

"Listen, A. G., we can't pass it up," he continued. "It's great. Let me buy the land and I'll make it work."

I couldn't recall a single land deal that George couldn't make profitable. He could just visualize what a potential building site could become. By the end of the phone call, I was convinced to try it his way.

The next Monday morning, my brother George, who was by now my company's attorney, drew up our formal bid papers and sent them to George Filios. Minimum bid for the land was set by the court at $516,000. George placed our bid at $500 over the asking price. I didn't expect results because our price was almost at a bare minimum; if the land was as good as George said, other buyers would surely bid at higher prices. Fortunately for us, we were the only bidders and were awarded the land. George called me immediately with the news. I would never question his judgment or his ability to scout out high-potential property again. That piece of property served as our entry to the Las Vegas market, where we have been ever since.

Our plan was to build the 50,000-square-foot Tropicana Plaza office complex on five acres and the 172 Tropicana Village Garden Apartments on the remaining eight. George Filios immediately

Evanthia Spanos and her children. Standing from left to right: Evanthia, Danny, and Alex. Seated from left to right: Stella, George, and Leo.

Gus and Evanthia Spanos with their six children.
From left to right: Leo, Stella, Gus, Madeline, Evanthia, Danny, Alex, and George.

Constantinos "Gus" Spanos (mid-1920s).

A family photo from the early 1940s.
Standing from left to right: Peter Spanos, Helen Spanos, Olympia Spanos, Mary Spanos, Charlie Spanos, Dan Spanos, Stella Spanos, Alex Spanos, George Spanos, Andonia Fotinos, and Gus Fotinos. Seated from left to right: Chris Spanos, Christ Spanos, Ourania Spanos, Gus Spanos, Evanthia Spanos, Peter Fotinos, Panayota Fotinos, and Rica Fotinos. Down in front: Madeline Spanos and Leo Spanos.

The older boys with their father, Gus Spanos.
From left to right: George, Danny, and Alex.

Left to right: Alex, George, and Danny showing off their baton skills.

Alex Spanos at twenty.

Alex with his mother, Evanthia.

George and Alex Spanos during their college years.

Alex Spanos and boyhood friends Bill Bianchi, Bert Mauer, and Bob Clark.

Faye in Florida in 1945.

Alex and Faye (circa 1946–47).

Left to right: John Mirageas, Nick Pappas, Nick Mahleres, and Alex Spanos on the Clearwater Beach.

Alex Spanos with Faye (second from left), her girlfriends, and Nick Mahleres on the Clearwater Beach.

The Roma Lunch Bakery on El Dorado Street.

Alex and Faye on their wedding day, August 22, 1948, at St. Nicholas Greek Orthodox Church in Tarpon Springs, Florida.

Newlyweds Alex and Faye Spanos working at the Roma Lunch Bakery in 1948.

Alex Spanos with friend Jim Kourafas holding his son Dean.

Alex with his first airplane, a Voltee Vibrator Basic Trainer 13 from the U.S. Army Air Corps. He bought it with an $800 loan in 1948.

Alex Spanos and George Filios (first from left) with construction and management personnel at an apartment development in Reno, Nevada, circa 1972.

Alex with former Bank of America chairman Dick Rosenberg and then–Bank of America chairman David Coulter, receiving a replica of the $800 loan check that started him on the road to success.

Alex Spanos, Bob Hope, and Andy Williams at the Ellis Island Awards in 1986.

Prime Minister Andreas Papandreou and advisor John Papanicolaou with Alex Spanos in 1986 in Athens, Greece.

Alex Spanos with his son Michael being welcomed by Greek defense minister Yannis Haralambopoulos (to the right of Alex Spanos).

Former mayor George Christopher (left) and Mrs. Alex G. Spanos look on as Mayor Dianne Feinstein (right) presents the key to San Francisco to Alex Spanos. Spanos was recognized for giving $250,000 to the M. H. de Young Memorial Museum for the Alexander the Great exhibit.

The city of San Francisco presented Spanos with this bust of Alexander the Great as thanks for his contribution to the Alexander exhibit.

Enjoying a night out: Alex and Faye Spanos with parents Gus and Evanthia Spanos and Bob Hope.

Left to right: Tip O'Neill, Alex Spanos, Mickey Rooney, Bob Hope, and President Gerald Ford at a golf tournament in Palm Springs.

Telly Savalas and Alex Spanos in Palm Springs at a golf tournament.

At the 1991 Bob Hope Classic with Bob Hope and President Ford.

Spanos and Hope practicing their dance steps in Florida.

Spanos and Hope practicing on the golf course at the Bob Hope Classic.

Spanos and Hope developed a song-and-dance routine that they performed at charity events around the world.

Spanos and Hope performing their song-and-dance routine.

The marquee advertising their song-and-dance act.

Alex Spanos with President George Bush, friend Alec Courtelis, and John Sununu on Air Force One.

To Alex, Faye, Dea Spanos
Thanks for all you do and have done for
us - Geo Bush

Me, Too - Barbara Bush

Left to right: Faye Spanos, President and Mrs. George Bush, Dea Spanos Berberian, and Alex Spanos.

Alex Spanos serving as honorary chair of the USO Fiftieth Anniversary Salute on April 5, 1991.
From left to right: Former Saudi ambassador Mohammed S. Al-Sabah, Dick Cheney, Alex Spanos, Dolores and Bob Hope, President George Bush and Barbara Bush, Colin Powell, Gerald McRaney, and President Ronald Reagan.

Alex and Faye Spanos with President Reagan.

Alex and Faye with George W. and Laura Bush in Stockton, California.

January 1997: After handing a donation to the Red Cross for flood victims in California, Spanos shakes hands with Red Cross executive Patricia Kennedy. Looking on are California governor Pete Wilson and Ann Veneman, secretary of the California Department of Food and Agriculture.

Former California governors George Deukmejian and Pete Wilson with Spanos at a Chargers game.

Super Bowl XXIX, January 1995.
Left to right: Alex Spanos, Pete Wilson, Rush Limbaugh, and Barron Hilton.

Jubilant over a Chargers win.

After the 1995 Super Bowl, enjoying the downtown parade in San Diego with Mayor Susan Golding.

Left to right: Alex and Faye Spanos with army buddies Jim Kourafas and Nick Mahleres and their wives, Pat and Helen.

Alex with his brothers and sisters.
Left to right: Leo, Alex, Madeline, Stella, and George.

Alex and Faye with their four children.
Left to right: Dean, Dea, Faye, Alex, Alexis, and Michael.

Left to right: Dean Spanos, Alex Spanos, Chargers linebacker Junior Seau, and NFL commissioner Paul Tagliabue.

Left to right: Michael Spanos, Alex Spanos, Al Davis, and Dean Spanos.

Left to right: Frank Gifford, Alex Spanos, and Jack Kemp at Qualcomm Stadium in San Diego, October 21, 1996.

Alex Spanos with sons Dean and Michael at the opening of the golf course, The Reserve at Spanos Park.

Alex showing affection for his friends Bob and Dolores Hope during an Easter dinner at the Spanos home.

Bob and Dolores Hope performing at a gala hosted by Alex Spanos on January 22, 1998, for Super Bowl XXXII in San Diego.

Alex and Faye on the way to a game.

Alex and Faye acknowledging friends and family at their fiftieth anniversary party, August 22, 1998.

A family portrait commemorating Alex and Faye's fiftieth wedding anniversary.

October 2001 at Qualcomm Stadium.
From left to right: Ron and Dea Berberian, Dean and Susie Spanos, Faye and Alex Spanos, Helen and Michael Spanos, Alexis and Barry Ruhl.

obtained the zoning permits for the projects, and that's how we started in Las Vegas.

When we opened the Vegas operation, we basically quit building in Reno. I appointed George Filios division manager of our Vegas office and told him, "Find more land!" George's English still left much to be desired, but it was no handicap to him. He began scouring possible sites, meeting realtors, bankers, and sellers, telling everyone he wanted to buy land to build offices and apartments. Few people took George seriously. They couldn't believe he had the financial backing. *Who was this man?* people thought. He couldn't speak proper English, and yet he was talking about multimillion-dollar deals. When George would tell them he was my representative, they wouldn't believe him. In those days, my name was known in Vegas, not because of development but for high-stakes gambling. Of course, gambling wasn't the best sport on which to stake a reputation, but that's the way most people knew me back then in Las Vegas.

A few months after moving to Vegas, George received a call from Vegas realtor Chuck Ruthie about a parcel of sixty-two acres on Sahara Avenue and Maryland Parkway. George had already made numerous attempts to buy the land, but the owner was asking an astronomical price. Ruthie assured George that he would give him a good deal. They negotiated a price of $5.5 million. But the owner of the property, Irwin Mylanski, owner of Paradise Development, which was then one of the city's three major developers, wouldn't take George Filios seriously.

George called me, saying he'd found another great piece of property but that I had to fly to Vegas immediately. "You have to meet the owner of the property, Irwin Mylanski," he said. The next day, George and I walked into Mylanski's office and I told the secretary my name. She went to the back offices and I could hear her say, "Mr. Spanos is here." A split second later, Mylanski and his partners rushed out of their offices, apologizing profusely for not taking

George seriously. They led us into the boardroom. I pointed my finger at George and told them, "This man represents me. When you're talking to him, it's the same as talking to me."

My experience with George Filios was an example of an important management strategy: if you take pride in the people who work for you, they eventually outdo themselves. At our meeting with Irwin Mylanski, we agreed to put down a $50,000 refundable down payment, contingent on getting proper zoning. A "Sold" sign was posted immediately on the property. The next day, our phones started ringing nonstop. Everyone wanted to buy the land. Offers poured in above and beyond what we had paid.

We built a total of 750 apartment units on the property. Of those units, 444 were three-story buildings, the rest were two-story. We also built a 72,000-square-foot office building, and left sixteen acres open for a shopping center. Eventually we sold the sixteen acres for $7 million, $1.5 million more than we'd paid for the entire sixty-two acres.

By the midseventies, my office walls were filled with newspaper headlines touting the arrival of my new offices, apartments, and shopping centers:

"GARDEN OFFICES BEING BUILT"

"CONCORD UNITS POPULAR"

"VILLAGE NORTH FILLING UP FAST"

"SITE PREPARATION BEGINS FOR $4.5 MILLION COFFEE COMPLEX"

But the headline perhaps most indicative of the time was, "High Flier Bucks Building Trends." While most developers were calling it quits or going bankrupt, I was prospering due in large part to my new philosophy of selling my projects as soon as possible. Sometimes, I bought and sold properties before actually taking possession in a process I call Triple Escrow. It involves closing the property purchase, the loan, and the sale to someone else simultaneously, before actual ownership and before putting anything down. Between 1968 and 1974, I built over three thousand apartment units during a period when the U.S. housing industry was experiencing a crippling recession and when many top builders were going bankrupt.

Other builders were going public in an attempt to raise needed funds. In 1971, I asked my accountant, Herb Bowman, whether we should also consider going public. Herb hired an investment banking firm to give us an assessment. Its verdict came back pretty quickly. No need to go public, the firm told me. The only reason to go public is to raise money, and I wasn't short of cash. That evaluation put the thought of going public out of my mind forever. We were a private company, and then we became a family company when my sons came of age.

In 1972, my oldest son Dean graduated from the University of the Pacific. He went to work for me full time, heading up my new Florida division. We had a second home in Tampa, not too far from Faye's childhood home in Tarpon Springs. Dean had always been very independent as a young man and had his own mind. I was strict as a father but always allowed him to choose his own life and friends. The only problem I can recall with Dean was when he was about thirteen. During an argument, he told his mother to shut up. It was the only time I spanked any of my kids. Afterwards, I went in my bedroom and cried. But from that point forward, Dean showed total respect. He knew that he had hurt my feelings as much as I had hurt his. I expected him to set an example for his younger siblings, and as a father I was proud when he finally showed maturity.

Like his best friend, Barry Ruhl, Dean had entered college believing that he wanted to become a dentist. But once he began taking business courses in college he realized that he loved construction. Every summer since he was fourteen, he had worked at our construction sites. First, he swept empty units before they were painted out. Before long, he had worked practically every job on a construction site: laborer, carpenter, plumber, and more. Dean joined me in my business full-time when he graduated from college at twenty-two, manning our new Florida division.

The Florida operation was my first big step out of California and Nevada. Dean and I arrived knowing nobody in Clearwater construction. I knew from my first construction experience that we needed a capable project manager. At that time, Dean was a business school graduate with little knowledge of Florida construction. He was going into a new state to start a new construction company with different building codes and different styles of doing business. Just as Al Toccoli had mentored me in my first Stockton project, Dean needed a project manager to show him the ropes in Clearwater.

Over a period of three weeks, I returned to Clearwater three or four times, driving from project to project being built by my soon-to-become competitors. I spoke to subcontractors and construction crews, asking them, "Who's the best project manager in Clearwater?" I added that I wanted a young man who could relate to my son. One name kept coming up: Charlie Raffo. At twenty-eight, Charlie was a University of Florida graduate with a bachelor's degree in building construction. He had passed his tests to become a qualified general contractor. Everyone spoke of his skill, diligence, and commitment to hard work and, best of all, his ability to bring a project in on budget.

I called Charlie Raffo. He not only didn't want the job; he didn't even want to meet with me about it. He was happy with the company he had only recently joined, he said. But I was persistent. After a breakfast meeting, Charlie Raffo agreed to fly out to Stockton and see our operation. After the trip, he agreed to work with Dean in the Clearwater office.

Charlie and Dean were a great team. Within two years, Dean became the real head of the Florida division, and I made him a partner in our first two Florida projects. Fresh out of college, he could not believe how easy it was to add zeros to his bank account. He started counting his money before he made it. But after a couple of years, the market turned and many of the tenants, who had leased up our projects so fast, faced the specter of going out of business and couldn't afford to pay the rent. Many tenants moved out, leaving us with empty buildings and no cash flow for debt service. We went from a positive to a negative cash flow within twenty-four months. Dean's head spun when he saw how quickly the zeros diminished. It was a valuable lesson for Dean to learn about how quickly economic conditions can change.

No one expected that Dean would stay with the company. Relatives and friends predicted that he would walk away because of my reputation for having a short temper. The truth is that it has not been easy for Dean. Although he has been in my shadow, he never gave up in anger or frustration. He stuck it out. Our professional relationship has become so close that others marvel at how we make it work.

The Belcher Plaza Office Building was our first Florida project. It would be set on twenty-one acres we'd purchased in the middle of Clearwater. The market value for the project was estimated at $12 million. The plans included a single-story landscaped office building and 324 units of garden-style rental apartments, all built in Spanish-style architecture designed by Clearwater architect Frank Morris. It was an ambitious project, and other developers thought we were crazy.

Clearwater wasn't recognized as a big city, so when we unveiled our plans our competitors thought we didn't know what we were doing. But I sensed that there was room for apartments and offices. It didn't take a genius to see opportunity in the traffic clogging I-15 and the motels standing side-by-side along the highway corridor that ran from St. Petersburg all the way down to Tarpon Springs. How could we go wrong?

There really is no foolproof method for predicting building trends or when one area becomes a "hot" site for apartment construction. I do it through my knowledge and experience. My foray into a new geographic market does not happen because somebody else told me that it would be a good area for development. By the time others are talking about a prospective market, it's probably too late to move. Sure, I watch what others say, but I try to make decisions on my own. I drive all over a city, study the growth patterns, the traffic, and other details, and then make up my mind whether to move in or not.

So far, my judgment has usually been right. I sensed that Clearwater could be a great market for us. Once we started the project, we quickly found buyers for the apartment buildings and enough tenants to fill the office building. The success of Belcher Plaza showed that our confidence in the Clearwater market was correct. Over the next four years, I would invest more than $40 million in four Clearwater apartment complexes. My expectations about the Florida market were rewarded in the seventies, and by 1980 we had built over 1,500 residential apartment units and over 250,000 square feet of commercial space in the cities of Clearwater, Largo, and St. Petersburg.

Clearwater brought me into contact with Jerry Reinsdorf. Today, Reinsdorf is the owner of the Chicago White Sox and the Chicago Bulls. But back then he was the thirty-six-year-old chairman of a new real estate syndication business called Balcor, a Skokie, Illinois–based investment company. Balcor grew out of the investment counseling activities of Reinsdorf and his partner, Bob Judelson, whose first public real estate limited partnership in 1971 turned out to be the start of something big. Partnering with Fidelity Mutual Life Insurance Company, they came up with a successful deal structure. Fidelity would put up money for down payments on properties, and Balcor would raise the remainder of the purchase price through public offerings. One day, I received a call from someone at Balcor asking if we had any apartment complexes for sale. Of course, I said, everything I build is for sale.

Soon after, Jerry Reinsdorf and Balcor purchased our 324-unit Star Crest Village apartment complex in Clearwater for $5 million. We closed on that property on May 1, 1973, which happened to be the day that Richard Nixon's key aides resigned at the height of the Watergate scandal.

Meeting Jerry Reinsdorf was a pivotal moment for me. Not only did he become a lifelong friend, but he also introduced me to real estate syndication. The real estate syndication boom of the mid-seventies and early eighties prompted me to expand my annual construction activity from approximately three thousand apartments to fifteen thousand apartments.

Real estate syndications were legitimate tax avoidance plans to help real estate owners keep their taxes as low as possible. With careful planning, it was possible to convert part of their ordinary, high-taxed income to lower-taxed capital gain income. The benefits were sizable: If the tax bracket for capital gains income was 25 percent, the property owner would be left with a $75,000 after-tax profit from a $100,000 investment. But if the tax bracket for ordinary income was 50 percent, then the investor would net an after-tax profit of only $50,000.

Another technique was to maximize the annual tax return deduction for operating losses through the use of accelerated depreciation methods, which produces tax deductions without any cash outlay. Accelerated methods of depreciation permit relatively large deductions in the early years. In the case of real estate, the depreciation deduction normally exceeds the actual decline in value of the property.

But syndication involves more than just buying properties and selling them off years later at a profit. It's a very hard, labor-intensive business. In the stock market, ten or twenty people can manage a $1 billion portfolio. But each rental income property is like a small business, with its own character and its own problems. Syndicators do not own the property held in their portfolios; they work as general partners for the masses of individual investors assembled by the real estate and securities brokers. Syndicators collect acquisition fees that can total as much as 30 percent of the money raised and management fees of about 15 percent. They also share in the profits when the funds are dissolved after five to twelve years.

Although syndication was a tremendous boon to my company, I didn't change my construction strategy. I had found my niche and I stuck with it, concentrating on two types of buildings: apartments and low-rise garden-style office buildings. I never built houses. I also found a successful formula for operating the projects. When most developers sold their projects, their involvement ended as soon as the contract was signed. Management and maintenance would be the buyer's responsibility from that moment forward. But syndicators brought passive investors to my projects, people who knew nothing about apartment or office building management and maintenance. I decided to retain management responsibilities to ensure that the properties were rented and cash was flowing. From the time the property commenced leasing to the end of a three-year contract period, I handled property management, was responsible for any rental operating losses, and took any net rental income. During the last year of the contract, I guaranteed the equity investors a mutually agreeable return on their investments. This formula made my investors happy and made them eager to invest in future projects.

Jerry and I did more deals, bigger deals, more expensive projects. Balcor bought my apartment complexes and office buildings in Las Vegas, Reno, Atlanta, and California. One year, we closed over $800 million in sales with Balcor. Jerry has shown more integrity than any other businessman I've known. We did multimillion-dollar deals on handshakes. But in 1974, recession hit again. Balcor had committed to buy $4 million worth of property from me. Real estate syndicators had to register their partnerships with the Securities and Exchange Commission (SEC); that year, the SEC was extremely slow in allowing Balcor to take the properties it had purchased from me to market. So Balcor couldn't raise the money in time to pay for the properties; Fidelity also couldn't or wouldn't come up with the cash.

Balcor ended up owing me $4 million.

Jerry called and asked if I could wait for the $4 million until the situation improved. In the time I'd known him, Jerry had inspired confidence as both a businessman and a friend. I told him I would wait as long as it would take for him to pay me. The $4 million was paid in three years. But my goodwill toward my friend Jerry paid even bigger dividends. Balcor was able to stay in business because I didn't foreclose on the $4 million. Eventually, Balcor became one of the dominant players in the real estate syndication business. By the time Jerry left Balcor, we had done well over a $1 billion worth of business together. Balcor was sold to American Express, and I was able to do even more business with Jim Robinson and Sandy Weill of Amex than I had ever done with Balcor.

American Express and its syndication subsidiary, Shearson Lehman Hutton, Inc., led me into the public, rather than private, syndication business. Private placement was bound by rules and guidelines that prohibited the sale of the interest in the partnership to individuals without a certain net worth. Additionally, you couldn't sell to more than a certain number of investors, which at that time was thirty-five, in one partnership. This limited the size of the deal. Public syndication had no such limitations. American Express's large network of brokers could bring in a broader base of investors with a lower net worth. As a result, I could raise more money and have a bigger and broader base of potential investors.

By 1977, thanks to associations with friends like Jerry Reinsdorf, I was the number one builder of apartments in America. In the fiscal year ending September 30, 1976, I built 3,730 apartment units valued at $69 million, and an additional 244 units valued at $4.6 million, which I kept for my personal investment. *Professional Builder* magazine ranked us twenty-third in total U.S. overall construction based on our additional $6.5 million in garden-style office complexes. That year, the total dollar value of our properties was in excess of $102 million.

With the opening of the Florida division, followed quickly by divisions in Atlanta and Houston, my Cessna was no longer meeting my travel needs. So I decided to buy a twin-engine Cessna Citation jet. Some of my associates balked at the $750,000 price tag, but the jet paid for itself in the first nine months. I could oversee every project and inspect every foot of land before purchase. On one occasion, I picked up clients from Chicago at the San Francisco airport and flew them over the property they were interested in buying. When an unanswerable question about financing arose, we landed at a small runway near the lender's office, picked him up, and confirmed the specifics at 15,000 feet. My ability to ferry staff back and forth to work sites without wasting travel time allowed me to keep my staff to a minimum. The jet also allowed me to have dinner with my family and sleep in my own bed.

By the midseventies, I had laid the groundwork for national expansion, with the exception of the Northeast, where winter weather conditions made it economically impractical for me to build. As a multistate real estate operation, our company was no longer dependent on the California economy. Overseeing my operation, I traveled an average of six thousand miles each week. Every Monday, I would hold board meetings with staff in Stockton, and then I'd hit the road on Tuesday morning, hopping from state to state and city to city, meeting with our separate division staffs and checking out projects under construction. I would return to Stockton on either Thursday night or Friday morning and spend the weekend with my family. It was a grueling schedule, but it has become my way of life.

By 1974, I had a Hawker and a Jet Star and my first Gulfstream. By 1980, my company owned four jets—two Jet Stars and two Hawkers—which were used to fly me, my sons, my sons-in-law, and other executive staff around the country for inspections of the projects.

When the Florida market began getting tight with the late seventies recession, I closed our offices for three years. I brought Dean back to Stockton and put him in charge of all of our divisions across the country. By then Dean had married Susie Lucas of Los Angeles. They had been married in the same Greek Orthodox church in Tarpon Springs where Faye's and my impromptu marriage had been celebrated twenty-five years before. Eventually, my daughter Dea would marry Ron Berberian, my friend Art's son. My daughter Alexis would marry Dean's best friend, Barry Ruhl, whom we all had met in 1962, when Dean and I, and Barry and his father, Phil, played in a foursome at Stockton Country Club. My youngest son, Michael, would marry Helen Boudin of Sweden, whom he had met when she was visiting a friend in Stockton. The moment Michael saw Helen, it was love at first sight. Today, between our four children, we are blessed with fifteen grandchildren.

With Dean's move back home, we were all back together again in Stockton, where Faye kept our home a haven. I like to say that "Faye did not raise four children, but all five of us." She gave us all a base, a bedrock, a place from which to grow, and from this place of security we were about to grow even stronger.

CHAPTER 9

Kane Kalo, Na This Kalo

For me, charity really did begin at home. I learned to give to others by following my parents' example. They never forgot that they had once been the recipients of the grace and goodness of others, and they tried to give back wherever and whenever they could. Dad came to America with the help of his older brother George, with whom he stayed in Haverhill, Massachusetts, and to Stockton thanks to his cousin Aristides Petropoulos, who put him to work in his restaurant. When Dad went back to Greece to find a wife, he returned not only with my mother but with other friends and family members, all of whom he supported and sponsored.

No matter how deep their financial difficulties, my parents managed to give. Sending money back to even less fortunate relatives in Greece was a ritual for my father, as was my mother's habit of giving money to the needy in our church and feeding the homeless who wandered up to our door from their camp beneath the Santa Fe Railroad bridge.

In Stockton, we were part of a large extended family, and my parents' home was always open to everyone. Their welfare was our welfare. On Sundays, everybody—aunts, uncles, cousins, friends—came to our house to eat after church, and my father would cook the Greek dishes from his childhood. Whenever I was without movie money, which was often, my cousins paid for my ticket. My godfather, Steve Chiarchanis, as well as my uncles, counseled, encouraged, and protected me. These men weren't part of my immediate family. But I grew up with a sense of a bigger family one that extended beyond the conventional boundaries of blood. I grew up with a feeling of responsibility, not only for my immediate family but also for my community, my city, my world.

"*Kane kalo, na this kalo*," my mother always told us in Greek.

It means, "Do good, so that good comes your way."

She also liked to say, "Do something good and then throw it in the ocean. Don't brag about it." The idea is that the waves bring the good deed back to the giver in another form.

I was named for my ancestors' spirit of charity and giving. When my godfather christened me Alexander instead of my given name of Leonidas, he knew what the name meant: Alexandros is comprised of the words *alexein* (to defend, to help) and *andros* (man). Hence, the name means "defender or helper of mankind." The name was borne by my godfather's hero, Alexander the Great, the Macedonian king and military conqueror who helped spread the Greek culture across Asia Minor, Egypt, and India, from 356 to 323 B.C.

I've spent my life striving to live up to that proud and noble name. Since my childhood, I've believed that giving is not just a one-time act of random largesse; it's a daily way of life. The word that comes closest to describing my philosophy of philanthropy is *sharing*. I consider myself the steward of the wealth I have assembled; it will outlast me. I believe I have a sacred duty to share my good fortune with my church, my community, my fellow Greek-Americans, and my family, not necessarily in that order. Giving just does my heart good.

When I made my first money in the catering business, I paid off my father's debts. When I made even more money in the mid- to late fifties, I began helping my community. "You make a living by what you get," an anonymous author once wrote. "You make a life by what you give." Or as Texas oilman Bunker Hunt once said, "Money is a lot like manure. Pile it up in one place and it stinks like hell. Spread it around and it can do a lot of good." So ever since I've had money, I've believed in spreading it around. Disaster victims, churches, hospitals, medical causes, children's charities, educational and athletic funds—the beneficiaries are endless, but they share one similarity: like I once did, they need a helping hand. My philanthropy is a personal passion, not a company project; I write the checks from my personal account. I consider myself fortunate that I can afford to do that.

In the fifties, I became aware of the obvious financial needs of St. Basil's, the Greek Orthodox church across the street from the house where I grew up. So I helped the church extricate itself from debt. As a child in this church's small and crowded classrooms, I spent what seemed like an eternity hunched over rickety desks, reading uncertainly and haltingly in Greek and learning about the language and culture of Greece from hand-me-down reading books. As an adult, I began a campaign of giving that continues to this day. First, I gave time; then, as soon as I was able, I began giving money.

In the early sixties, I was made aware of the serious lack of athletic programs for Stockton kids. I had been one of those needy kids—a poor baker's boy who dreamed about athletics but could afford neither sports equipment nor time away from my bakery job to play. On the advice of my high school friend Tony Morelli, I first sponsored a local softball team, which became one of the best in the country. Then I supported a basketball league for Stockton kids ninth grade and younger. Tony was the driving force behind it all. He was one of the most trusted friends I had, and he loved sports as much as I did. Sadly, in 1987, an intruder killed Tony in his home. To this day, I feel a deep sense of loss.

I saw a need to help athletes at my alma mater, the University of the Pacific in Stockton. In 1969, I got a call from the university's athletic director, Cedrick Dempsey, who is now the executive director of the NCAA, the governing body of all intercollegiate sporting events in the United States. Overseeing 1,200 collegiate institutions, he's one of the most influential men in collegiate sports. But back then, he had a problem: the university sorely needed funds for its football team and, just as importantly, it needed a building that would serve as the center of all university athletic activities. I wholeheartedly offered my support. In 1973, we opened the university's Pacific Athletic Foundation building. Later, in 1981, the Alex G. Spanos Center, an auditorium for athletic and citywide events on the University of the Pacific campus, was officially inaugurated. In 1972, I was invited to serve on the university's board of regents, a position I held until taking the title of honorary regent. After that, my son Dean was appointed regent in my place. After Dean, my son Michael served as regent. Today, my daughter Dea represents our family's commitment to the school.

More and more needs in Stockton and beyond began to command my attention: schools, charity crusades, youth funds, scholarship funds, medical societies, research foundations. Then, in the early seventies, I found a deep and ongoing need that couldn't be remedied with a simple donation. I got a call from Father Leon Pachis, founder of Guadalupe Homes for Children. Father Pachis told me that one of his homes, St. John's School for Boys, which served the handicapped and learning-disabled in Whitewater, California, desperately needed help. More than three hundred children passed through St. John's annually. They had no gym or school buildings, just makeshift rooms in a ramshackle dorm complex. The kids played basketball and other sports in an open field. The father wanted to raise money for a gym and a school building for the boys.

I immediately offered to donate $10,000. "Alex, I'm very grateful," Father Pachis said. "But why don't we use the ten thousand to raise even *more* money for the children?" The father planted the seed for a series of fund-raising events, which would allow others to donate and supply the school with a regular infusion of cash.

We called the event, which we first held in 1973, "An Evening of Elegance." I underwrote all costs so that 100 percent of all proceeds would go directly to St. John's School for Boys. This gala, with entertainment by Bill Cosby at San Francisco's St. Francis Hotel, raised almost $70,000. The second event, with entertainment headlined by Bob Hope, made more than $100,000. By the third event we had raised more than $300,000, enough to build the school building and athletic center at St. John's. Today the Guadalupe Homes are known as Trinity Children's and Family Services, with fifteen centers for emotionally disturbed and handicapped children across California. The success of our fund-raising gala made me realize that I'd found a vehicle to raise great sums for other charities. All we had to do was identify more needs, which we found in Stockton's Dameron Hospital, the Eisenhower Medical Center, and several other institutions across California.

By 1985, we had held seven Evening of Elegance events. Our final one, held in 1985, raised $1 million for various charities. At each Evening of Elegance, Bob Hope entertained with the same spirit of generosity he always had when charity was involved. "If you haven't got any charity in your heart, you have the worst kind of heart trouble," Bob once said. He always performed without charging for his work. First, he would do his stand-up comedy act, then a little soft-shoe and tap dancing, and then his wife, Dolores, would sing some lovely melodies from the forties and earlier in that wonderfully lyrical voice of hers. Thanks to Bob and Dolores, my benefits became a great success; they gave the high-paying audience a show to return to repeatedly, every two years.

Bob is, of course, the ultimate showman and I consider myself blessed to be his friend. As I traveled around the world playing golf with Bob, I got a chance to watch him practice and perform his routine. I marveled at his talent, style, and agility. He was not only young at heart but in fact one of the most youthful men I have ever met. A stand-up comedian and showman practically twenty-four hours a day, he lived his life before the public. I was just the opposite. Although I had performed publicly with my brothers and sister in school, I was uncomfortable with public speaking. The first time I tried to speak publicly, before my old alma mater, Cal Poly, in the early seventies, I could barely get the words out.

One day, when Bob and I were flying in my plane to another golf game and one of his charity performances, we stopped at the Denver airport to refuel. While we were on the ground, the weather changed abruptly, and we were told that we couldn't take off until it cleared. Bob and I were stranded. We went inside the terminal and sat down in the waiting area. I began to fidget, like any other high-strung guy would do. But not Bob. He sat calmly and began humming to himself. Before long, much to the astonishment of several fellow travelers and airport personnel, he stood up and began practicing his soft-shoe routine. "I wish you'd show me how to do that," I told him.

Growing up in Ohio, Bob had taken tap-dancing lessons as a teenager. His instructors included entertainer King Rastus Brown and Vaudeville hoofer Johnny Root. A natural, Bob took over some of his teachers' classes. Before becoming a comedian, Bob performed with several partners in Vaudeville song-and-dance routines.

In the Denver airport, Bob asked me to stand beside him. Right there in the terminal, he showed me how to do one simple step, then another. Suddenly, I didn't care if the plane ever took off again. We practiced the steps during what turned out to be a two-hour layover.

I was completely captivated. I knew how to tap-dance from my childhood, but dancing with Bob Hope was a thrill like I'd never known. This was *professional* dancing, and I loved it. "I want to learn more!" I told Bob.

"Well, Alex, let me set you up with some dance lessons," he said.

At first, Bob taught me himself. We practiced together in hotels while he was on the road and in his living room in the Los Angeles suburb of Toluca Lake. Then Bob's choreographer, Louis DaPron, took over my lessons. For the next few months I practiced regularly with Louis. I was a diligent and hardworking student. I got so hooked that I installed a parquet dance floor in my office and floor-to-ceiling mirrors for my strenuous daily practice sessions.

Bob got a big kick out of how I put my entire heart and soul into dancing. He checked on my progress regularly. He must have thought I was doing okay, because one day he called his manager, Ward Grant, and said, "Get me two straw hats and two canes!" He told me we were going to do something together. He asked Louis DaPron to develop an act for the two of us; pretty soon, I was not only dancing but singing, too. "For your next benefit, we'll do a song and dance routine, and it'll tear them apart," Bob said. My next Evening of Elegance benefit was scheduled for late 1979 at the St. Francis Hotel in San Francisco. The thought of performing with Bob Hope before a live audience was heady. It also made me practice twice as hard. I had no intention of making a fool of myself before a thousand people. Bob and Louis reassured me that I had made great progress. Until that time, I had never thought there was a ham in me, but now I couldn't wait to show the world my new skills.

Bob leaked the news to the local papers. "Alex and I have rehearsed in at least twenty-five different places—on the first tee at the Bobolink Golf Club, on the tarmac at Midcoast Aviation in St. Louis while they were refueling his jet, and on the stage of the London Palladium during a break in the taping of one of my shows," he said. "We're going to let the audience decide whether he should give up real estate for a life on the stage."

All one thousand tickets sold out two months in advance. The entertainment would include Hope and Spanos, Paul Anka, Les Brown and His Band of Renown, and, per tradition as master of ceremonies, the one and only cigar-smoking, lollipop-licking Aristoteli "Telly" Savalas.

What can I say about Telly? He was larger than life. From the night when we met over baccarat in Vegas, we became friends forever, two heart-and-soul Greek-Americans. Two weeks after we met, Telly called me and roared, "When you coming down to see me, baby?" We arranged to play golf in Los Angeles, then have dinner at Chasen's afterwards. Telly was living in the Sheraton Hotel in Universal City, where he kept the same suite of rooms for as long as I knew him. We played golf together often, frequently with Bob. One year, the three of us traveled to the Bob Hope British Classic in London. Telly had spent a lot of time in London and knew all of the Greek restaurants, where everyone made a big fuss over him. Pretty soon, he was part of my family, visiting us in Stockton, where everyone—especially my parents—fell in love with him.

A few years into our friendship, Telly called me with an idea born of his passions, which might be ranked in the following order. First and foremost, he was passionate about his family. He doted on his large and extended clan, including his two ex-wives and his lovely current wife, Julie. He did everything he could for all of them and never waned in his devotion. Telly was also passionate about his Greek-American heritage, and he was a true champion of our community. His next passion was, of course, acting. Then came gambling, at which he was so talented that some casinos barred him from their tables. Telly's idea for me involved another one of his passions—horse racing—at which Telly was convinced we could strike gold.

"Alex," he said to me, "I've got some horses and I've got a stable, and I'd like to have you as a partner."

He had facts and figures showing how it could be a great deal. I couldn't say no. Telly had been extremely generous with his time at my Evening of Elegance and other charity and civic events. So we formed a 50/50 partnership, which Telly ran without my participation.

Telly's horse, Telly's Pop, which he owned with movie producer Howard Koch, had won $350,000 in purse money in the midseventies. He was as proud of that horse as if it were his own child. But I didn't have a piece of Telly's Pop. Our partnership produced three other racehorses: Grand Pierre, Maharina, and Telalex, a combination of our names. The horses ran under the Greek flag at the Santa Anita racetrack in Palm Springs. We never won a race. Actually, I never even saw our horses. I wasn't really interested in the sport. But Telly was happy and totally involved in horse racing. We remained partners, brothers, and lifelong friends.

You couldn't help but love Telly Savalas. His spirit was infectious. He had a great innate gift for impromptu speaking and entertaining. He would make audiences roar with laughter, and his introductions as emcee at our Evening of Elegance events were always appropriately dramatic, capturing the spirit and essence of the occasion. He never practiced, never rehearsed. But he was a perfectionist. When told by a reporter that Frank Sinatra rehearsed for a month before he performed, Telly, as always, cracked wise: "It's too bad Sinatra has to work so hard and needs all that practice time." Telly had so much natural talent that when it was time to get on stage and start the show, he would glide into his act effortlessly, as if he had worked at it for hours. "Ladies and gentlemen, we have a special announcement to make," Telly roared at the 1979 Evening of Elegance. "A special act will be playing this evening, direct from a smash performance at the Palladium in London!"

He signaled for a drum roll, then: "It's my pride, my pleasure, my honor to present to you . . . *Spanos and Hope!*"

The orchestra struck up "Gimme That Old Soft Shoe," and Bob and I walked onstage. "This is the greatest break we've ever had," Bob told the audience as we launched into our thirteen-minute act. When we did "There's No Business Like Show Business," the song said everything about why I was onstage.

I sang the first verse:

> *The butcher, the baker, the grocer, the clerk*
> *Are secretly unhappy men, because...*

Bob sang the second:

> *The butcher, the baker, the grocer, the clerk*
> *Get paid for what they do, but no applause.*

Then I sang the next:

> *They'd gladly bid their dreary jobs good-bye*
> *For anything theatrical, and why?*

Then, together:

> *There's no business like show business...*

I was the number one builder of apartment complexes in America. I loved and cherished my work. But once you're onstage, especially with a legend like Bob Hope, there is indeed no business like show business. "Here's twinkle-toes Spanos!" Bob said, introducing one of my solos. We sang and danced, even holding hands and dancing side-by-side in syncopation for one song. Our act brought down the house, and, best of all, the charitable contributions soared through the roof.

We later took our act around the world at different charity events, from New York to London to Moscow. Then, on November 28, 1984, I experienced the thrill of a lifetime when Bob and I performed at a sold-out benefit for the New York Zoological Society at the capital of international entertainment, Carnegie Hall. The beloved Muppet Big Bird was the emcee, and the performers included the Dance Theater of Harlem, Imogene Coca, Julie Stein, Adolph Green and Betty Comden, Dolores Hope, and Hope and Spanos. Our song-and-dance act preceded speeches by Secretary of Agriculture John R. Block, Mayor Ed Koch, and former governor Hugh Carey. Bob and I walked by Carnegie Hall on the night before our performance. The marquee blazed "BOB HOPE" in block letters.

"Hey, where's my name?" I asked Bob.

"Your name is on your apartment complexes," he laughed.

Next thing I knew my name was on the marquee right under his. Bob always brought me back to earth fast. Wherever we performed, his act included plenty of ribbing. "Flying free on Alex's plane is not only convenient and economical, but he's never lost my luggage," he'd tell audiences. "That was a heck of a plane that Alex gave me," he'd say. "It flies on ouzo." Or: "I'm not sure what Alex calls his airplane. But I call it Bob Hope One."

Actually, I did give Bob an airplane. At first, I just let him use one of mine anytime he wanted. I loved the man. He was my best friend. There wasn't anything I wouldn't do for him. One day, my company board and I were talking about cutting costs, and the subject of the Hawker jet that I had permanently lent to Bob came up. My son Dean said, "Dad, why don't you just give it to Bob?"

"Deno, what a great idea!" I said, knowing that giving Bob the jet would be considerably less expensive than the costs for pilots, fuel, and maintenance.

I brought the plane up to perfect standards, and a week or two before Christmas I put the airplane in Bob and Dolores's name. They couldn't have been happier. But later, the plane had a minor problem and needed servicing. I got an urgent call from Bob when he got a bill for $29,000, which, relatively speaking, is like a $500 service charge on fixing an automobile. "The plane you gave me is broken, and they want $29,000 to fix it!" Bob said over the phone. "What do I do?"

He decided that he liked the loaner much better, but the plane was Bob's to keep.

In the fall of 1980, Bob asked Faye and me to accompany him and Dolores to the Soviet Union, where he was going to entertain 250 members of the American Embassy staff stationed in Moscow. It would be a very tense visit. Earlier that year, President Jimmy Carter had announced a boycott of the Summer Games of the XXII Olympiad, which were held in Moscow from July 19 to August 3. The reason for the boycott was the Soviet Union's December 1979 invasion of Afghanistan. When Russia's leaders missed Carter's deadline to pull out of the country, the United States boycotted the games and encouraged other countries to do the same.

The embassy staff desperately needed some laughs, and Bob, always eager to heed his country's call, accepted the invitation by U.S. ambassador to the Soviet Union Tom Watson. Bob, Dolores, Faye, and I, as well as Attorney General Clark Clifford and his wife, and Bob's friends, former secretary of the air force Stuart Symington and his wife, Nancy, were guests at the residence of Ambassador Watson.

We all stayed together at the embassy and were cautioned not to talk too much because the place was bugged. We were treated royally with tours of the city and choice seats at the famous Russian circus and an unforgettable puppet show. On Saturday night, Bob entertained at a gala dinner. His act was spectacular as always and he had the crowd in stitches. At the end of his act, Bob called me up to the stage for our dance routine. Once again, we brought down the house.

Immediately upon returning to the States, Bob recounted our adventures in Moscow while promoting his 1980 "Bob Hope for President" TV special. "After dinner, Alex and I were taking a walk down a Moscow street, deserted in the early morning hour, and he complained of a backache," he told the press. "I started showing him an exercise that looks like a ballet step. Alex said, 'But it hurts here,' and placed my hands on his fanny. Just then, we noted a Moscow police car following us. We hurried back to the embassy as they put their spotlight on us. I could have wound up doing my act in Siberia. *I wish I had a picture of that!*"

While globe-trotting with Bob Hope, I remained closely involved with various causes that needed my assistance.

In 1980, I was made aware of a need emanating from Greece. It was an art exhibit called "The Search for Alexander," consisting of more than 150 works representing the age of Alexander the Great and his influence on later ages. The exhibit was scheduled for the Art Institute of Chicago and New York's Metropolitan Museum of Art in 1983—but nothing west of Chicago. It was the first time these incredible objects, including treasures from the royal tomb of Vergina only recently discovered, in 1977, would be seen outside of Greece. The exhibition was the most important assemblage of ancient arti-facts ever to leave Greece. Among its treasures were a gold wreath of oak leaves and acorns, a solid gold casket, and small ivory heads thought to be portraits of Philip and Alexander. My San Francisco friend Dodie Rosekrans was amazed when she saw the opening of the exhibition in Thessaloniki, Greece, and she returned home singing its praises and twisting my arm to give in support of the program.

I felt the exhibit represented a rare opportunity for northern Californians to experience one of the greatest periods in the history of the world and glean a greater understanding and appreciation of

Greek culture and civilization. So I arranged to bring "The Search for Alexander" to San Francisco's M. H. de Young Memorial Museum. Current U.S. senator Dianne Feinstein, who was then mayor of San Francisco, played a key role in supporting the exhibit and welcoming it to the city. I was impressed with her and knew that she would have a long political career. We still maintain a cordial relationship.

The opening preview included a black-tie dinner given by Dodie and John Rosekrans for Faye and me and Margaret Papandreou, the wife of Greece's prime minister. What a night! The sound of bouzouki music and traditional Greek food and festivities filled the museum. Telly, who narrated the exhibit's self-guided audio tour, came up for the opening events. He hammed it up with the press, claiming to be "astounded" to discover that the exhibit was in honor of "Alexander the Great, the ancient Greek ruler, and not Alexander Spanos, the great Greek-American builder."

Soon, I became aware of another need, this one in Greece for the restoration of the Temple of Zeus at Nemea, a five-story sanctuary built in 330 B.C. It was hard for me to fathom that the temple where the gods of Greek mythology were worshiped had fallen into disrepair. This was, after all, the sacred temple named for Zeus, the leader of the twelve mythological deities, whose symbol was thunder and who appeared in many statues clutching a lightning bolt (which, ironically, is also the logo of the San Diego Chargers). The temple was the site of four panhellenic athletic festivals, which were to the Greeks what the Olympics are to modern times. But by 1984, only three of the original thirty-six columns remained. My donation didn't cover the entire reconstruction, but it got the reconstruction project off to a good start. Today, the Temple of Zeus is once again majestic.

I never wanted, and never expected, anything in return for my contributions. But in 1982, I became one of the ten annual recipients of the Horatio Alger Award. Named for the New England–born writer whose works emphasized the American rags-to-riches phenomenon, the award recognizes "men and women whose successes were born of adversity." In my acceptance speech, I recognized Faye and my four children and their families, and made reference to opportunity, to the constant striving for excellence, and to the ever present possibility of fulfilling the dreams each of us carries in our heart and mind. But throughout the ceremony, I thought most of all about my father. The fact that Dad never spoke one word of praise to me left me with a lingering sadness. I had longed to hear him say that he was proud of me and that I had achieved all that he expected of me—that he was pleased with the success I had made of my life. But he never spoke such words. Accepting the award, I could not help wondering whether the auspicious event would have made him express some pride—or if I would forever remain the son who had walked out on him.

It would have been great to have Dad in the audience at that award ceremony. But by then he had already been dead for six years, having died at eighty-five in 1976 after complications from a broken hip, although the cause of his death was listed as acute leukemia. Dad and I spent considerable time together with our families in his latter years. But we were never able to speak heart-to-heart with each other.

I learned many important lessons from my father. But perhaps the most important is that family comes first. Like Dad, I have taken on the responsibility for the welfare of my entire family. The English proverb "Charity begins at home" expresses everything for me. I'm as passionate about giving to my family as I am about giving to my world. Most successful individuals wait until after their death to give their children their inheritance. I believe in a living inheritance, in building a life together—in passing on responsibility, and good fortune, early. This philosophy has proved to be another cornerstone of my success story.

During the early seventies, I set the structure and organization of my growing construction activities. It was based on nepotism. First,

I hired my brother George and Faye's brother, Michael. I hired my children after they graduated from college, and when my daughters got married, I hired their husbands. Nephews and nieces worked for me for as long as they wanted. If we had been a public corporation, where nepotism is not easily justifiable and not always defensible, I probably couldn't have hired family members. But we're family-owned, privately held, and family-run. Unlike my father, I wanted my family to be partners in my business. Because family is the most important thing in my life, I felt that my family members were the best people to run my company.

I learned through experience that hiring your family to work for you while simultaneously trying to run a smooth operation isn't easy. But I eventually devised a formula that worked. By the early eighties, with our business interests and construction activities spanning from California to Florida, I created division offices by geographic area. I put my sons and sons-in-law in charge of the divisions, each of them supervising a division independently of the others, but all of them personally accountable to my company's board and me. The board included all of our division heads, my brother George, our company's lead counsel, accountant Herb Bowman, and me as chairman. Neither my sons nor sons-in-law had the authority to correct or reprimand each other outside the confines of their role as equal members of the board.

My oldest son, Dean, heads the management and supervision of all division offices, and my son Michael assists Dean in that task. I always try to remember that my kids grew up differently from the way I did: I grew up wanting and needing, they grew up having everything they needed and more. They never had to struggle. My friend Barron Hilton, son of Hilton Hotel founder Conrad Hilton, who began with a single West Texas hotel and built it into an empire, told me a great story. When Conrad Hilton was still alive, he often reprimanded Barron and his older brother, Nicky, for spending too much money on alligator shoes and other nonessential items. "Dammit, don't spend it like that," Conrad Hilton admonished his sons. "I've worked too hard for it." One day, Nicky answered his father by saying, "What can I tell you, Dad? You never had a rich father like we do."

On the subject of family, Barron has always been most complimentary of mine. Once when he was at our house for dinner, he looked around at Faye's and my four children and our grandchildren, and said, "My God, what a lucky man you are." He wasn't talking about my house, its furnishings, or any kind of material wealth; he was talking about my family.

Having my family involved in my business guarantees loyalty, which I believe to be, next to attitude, paramount in achieving business success. I also believe in running lean on the executive end. The total number of all my executives nationwide has never exceeded thirty, including the legal department. We are one of the largest builders in America and yet we operate with a very small core of executives.

From 1960, when my construction company was formed, up until 1983, I built almost 46,000 residential units and over 2.5 million square feet of commercial property. By 1985, we had division offices in fifteen states and were employing almost nine hundred people, not counting construction crews we contracted to do the projects.

By the mideighties I sensed dark skies ahead. The signs were subtle, a succession of foreboding events—all entirely unexpected and seemingly unconnected to anything I was doing at the time. But I suddenly felt as if I was completing one of those connect-the-dot puzzles, connecting dots from one to the next until I could see the emergence of a pattern I hadn't seen before.

The first dot emerged early in 1984 in a meeting in New York with Balcor, my friend Jerry Reinsdorf's real estate syndication company, which bought many of our apartment complexes. At that meeting, for the first time ever, Balcor's executives seemed hesitant about buying our properties. They gave no specific reason, just appeared uncomfortable at the thought of spending so much cash.

I could have attributed Balcor's attitude to unrelated internal problems. But then another one of our major clients, Fox & Carskadon, displayed the same tentative attitude. The company appeared reluctant to proceed with any new investments. Fox & Carskadon's CEO, Pat McDowell, and one of his top associates seemed unnaturally controlled and reserved. Then I connected another dot in the puzzle. I began hearing talk that the Reagan administration was contemplating a major tax overhaul, which could significantly affect the housing industry and its profit structure. Of course, no one knew for sure how serious Washington was about such a drastic proposal. But these three "dots"—the twice-confirmed tentative mood of two major clients, the rumors from Washington—began to weigh heavily on my mind. Was it coincidence that these three events occurred at the same time, or did they indicate something more serious?

I acted fast. I immediately divested my company of all of its unsold properties, including $40 million worth of land where we had planned to build apartment complexes, and converted our assets to cash. It was one of the best decisions I ever made. In 1986, the Reagan tax reform act took away many of the tax benefits for owning real estate, leaving real estate syndicators like Balcor and Fox & Carskadon without lucrative tax benefits to offer their clients. The new law insisted that an investor's share of losses from "passive activities," such as the rental activity of apartment projects, could not be deducted against active income such as salary, business income, interest, and the rest.

Looking back now, I believe that my life has been full of such fortunate turns of fate: meeting my wife, quitting the bakery, going into business on my own, traveling to Mexico, semiretiring to play golf, and many more seemingly unconnected dots that eventually led me to success and, in the case of my wife, true and lasting love and family. In recognizing these dots and following hunches with action, I once again realized that life is filled with chances and opportunities. You can either take advantage and make something of them, or fail to recognize them and walk blindly by.

The cash I raised from selling my real estate holdings would come in handy soon, because in 1984 another dot appeared in my field of vision. This one wasn't foreboding. Just the opposite: it was an opportunity I'd dreamed about since my boyhood. After years of searching, I finally got my shot at buying an NFL team.

CHAPTER 10

Chasing a Dream

Maybe the dream was born in my boyhood, when we didn't have time for sports or money for equipment; or when I was a young man stuck in the bakery, about as far away from an athletic field as one could get. But somewhere, somehow, I was left with an almost desperate longing to achieve a once inconceivable dream: not to play professional sports, but to *own* a professional sports team, ideally a football team.

In the early seventies, I set out to fulfill my fantasy, embarking upon a long and convoluted journey that would teach me another valuable lesson of success: the principles of one business enterprise do not always apply to other enterprises. But learning this lesson would take many years, and tremendous heartbreak.

I had been systematically achieving each of the business goals I set for myself. I hadn't given much thought to *anything* but my family and my business—and, of course, golf, philanthropy, and singing and dancing with Bob Hope. I was wealthy enough to realize my dream of owning a professional football team, but I knew that actually buying a team would be difficult. I had tried for years, chasing practically any sports franchise that became available.

I had begun with basketball in the midsixties. I heard rumors that a new team would be franchised out of the city of Oakland as part of the newly formed American Basketball Association (ABA). Entertainer Pat Boone, who had along with others taken ownership of the Oakland franchise, had publicly announced that he would be seeking to broaden his partnership base. Wanting to be the first to get my offer on the table, I flew to Reno with my brother George, checked into the hotel where Pat was performing, introduced myself to Pat, and made an offer to become a partner in his Oakland team. My offer was predicated on the idea that Pat and I retain majority ownership of the team between us. I wanted to take an active role in running the club.

Pat came to Stockton for a meeting, where we posed for photographers by the pool in my backyard. I had my doubts whether the ABA would survive, so I came up with a strategy. If we could sign stars Rick Barry and Nate Thurmond of the San Francisco Warriors to personal service contracts, we would be in business. I believed that the birth of the Oakland team hinged upon signing Barry and Thurmond, who would give our new league a following. Rick Barry met with me in Stockton with his father-in-law, Bruce Hale, who had been signed to coach the Oakland team, and Hal DeJulio, the team's prospective general manager. Nate Thurmond's representative was a crackerjack attorney by the name of Willie Brown, who went on to become the longest-serving speaker of the California State Assembly and the current mayor of San Francisco.

Their lawyers were examining the legality of jumping from the National Basketball Association (NBA) to the ABA. But the deal quickly disintegrated. The ABA lost credibility when several NBA stars that had committed to coming over backed out at the last minute and returned to their former clubs. We were unable to sign Thurmond and Barry, and without the prestige those two players would have brought to Oakland, the deal was no longer attractive to me. Reluctantly, I stopped negotiations and rescinded my offer.

This, however, wouldn't be my last attempt to own a pro basketball franchise. On July 16, 1969, formation of the Western Pro Basketball Association (WPBA) was announced. The league's opening date was set for November 6 of that year. I was slated to be one of the new owners. My team, the Stockton Aces, would have a working agreement with the Phoenix Suns and receive help from the San Francisco Warriors and the Oakland Oaks. The premise was that NBA and the still-surviving ABA teams would lend players to the WPBA if we agreed to help pay their salaries. To keep player salaries to a minimum, we were also investigating the possibility of finding part-time jobs and homes for our players.

When the ABA designated its franchise for Oakland, instead of Stockton, Oakland became our top choice for a WPBA franchise. But I felt that the cost of operating there would be prohibitive. The Oakland Coliseum rented for $1,000 a night, which made it the most expensive venue in the new league. Other teams were slated to play in high school gymnasiums or small civic centers. The league asked that each franchise ante up $5,000 in earnest money. Considering that the entire league only had a treasury of $20,000 for administration and officials, I didn't think the WPBA could be self-sustaining. So my discussions with the WPBA fell apart, as did the entire league eventually.

Next, I turned to horse racing. This was long before I got involved in Telly's horses, which were a bargain compared to my first experience with horseflesh. In 1971, I was approached by Peter Marengo III, a member of one of Stockton's oldest families, to take over the California Trotting Races, called Cal-Cap Trot, held at the California Exposition grounds in Sacramento. Marengo brought me facts and figures showing that we could make a good profit.

Marengo would be the general partner and manager of the race-track. I would be the investor, the front man. Peter ran the whole operation. He assured me he knew everything about racing. His family had owned horses and had been around the horse racing business all their lives. I liked Peter and had faith in him, but we immediately ran into trouble. After the state took its cut in fees and taxes, our only profits came from concessions. With marginal attendance, concessions could not carry us over the profit line and our operation was soon drowning in red ink.

We tried proposing changes like automatic multiple-tote boards, which would figure winning wagers within sixty seconds after the finish. Nothing helped. Things eventually got messy, and I bought out Marengo, doubling my headaches.

Sports editor Bill Conlin wrote the following in the *Stockton Record*:

> Peter J. Marengo III had a toothache yesterday in Stockton, and it excruciated all the way up to Sacramento, which is 40 miles as the deepwater seagulls fly. Wednesday was supposed to be the day the "One-Eleven" settled his financial differences with Alex G. Spanos. For a cash consideration, Marengo was to sell his stock in Cal-Cap Trots to Alex, giving the latter exclusive control.
>
> But Marengo had three teeth pulled, including one wisdom, which might influence his judgment, and so the final lawyers' settlements were forestalled. The agreement, however, has been formalized. It, naturally, involves a complete transference of the Marengo stock to Spanos. This involvement, and at the right price, was settled upon a month ago. But there were details involved. One, of course, was a harsh stipulation, which the Spanos interests intended to exert. It was, e.g. and to wit, that Marengo The Third couldn't go

back into the harness racing business in the immediate area for four years. It was standard, as a matter of contractual form, and very much routine. But it is an issue upon which the erstwhile partners, and one-time fast friends, have lately been bogging down about.

When I took over, I promised that we would clean up harness racing, which had a reputation for fixed races. We joined the Harness Tracks of America, which had a strong security division. I made it my personal mission to get Cal-Cap Trot into the black.

I appointed Ron Weidman, my former pilot and assistant, general manager of Cal-Cap. He devoted his efforts to making our organization profitable, resulting in the biggest percentage gain in both attendance and winning purses of any track in the nation. Raising the purses brought in better horses, but soon our attendance numbers were sliding again. We had projected losing money for the first two years, but that estimate turned out to be conservative. After two years, having lost $1 million in harness racing, I put the operation on the market at an initial asking price of $1.5 million. No buyers came forward. I reduced the price to $1 million. Still no takers. But I didn't give up hope.

Then, in 1974, against all odds, the opening of the new season was unbelievably successful, so successful that we reopened the top-level pari-mutuel betting windows, which we had closed to cut costs. But it was too little, too late. Attendance soon dwindled again. At the end of the 1974 season, a group of horsemen, incorporated as Golden Bear Raceway, assumed operations at a price that represented enormous losses for me. I put the entire experience—and the losses— behind me and moved on.

My focus on horse racing had taken a toll on my golf game. Soon after the sale, I flew to Monterey to see my pro, Art Bell, at Pebble Beach. We hit a couple of buckets of balls, and my game seemed to be straightening out. Art suggested that we play a few holes. On the par 3 fifth, a 165-yarder, I decided to hit straight to the green. Pulling a five iron, I must have hit some kind of sweet spot, because my ball went soaring higher and higher, landing not only on the green—but right in the cup.

Maybe, I thought, it was foreshadowing better things to come.

I soon realized that I wouldn't rest until I owned a pro football team. It didn't matter which team, as long as I could get one.

My growing network of friends took me straight to the top, which in the early to midseventies meant the great Al Davis, majority owner of the Oakland Raiders and one of the most colorful characters in pro football. Al had served in almost every job in football: player, assistant coach, head coach (NFL Coach of the Year), commissioner, manager, owner, and member of the Pro Football Hall of Fame. His philosophy of "Just win, baby," pushed the floundering Raiders from 1–13 upon his arrival in 1962 to becoming the winningest team in football. Al was a fierce enemy: "He makes Darth Vader look like a punk," wrote Hunter S. Thompson. But he was a ferociously loyal friend. "If I were in any kind of trouble, and I had one phone call to make... it would be Al Davis, and that's it," said coach and later sportscaster John Madden.

I met Al through my assistant, Paul Christopulos. Paul told me that if I ever got serious about buying a football team, I should talk to Al Davis. I told Paul I had been serious for years, and he set up a meeting. One day, I went to see Al, who was staying in a Las Vegas hotel, with my friend Jerry Reinsdorf, who was also interested in getting into professional sports, and would soon become owner of the Chicago White Sox and the Chicago Bulls. Al had told us to meet him by the pool. So there we were, Jerry and I in our business clothes, staring down at Al Davis, who was sprawled out on a chaise longue in full suntan mode. He took us up to his suite, which was equipped with a blackboard that he had set up for us. Right then and there, Al Davis gave us a lesson on how to buy a professional football team.

A real estate syndicator, Jerry was interested in the economics of syndicating a team. Instead of assembling a group of investors to buy real estate properties, he wanted to assemble them to buy a professional football team. Long before the public understood the advantages of sports syndication, Al could foresee the potential. Writing furiously on the blackboard, Al took us through the specifics of syndication. In those days, a team might cost between $15 and $20 million. Al showed us how Jerry or I, as general partner, would put up 15 or 20 percent of the purchase price, around $1.5 million, and nine other investors at 10 percent each would supply the rest. He showed us the tax ramifications, which were fantastic.

It all sounded fine, but I wasn't interested in syndication.

"I want to own a team on my own," I told Al. "Total control. No partners. I don't want any problems down the line."

Al said he didn't know of any NFL teams for sale. "If you ever come across anything, please call me immediately," I told him. Al said he'd keep in touch, and he did, quickly becoming a trusted friend.

In 1974, the newly created Tampa Bay Buccaneers were put up for sale. The NFL had assembled two expansion teams, one of them in Tampa, the other in Seattle. Tampa seemed like a great deal: a brand-new team in search of an owner. I saw the Bucs as an opportunity to shape a team from its inception. Faye and I had strong family ties in Florida, especially in her hometown of Tarpon Springs. We took at least one trip there each year to visit friends and relatives. I put in my bid, becoming one of fifteen "owner-candidates," and announced my intentions at a Tampa press conference. I was willing to pay up to $16 million and expected that it would take another $20 million to get a team on the field. But I jumped in too late. I learned along with everyone else that an agreement had been reached with Hugh F.

Culverhouse, a Florida-based attorney, who ended up buying the Bucs for $12 million.

I was disappointed but undaunted. My timing may have been off for the Bucs, but I knew that another opportunity would eventually come along. It did in 1976 when I got a call from Al Davis. The San Francisco 49ers were for sale, he told me. The price was around $12 million, and he had been commissioned by the majority stockholders, the widows of the late Tony and Dick Morabito, to find a buyer. I couldn't have hoped for anything better. I loved the 49ers; they were my hometown team, although in 1976 they were the worst draw in the NFL. The 49ers' financial statement indicated that they'd earned only $100,000 profit the previous year. Still, I wanted the team. But I'd have to wait a year to make my move. The sale was contingent upon the concurrence of all of the team's limited partners, one of whom, Franklin Mieuli, was on a sailing vacation and could not be reached. By the time he returned from the high seas, it was the beginning of the new football season, and the Morabito family thought it unwise to sell until the season was over. By then, the asking price had escalated to $18 million. "I still want the ball club," I told Al Davis.

He invited me to his house in the Oakland suburb of Piedmont to discuss the deal. I drove to the meeting with my brother George and my assistant, Paul Christopulos. Al met us at the door and led us into his den, whose interior design scheme was exclusively in the Oakland Raiders' colors of black, white, and silver—everything from wallpaper to furniture to Al Davis's clothes. "We have a buyer from back east, but the widows would rather have somebody local," Al told us. "I'm getting $200,000 for helping them find a buyer and I'll get the same price no matter who buys the team. But I want you to buy it, Alex, and the widows would rather you buy it because you're from California."

From 10 A.M. until 7 that night, Al laid out the terms of the purchase and made predictions (which turned out to be absolutely dead-on) about the future of professional football—the tax ramifications and the television prospects, which Al predicted would send the value of NFL teams soaring through the roof. "If you buy the 49ers for $18 million today, the team will be worth $100 million ten years from now," Al predicted. He was friendly, informative, optimistic, and sincere. "Alex, you are the only one that should own this ball club," he said when we got up to leave.

"I'll get back to you in twenty-four hours," I said.

Al told me that I had until 5 P.M. the next day to bid the $18 million. "Call me, and the ball club is yours," he said. "After five, it's gone."

Driving back to Stockton, I just couldn't believe that anyone would pay $18 million for the 49ers. "The ball club's losing money," I kept saying. "No way it's worth eighteen million. We'll get it for twelve if we hold tight."

I took the deal to my board, which included my four children, my sons-in-law, my brother George, and my accountant. Everyone was against the purchase. I called Al the next day and told him that I thought the price was excessive. "I can see an increase of one or two million from last year's eleven million price, but not a seven million increase," I said. I stubbornly held fast to $12 million.

"The Morabitos won't sell for anything less than eighteen," Al told me.

I held my ground, thinking there couldn't be *anyone* who would pay $18 million. The next afternoon, I was watching the 5:30 P.M. TV news when a special report flashed on screen: the DeBartolo family from Youngstown, Ohio, had bought the San Francisco 49ers for $18 million. I felt nauseated. As always, Al Davis was right; I should have come up with the cash.

After two losing seasons, Eddie DeBartolo hired Stanford head coach Bill Walsh and ushered in a new era for the 49ers. Over the next fifteen years, DeBartolo and Walsh would become the architects of the most victorious franchise in sports. DeBartolo upgraded the organization's front office administration and its on-field talent, including drafting a quarterback named Joe Montana from Notre Dame in the third round of the 1979 draft. The 49ers would go on to earn the moniker "The Team of the Eighties" after claiming four Super Bowl titles during that decade. They extended their dominance into the nineties, becoming the only NFL team to produce ten or more wins for sixteen consecutive seasons (1983–1998). Since 1981, they have won thirteen division titles, five conference championships, and five Super Bowl championships. By 1999 the team that I could have bought for $18 million was worth an estimated $371 million. Regrets? You bet.

On the day that I lost the 49ers, I should have learned the first lesson of professional sports ownership: conventional business standards don't apply. I didn't take that lesson to heart, not yet, anyway. But I vowed never to miss another opportunity. Al Davis had predicted the future of the NFL for me, and I hadn't believed him. After that point, everything Al Davis said was gospel to me. If I wanted to own a ball club, I'd have to pay the price.

In 1978, Faye and I were in Europe with Bob and Dolores Hope, playing in the Bob Hope British Amateur tournament, when I got an urgent call from my office. I was told to call Al Davis immediately.

"I see a situation here in Oakland that I think would be terrific for you," Al said.

"You mean a ball club?" I asked.

"Yeah, a ball club," Al said. "Baseball. It's a terrific deal. You can buy the Oakland A's for about $9 million."

"But I want football," I told Al.

He insisted I call Charlie Finley, who owned the A's. I did as Al instructed. Charlie told me that the price for the A's was $8.2 million.

I told him I'd get back to him when I got home in a week. When I returned, I called another meeting of my board. "We have the chance to buy the Oakland A's for $8.2 million," I said. "What do you think?"

Today, I would estimate that the asking price for the A's is more than $150 million. Had I made that investment, it would have been among the most lucrative of my business career. But nobody on my board was interested in baseball, including me. So, once again, I walked away.

It would be several years before my next pro football opportunity, and it was another backdoor deal at best. In 1982, David Dixon, a successful New Orleans art and antiques dealer, founded the new United States Football League (USFL) to supplement football during the NFL off-season. The original launch included twelve teams from major markets, including New York, Los Angeles, Detroit, Chicago, Boston, Tampa, Oakland, Denver, Washington, Birmingham, Philadelphia, and San Diego. The USFL was designed to run cheap: except for two or three stars, no player would earn more than $40,000 a year. To further keep costs to a minimum, the number of players and coaches would be fewer than NFL standards. David Dixon had heard of my dream of owning a football team and called and asked me if I'd be interested in participating in the USFL. He told me that he thought there was a great potential television market for off-season games.

I agreed to take the USFL's Los Angeles Express franchise and attended USFL meetings in Chicago, New York, and San Francisco. It soon became apparent to me that the USFL would not abide by its own original guidelines. The leadership seemed to be succumbing to player and coaching pressures for higher costs than originally envisioned. I began to doubt whether the USFL had sufficient financial backing, and questioned whether it could survive in the long run.

The end for me came during a USFL owners meeting in Chicago. I suggested that all of the owners put up a substantial amount of cash to ensure that the new league would have operating funds for three years. "No IOUs, no letters of credit," I added. Only one other owner offered to join me in putting up the cash.

Then someone stepped up to save me, in the place where I had made so many critical contacts: on the golf course. I met Barron Hilton in 1981 through our mutual friend Jim Mahoney, a Los Angeles public relations executive who also represented Bob Hope and Johnny Carson. I'd also met Mahoney on a golf course, when we won the Bob Hope Classic in Palm Springs. Being in public relations, Jim spent part of his time introducing people. He invited me to play with him and Barron Hilton in Los Angeles.

I liked Barron immediately. After we hit our tee shots on the eighth hole at the Bel Air Country Club in Los Angeles, Barron and I rode together and talked about our mutually favorite subject: professional football. Barron's involvement with pro football dated back to 1959, when Texas oilman Lamar Hunt approached him with a plan to form a new professional football league, the American Football League (AFL). Hunt asked Barron whether he would be interested in taking the Los Angeles franchise. The idea appealed to Barron, and he agreed to take what were then the Los Angeles Chargers.

During his first year of ownership, Barron lost close to $1 million. Convinced by San Diego sportswriters Jack Murphy and Gene Gregson that San Diego would support a major league sport, Barron moved the team to San Diego for the following 1961 season. Lightning struck! In the span of five years, the San Diego Chargers won four Western Division titles and one AFL championship, producing stars like Keith Lincoln and Lance Alworth. During that period, Barron served a term as president of the AFL, initiating the first steps toward the new league's goal, a merger with the National Football League. At the same time, Barron was elected president and CEO of the Hilton Hotels Corporation. Because that business required his full attention, he sold his majority interest in the

Chargers to car salesman-turned-junk-bond-pioneer Gene Klein in 1966 for $10 million. However, Barron opted to remain a minority partner in the team.

When I met Barron on the golf course, he still owned 30 percent of the Chargers. "Alex, I understand you are interested in going to the USFL, but I don't think you belong there," he told me on the golf course. What he said next effectively ended my involvement in the USFL. "I own 30 percent of the San Diego Chargers, and I'd like to see you get involved in the NFL. I'd like to sell you 10 percent, and with the 10 percent you'll have right of first refusal should Gene Klein ever want to sell the team. What do you think?"

What did I think? I would have rather owned 10 percent of an NFL team than 100 percent of the Los Angeles Express. I asked Barron what price he'd put on the 10 percent.

"Four million dollars," said Barron.

"You've got a deal," I said, and we shook hands on it. From teeing off at the eighth hole to arriving on the green to putt, the deal took no more than eight minutes. I sent him a check for $4 million. No contract was needed. I trusted Barron implicitly.

Barron and I went to see Gene Klein at his big, gorgeous home, which sat on a hundred sunny acres in San Diego. Klein was a character, to say the least: a Bronx-born, self-made former encyclopedia salesman who moved to California, where he pitched used cars on TV as "Cowboy Gene," proclaiming that his vehicles were "cheaper by the pound than hamburger." But Klein was no joke. He parlayed that used car business into a multimillion-dollar empire. He bought and sold Bantam Books, National General Theaters, and the Great American Life Insurance Company before getting into pro football with the Chargers.

The purpose of our visit with Klein was to get his approval for my 10 percent buy-in and his acceptance of the provision that would grant me the same right of first refusal as the other limited partners, should the team ever come up for sale. Barron introduced me, telling Klein that he'd sold me 10 percent of his interest in the Chargers. I didn't feel that Klein particularly cared for Barron's move; the more partners, the more potential for grief. But Klein appeared friendly during our meeting and congratulated me on my acquisition. After the sale of the 10 percent was announced, Klein told the press, "Alex Spanos is a man of impeccable credentials, and we're delighted to have him as a minority shareholder."

In June of 1982, after securing the approval of the other Charger stockholders and the NFL, I officially became a limited partner in the San Diego Chargers. I began to attend games in Klein's box. It was a thrill to watch the famed Charger offense during those years. I began to follow the team's fortunes closely and kept alert to any opportunities to acquire more control.

Soon, it became clear that Klein was toying with the idea of selling his majority interest in the team. He was frustrated with the fifty-seven-day player strike during the 1982 season and fed up with the protracted legal battles of the NFL, which had been ordered to pay Al Davis and the Los Angeles Coliseum damages of $48.9 million, plus interest and legal fees, after failing to prevent Davis from shifting the Raiders from Oakland to Los Angeles. If the NFL lost its appeal of Davis's lawsuit against all NFL owners, Gene Klein would be responsible for a portion of that settlement, and Klein hated paying anything to anybody—especially Al Davis. Klein was also sick of the NFL-USFL salary war and the Chargers' much publicized drug problems. And he was also becoming increasingly involved in thoroughbred horse racing.

In 1982, Klein complained in an interview that the continuing problems with the team and football in general had taken much of the fun out of the game. Furthermore, the team's elimination from the 1982 playoff picture by the Miami Dolphins appeared to increase

Klein's outspoken and growing disenchantment with pro football. Klein's deteriorating health was the last straw. While on the witness stand during the 1981 antitrust trial of the Oakland Raiders–Los Angeles Coliseum against the NFL, Klein had suffered a heart attack. In April of the following year, he suffered another heart attack while taking his daily walk. In 1983, I approached Gene Klein about buying 50 percent majority interest in the ball club.

"Come on down and we'll discuss it," Klein replied. We spent the day together, just Gene Klein and I. He said he had arbitrarily put a price of $60 million on the team, which meant that his 56 percent would cost me somewhere around . . . *$33.3 million*. I almost had a heart attack of my own.

Having had the opportunity to buy 100 percent of the Bucs for $12 million and the 49ers at $18 million, I was unprepared for $33 million for 56 percent of the Chargers. But determined not to let another opportunity slip away, I offered $50 million for the club or $28 million for Klein's 56 percent. After some haggling, I said I'd pay $55 million, or $30.8 million for Klein's 56 percent, provided that there would be no interest on the balance once a down payment had been made. Klein refused my offer, insisting on interest. We haggled for almost five hours. Finally, unable to get Klein to go lower, I agreed to his $55 million price on the entire team, or $30.8 million with interest for his majority share.

We shook hands on the deal, and I immediately flew to play in Barron Hilton's golf tournament in Las Vegas, where Barron congratulated me on the sale. But that same night, Klein left a message with my wife, Faye, who immediately called me in Vegas. "Gene Klein called to say the deal's dead," she said.

I called him back immediately.

"Hey, we made a deal," I said. "We shook hands on it."

"Sorry," he said. "I've got problems I didn't realize."

He mentioned a just-released *Sports Illustrated* article about rampant drug use among the Charger players.

"We made a deal," I repeated. "We shook hands on it. I'll deal with the players' drug problems. Let's move forward."

But Klein refused to sell the Chargers until he had resolved the drug problems.

I thought that the team's drug problems were only an excuse and that Klein was holding out for more money. My suspicions would soon turn out to be true.

I've always felt that in doing business, or anything else, a person's word should be his bond. Up until this experience, if someone gave me his word and then turned around and broke it, that would have been the end of our relationship. I've made multimillion-dollar deals on handshakes alone and never backed off even when circumstances changed. A few years back, I was at a social event when an investor I knew asked me about a project I had for sale. He said he wanted to buy it, and we agreed then and there on the price. We shook hands and agreed to meet the following week to draw up the contract. The very next day, I received a call from a group of investors who offered to buy the same property for $2 million above the price I had agreed to the previous night. I hadn't signed a contract, so I was legally free to accept the new offer and pocket an extra $2 million. But I turned it down, because I had already given my word to someone else.

But, as I would learn again and again, football is not a conventional business. Klein had a legal right to change his mind. But, in principle, he had reneged on a deal. Klein had several excuses, but I never believed any of them. I believe he reneged on the deal because he thought he could get more money later. I couldn't do anything about it. It would be his word against mine, since no one else was at our meeting in his home. I didn't pursue the matter further. I was a limited partner in the Chargers and had to live with Gene Klein for as long as that business relationship lasted. I also still harbored the hope that he would sell me the team in the future. I walked away from the experience irritated, but careful not to burn bridges behind me.

Almost a year later, in March of 1984, I got a second shot. A flurry of *San Diego Union* articles indicated that Klein was once again considering selling the team. Perhaps now he felt the time was ripe. The Dallas Cowboys had recently been sold for a reported $80 million, which included the team's lease on Texas Stadium, valued at $20 million. The Denver Broncos had been sold for a reported $70 million. Once the news of Klein's interested in selling hit, reporters telephoned my Stockton headquarters asking me if I planned on buying the Chargers. I made my intentions clear in the *Stockton Record*: "I'd be crazy if I told you that I wasn't interested in purchasing controlling interest of the Chargers. As far as negotiations are concerned, I really can't make any comment on that. I'd prefer you spoke to Gene Klein. Any comment by me would be far too premature."

About a month later, Gene Klein held a press conference at Jack Murphy Stadium in San Diego to announce that he would entertain offers for the team. "Over the past couple of years there have been many inquiries by many different people who would have liked to purchase a majority interest in the Chargers," he said. "For some reason, that activity has substantially increased in recent weeks."

His criteria for selecting a new owner seemed simple. "I would not, under any circumstances, consider anyone who would not come in with the same enthusiasm for the organization and this city that I have," he said. "That is my primary consideration."

Klein's press conference opened the floodgates; a half dozen parties stepped up to pitch proposals. San Diegan Al Harutunian pushed a plan that would make the San Diego Chargers a publicly held corporation like the Green Bay Packers. Harutunian had served as the first chairman of the San Diego Stadium Authority after the stadium was constructed in 1967. He wanted to examine the feasibility of having one or more major brokerage houses serve as underwriters in taking title to the Chargers and conducting a public sale of stock. Harutunian admitted that the process would be "quite involved," which was an understatement.

Gene Klein expressed doubt that the NFL would approve any transaction that involved the sale of stock. The NFL insists that franchises have single-voice ownership. But Harutunian said single-voice ownership could be accomplished by electing a president. "If the stockholders don't like him, they just remove him," he was quoted as saying. Harutunian also said that he didn't want to lose local enthusiasm. "We wooed Gene Klein, and he's a San Diegan; he's not from Beverly Hills anymore," he said. "We want the fan to be dominant. That's my point. I see teams up and down the coast where the fan is not dominant. The owner is."

Rumors that Klein was selling the Chargers subsided over the next three months while attention shifted to the NFL meetings in Washington, where Klein and a San Diego delegation were lobbying hard, and successfully, to bring the 1988 Super Bowl to San Diego. But soon the newspapers were once again filled with rumors and reports of interested buyers, including Willametta Keck Day, the heiress to the Houston-based Superior Oil Company fortune. Superior Oil was in the process of being absorbed by Mobil Oil, which would result in a more than $1 billion payment to Day for her shares. But Klein told the *San Diego Union* that there was "zero" truth to published reports about Ms. Day. "I have never met the lady, I don't know the lady, and I don't know how these things get started," he said.

I kept in touch with Klein, but so did others, including Dallas real estate developer Carl W. Summers Jr., who had failed in an earlier bid to buy the Dallas Cowboys. Summers's interest proved to be real. In July of 1984, Summers and Klein met with NFL commissioner Pete Rozelle in New York. Afterwards, Summers told the press, "It wasn't really anything," and that he was there on "financial matters and real estate business." He said his meeting with Klein and Rozelle was "totally social." Despite Summers's denials, it was widely believed that at the meeting, or shortly thereafter, Summers made a formal offer to Klein to buy his 56 percent of the club. His bid was $40.7 million, which raised the team's value to approximately $72 million for the entire 100 percent.

I called Al Davis, who had once coached the Chargers, for advice.

"Can you afford it?" Al asked.

"Yes, we can afford it," I said.

"It's a bad deal, economically, right now," Al said. "But you'll make it up down the road." This time, I took Al Davis's advice to heart.

Summers knew he would have competition to buy the Chargers. "When I first met with Gene, he informed me at that time—and the understanding from day one was—that his partnership agreement called for whatever I did to be subject to his partners having the right of first refusal," Summers told the press. "He also told me who they were so that I had the understanding coming out of the chute that there were three or four capable of doing it, that is, of buying the team. So, it was not a surprise or shock to me. Obviously, Barron Hilton and Spanos are capable of meeting the offer."

In early July 1984, I received a letter from Klein mailed to all limited partners announcing that a formal purchase offer for the team had been made by Carl W. Summers Jr. However, as limited partners we could exercise our option to match the existing offer. My initial reaction was that the $72 million price tag was so high that maybe Summers was actually a pawn to get me to buy the team at an artificially high cost. When I realized that Summers was intent on buying the team, I called a meeting of my board to discuss the acquisition.

There were problems. The San Diego Chargers weren't merely a loser in the NFL. Then the highest-priced team in the league, the

Chargers were a bigger loser financially than on the football field. I'd always taught my four kids one hard-and-fast rule: *Don't ever invest a dollar unless you know you can get a good return on it.* The San Diego Chargers, with a total price tag of $72 million, represented the ultimate bad deal—to most people.

I had already received plenty of skepticism from my friends.

One night, my wife and I had dinner with our friends Dolores and Bob Hope and Barbara and Marvin Davis. At the time, Davis was the majority owner of Twentieth Century Fox. He and I talked for more than an hour about football. When I told him I was hoping to buy the Chargers, he looked me straight in the eye and said, "Alex, you're crazy. Let me tell you something: show business is a headache. When you buy an NFL team, you're in show business. You'll regret the day you buy a football team forever."

Bob, who had been part owner of the L.A. Rams and genuinely loved the game, was supportive. But Dolores Hope tried to talk me out of it, saying, "Oh, Alex, why do you want to get involved in football?"

As I expected, my board was skeptical as well. Except for my financial officer, Jerry Murphy, the board members considered the price excessive. They studied the team's past, present, and future financial condition and felt that we could not expect the kind of return on this investment we were used to getting from our other business projects. Jerry, on the other hand, saw the same potential I had envisioned. Granted, the return on investment would not be as great as with our construction projects, where we expect a rate of return on capital of anywhere between 20 and 25 percent, but we could reasonably expect profits in the range of 4 to 5 percent. I directed Jerry to use all available figures in order to present a convincing case to the board. He didn't fail me. He reviewed the balance sheets and came back showing long-term potential for television and ticket revenues. But we failed in convincing the rest of the board to change their mind. They voted 10–2 against the deal.

After one particularly confrontational meeting, my son Michael reminded me of the business lessons I had given him. "Dad, you are asking us to approve what you taught us never to do," he said.

"What's that, son?" I asked.

"You've always said that unless a venture promises a reasonable return going in, it's not worth pursuing. You are asking us to abandon that."

I wondered whether I was acting recklessly in my desire to buy the team. I went home and talked it over with Faye, always my greatest ally in facing my self-doubt. She understood what owning the team meant to me and encouraged me to move forward, as always giving me confidence and never expressing doubt.

But in spite of her encouragement, I seriously reconsidered the merits of the transaction. Owning a football team was my dream of a lifetime, and I couldn't abandon that dream. I suffered many sleepless nights reevaluating the wisdom of my inclinations, which prodded me to act on my instincts and disregard the advice of those I respected and loved. My internal struggle continued until everything became crystal clear.

I knew I had to move forward.

At the next board meeting, I stood up in front of my kids, my staff, my longtime accountant, my advisors and attorneys. "I know I'm going against what I taught you and what I told you we should be doing," I said. "But I want this more than you can believe. I'm sixty years old. We don't have to borrow money to buy the ball club, and I want to buy it. I'm sorry, but I'm overruling all of you."

When Carl Summers made his bid to buy the Chargers, Klein's representative sent a letter to all partners summarizing the terms of the purchase. With thirty days to match the offer, I asked Klein's reps for a complete package regarding the deal.

We retained an attorney with NFL experience and visited Klein's accounting firm, Price Waterhouse in San Francisco, to review financial documents—all without Klein present. We then submitted notice that I was going to exercise my right of first refusal. I later heard that Klein was surprised when I exercised my right of first refusal to buy the team.

No negotiations with Klein were required. My right of first refusal required only that I match the Summers offer. Although the official purchase price for the 56 percent was quoted at $40.3 million, I would be making an investment closer to $49 million, since in July 1984, the team had a deficit of $8 million. Apparently, management would pay the previous season's bills out of the current season's incoming revenues. So the revenues for my first 1984 season had already been spent to pay the bills of the 1983 season. It was annoying to have to come up with an additional $8 million to cover the deficit, but not annoying enough to dissuade me from the deal. I accepted the liabilities and moved forward with the purchase.

Under the terms of the sale agreement, I was to pay $30 million at the close of the deal and the balance over a five-year period. As a condition of the sale, Klein offered to remain on as a consultant, but we decided not to accept his offer. I wired the funds from my personal bank account. On August 1, 1984, I issued the following press release:

> I am very pleased and proud to announce today that I have exercised my first right of refusal to purchase the controlling interest in the San Diego Chargers of the National Football League.
>
> I have always believed in the pursuit of one's dreams. For me, it has been a lifelong goal to own an NFL team.
>
> I look forward to my new responsibilities with excitement and enthusiasm. It is my plan to become actively involved in the management of the team, and I believe my business experience and enthusiasm for the game will keep the Chargers a strong and viable team.

I also wish to mention that I am particularly glad the Chargers' home base is San Diego. I have always had a deep affection for the City of San Diego, and I am glad my new interest will demand I spend a great deal of time in this beautiful city.

One of my attorneys, Max Freeman, accompanied me to sign the mountain of contracts and paperwork. When we were leaving, Max, Gene Klein, and I were in the elevator when the conversation turned to Gene's highly successful thoroughbred horses. "At least horses don't have agents," Gene said. "They'll drive you crazy in this business."

In his autobiography, *First Down and a Billion,* Klein ends practically every chapter with the words, "Thank you, Alex," expressing endless thanks for my buying him out of the Chargers, which, he writes, was the biggest headache of his life. (Six years after selling the team, Klein died on March 12, 1990, from a host of medical problems.)

With the deal finalized, I triumphantly flew to San Diego with my two sons. There were billboards and banners and a feeling of excitement that I had never known. My first press conference would be held in the dining hall at the University of California at San Diego. About one hundred people were crammed into the dining hall. It was the proudest moment of my life, and my excitement showed. "He couldn't have fidgeted more if he were a rookie who just had been ordered for the first time to sing during dinner," one reporter wrote.

I rose to speak. I said I thought the Chargers were the best ball club in the NFL. The press reminded me that the team had just finished a 6–10 season. "Well, we'll make them the best club in the NFL," I said. I assured the press that I would not be an absentee owner. Any problems and I'd be there in a heartbeat. I promised to maintain a second residence in San Diego and that I'd consider moving my home and business headquarters to the city. Until then, because we needed a local presence, my son Dean and his wife and children would move to San Diego to represent our family and handle the day-to-day duties of running the team.

I assured everyone I wasn't going to make any changes in club management, since one of my strongest reasons for buying the franchise was the staff that Gene Klein had assembled: legendary head coach Don Coryell, general manager Johnny Sanders, assistant general manager Paul "Tank" Younger (the first athlete from the predominately black Grambling State University to play in the NFL, who earned his nickname by running over everything in his path), and publicist Rick Smith. I intended to give these men even more responsibility and authority, I said. I applauded Gene Klein's ability to minimize player salaries, putting the Chargers twenty-third in the league in average player salaries, even though I would soon discover that this statistic was nothing to cheer about. But back then I still thought it was possible to run the team lean and win. I would soon find out the hard way that unless you go out on a limb and spend money on players, you're destined to lose. But on the day of the press conference I was so full of enthusiasm that I could paint only the rosiest of pictures.

The press began firing questions:

"What's your personal background?"

"What have you done in your business?"

And finally, "Who is Alex Spanos?"

I knew that most of them didn't really care who I was or where I came from. All they wanted to know was *When are we going to win?*

I had achieved my longtime goal of owning an NFL team. I had every reason to be optimistic. The public perception was that the Chargers had great potential for victory. We had star players like legendary quarterback Dan Fouts, running back Chuck Muncie, tight end Kellen Winslow, and coach Don Coryell, designer of the awesome Air Coryell offensive machine. With my own determination for victory, how could I not be optimistic? I would soon discover that the team's stars were past their prime and major changes were needed in the coaching staff. But my enthusiasm rose up within me at the press conference and I spoke before common sense could intervene. "The San Diego Chargers will be in the Super Bowl within *five* years," I promised.

The crowd erupted in a crazy cheer. I had told them exactly what they wanted to hear. For forty years prior to that moment, I had set and achieved many five-year goals. Starting my catering business in 1950, I'd made my first $1 million by 1956. I began playing golf in 1955; by 1960, I was one of the top-ranked amateurs in America. I began my construction business in 1960; by 1965, that business was thriving. Between 1965 and 1970, I achieved my five-year goal of statewide California expansion. Between 1970 and 1975, I achieved my five-year goal of expanding across the western United States. Goals set, goals achieved. Up to this point, that was my success story. Professional football would be depressingly different, but I didn't know it back then. As Al Davis told me: "You can control your will to win. But you can't control the team."

I would soon discover why Gene Klein was so thankful that I'd bought him out of the San Diego Chargers.

CHAPTER 11

Learning by Losing

My life changed completely after I bought the San Diego Chargers. Until that moment, I had been one of the top builders in the country, but nobody outside of my community and industry knew me. The moment I became the newest owner of an NFL team, everybody, at least in San Diego, became familiar with my face and my name.

One night shortly after I bought the team, Faye and I visited Bob and Dolores Hope at their home in Palm Springs. We would always take one- or two-mile walks after dinner. On one of our walks, a couple of kids with pens and paper came running up, saying, "We want your autograph!"

"Okay, okay," Bob said.

"No, not you," said the kids. "Mr. Spanos. We're Charger fans."

The city of San Diego and the Charger fans gave me a great welcome. My entire family was thrilled to be part of the team. Faye became one of the most vocal spectators at Charger games, and our life began to revolve around the football season. For the first couple of years of my ownership I enjoyed every minute of the experience. I would fill our company planes with family members and friends and fly down to San Diego for the games. It would be a weekend event, a celebration. The guests always included Bob and Dolores Hope and Telly and Julie Savalas. Bob was an avid fan. He would call me with suggestions, including which players I should recruit. After one such conversation, when he suggested I sign up a wide receiver that had already been drafted by Seattle, I told him, "If you know of somebody else I can get, Bob, let me know." He assured me that he would, and he soon called with other suggestions. Even during the worst losing seasons, we continued the Sunday game-day tradition. The team became essential to my family, our friends, and me. Bob, Barron Hilton, and I, all of us wearing Charger jackets, would sit in the front row of my box. Bob would watch quietly while Barron, chomping at his cigar, would periodically erupt in verbal missives. As for me, I would loudly go crazy in my own way with each and every play. "You can always tell when you're at a Chargers game," Bob Hope would tell audiences. "They serve the hot dogs wrapped in grape leaves."

But the fun began to fade fast.

In the 1983 season, the year before I bought the team, the record of the team's respected coach, Don Coryell, began sliding. The 6–10 1983 season, with two blowout losses to the L.A. Raiders, was Coryell's second losing season in thirty-one years of coaching—and the beginning of the slump to come. Within the first three months of my ownership, I contended with player disputes, including Chuck Muncie's drug suspension and Kellen Winslow's contract standoff. Injuries had decimated the defensive backfield and many of the receivers.

My baptism into the complicated process of signing pro football players involved a player named Mossy Cade. I had just taken over as majority owner in early August 1984 when I walked immediately into the crisis. Both the press and the fans were clamoring for us to sign Cade, a cornerback from the University of Texas whom the Chargers had drafted in the first round (sixth overall) and who was in the midst of a holdout. Cade wouldn't accept anything less than any player picked after him in the draft. Since the eleventh pick, linebacker Wilbur Marshall of Florida, had signed a $3.1 million, four-year deal with the Chicago Bears, Cade insisted that we match the $3.1 million. Gene Klein had offered him $1.6 million for a four-year contract, but Cade turned it down. When I took over, I also refused to go higher than $1.6. Player salaries had already increased an average of 30 percent that year, and I felt I was running a business and could not justify that kind of money on one player.

But the pressure was on to sign Cade. At the press conference to announce me as the new majority owner, the first question was not about the plans for the future but about our holdout. "What are you going to do about Mossy Cade?" asked Jerry Magee, a veteran football writer for the *San Diego Union*, who was adamant that we sign the cornerback.

If we didn't come close to the $3.1 million, Cade's agent insisted that he'd defect to the USFL. With the press in hot pursuit of the story, Cade and his agent were staying in a secret location. We agreed to meet. Flanked by his agent and others, Cade, barely twenty-one, walked into my new office. Cade was wearing large dark sunglasses, which he never removed. He leaned back in a chair and kicked his feet up on the desk, as if to say, *Okay, let's talk money.*

What the hell is this! I thought.

We talked, or at least his agent and I talked. But I refused to go above the $1.6 million that had been on the table throughout the holdout. It was my first public relations nightmare. Cade jumped ship to the USFL Memphis Showboats, getting a four-year deal worth $2.25 million. The press blasted me for being "cheap," unwilling to back my commitment to victory with my checkbook. Looking back now, I realize they might have been right. Coach Coryell was also frustrated with my reluctance to open my wallet wide. "I've learned in my late years just to blank things like this out," he told the press. "I'll go on and do the best I can with what I've got."

It turned out to be a blessing in disguise. We ended up trading the NFL rights to Cade to the Green Bay Packers for first- and fifth-round draft choices, and Cade would play just two seasons in the NFL before off-the-field problems landed him in jail.

I made many mistakes after I bought the Chargers, but the biggest one was not replacing all the executives, including Coach Coryell, with my own people. I had felt that the change of ownership had caused enough of a disruption, and I didn't want to add to it by making personnel changes. But my staff's loyalty remained with Gene Klein, and I learned, much too late, that a football team cannot win without complete and undivided loyalty. Jerry Jones, who bought the Dallas Cowboys in 1989, was right. Immediately after his purchase, he cleaned house, firing everybody, including the great coach Tom Landry, and brought in his own people. The press crucified him, but within three years his Cowboys won their first of several Super Bowls. Unlike Jones, who fired everyone in one fell swoop, I was forced to do my firing over a long and excruciating period. I had reason to believe that their loyalty was not totally with me. We were soon plagued with numerous press leaks, and it eventually became apparent that some members of the staff were still in constant communication with Gene Klein about what was going on within the Chargers organization.

Pretty soon, the headlines began singing dirges:

"CHARGERS HAVE NEW OWNER, BUT SAME OLD PROBLEMS ON DEFENSE"

"CHARGERS ARE A $72 MILLION QUESTION MARK"

"THE CHARGERS FUTURE MIGHT VERY WELL BE BEHIND THEM"

When the 1984 season began, none of the preseason media prog-
nosticators felt the Chargers could win the AFC West, as they had
done in 1979, 1980, and 1981. A playoff berth would be a very long
shot. Victory came early, but it was fleeting. In my very first game as
owner, we faced the Minnesota Vikings on their home turf. In the first
play of the game, quarterback Dan Fouts fired to Kellen Winslow,
who pitched the ball back to Wes Chandler, who sped to a twenty-
four-yard gain. We slaughtered the Vikings, 42–13, and I thought to
myself, *How hard can this be?*

By October we were 4–2, with wins against Minnesota, Houston,
Detroit, and Green Bay. But by early November, 4–2 had become
4–5, with three straight losses to Kansas City, the L.A. Raiders, and
Seattle. The prospects were slim for finishing even a barely respec-
table 8–8, as our final six weeks included two outings against the
division-leading Denver Broncos, undefeated Miami, the Steelers at
Pittsburgh, Chicago, and Kansas City. We managed to beat Miami in
overtime, 34–28, and Chicago by a score of 20–7, but lost all the
other games. The Chargers finished fifth, otherwise known as last
place, in the AFC West with the same 6–10 record as the year before.

I once relished my daily walks through the streets of San Diego.
But when we began losing and continued to lose, I began to dread
facing anyone. I was the owner of the perpetually losing San Diego
Chargers, and that was not a pretty image to bear. I began to understand Gene Klein's frustration. I didn't blame the press, and I couldn't
blame the fans. They wanted a winning team as much as I did. The
worst part was that, unlike my construction business, which I know
how to run extremely well, I didn't have the knowledge or control to
make a difference in the Chargers. I wasn't a player, I wasn't a scout,
and I wasn't a coach. Of course, while running my construction business, I don't personally draw the blueprints or pour the concrete. But
at least in that business, I know how to lead the people who do the

work. In football, I had to rely on other leaders and I had to rely on the team.

We finished the 1985 season 8–8, rising from fifth to fourth place in the AFC West. The highlight of the season was a 40–34 homefield victory over the Raiders in overtime. Just two weeks earlier, we had lost 34–21 on their home turf.

But the worst was still ahead. The 1985 season, when we finished 8–8, would become the highlight of my first three seasons of owner-ship. The year 1986 was agonizing. We won our first game against the Miami Dolphins convincingly, 50–28, but lost the next eight games just as convincingly:

20–7 at New York Giants
30–27 vs. Washington
17–13 at L.A. Raiders
33–7 at Seattle
31–14 vs. Denver
42–41 at Kansas City
23–7 at Philadelphia
24–23 vs. Kansas City

I took everything personally, especially the losses. The team's failures were my failures. I became obsessed with the Chargers. The staff began calling me "a live volcano" for my penchant for screaming. The press began calling me "Dr. Jekyll and Mr. Spanos." Their questions were always the same: Why were we so consistently losing? I would decline interviews so as not to have to make the same tired excuses for myself and the team. Watching games became extraordinarily frustrating. I lived and died with every play. I'd try to keep a positive face before the media, but in the privacy of my box (which was never truly private) I would slap my palms on the counter or throw them up in the air depending on what was happening on the field. I bellowed, bawled at the players below, and cursed the television replay. My family and friends knew not to get too comfortable if a game wasn't going well. The tragedies on the field would just become too painful for me to watch. If things didn't improve by the third quarter I'd bellow, "They're playing like bums!" and leave. My friends and family would follow or be left behind to find their own way home. On more than one occasion, as I walked out of a game, fans pulled down their pants and shot me the moon. I winced but just kept walking.

These were days of intense personal humiliation for me. I thanked God that I didn't have to face the fans every single day. When I bought the Chargers, I had considered moving my family and entire business operation to San Diego. It would have been a logical move. Owning an NFL franchise is an all-consuming occupation; most owners live in the same city as their team. Maybe, I thought, it was time to leave my little town for the big city. I mentioned the move to Faye. "I'd rather not," was all she said. Once again, my wife saved me. I really didn't particularly care to move, either. When fans began booing me in the street and reporters kept hammering at me in the newspapers, I was especially grateful to be able to go home.

During these frustrating times I would fly back home to Stockton and to the refuge of my family, who were all there, except for Dean, who lived in San Diego. As I've said before, we are a very close-knit family. When our children got married and started having their own children, it was as if they never left home. Four days a week we all eat dinner together at our house. Until eight years ago, Faye would regularly prepare meals for fifteen to twenty people. When the number of grandchildren kept growing and the number of friends invited to dinner increased, Faye finally agreed to hire someone to help with the cooking. I still relish family dinners: any evening my children and grandchildren visit us, the house is filled with their laughter. On the days when they didn't come, usually on weekends, we would visit them at their homes, which were just a block away from ours. These occasions were my only respite from the intensity of having to deal with endless Chargers problems.

In retrospect, I have realized that I was part of the problem. After losses on Sunday, I'd barrel into the Chargers offices first thing Monday morning, erupting. I'd unleash tirades and leave quaking staff members in my wake. "What the hell happened?" I'd yell at managers, coaches, and players. "If I were younger, I'd get on the field and show you how to win myself!" I realize now that I sounded like a maniac, and I probably was. I was driving myself and everyone around me crazy with my frustration. It took me a long time to realize that I was doing more harm than good.

If I could have found a quick fix, I would have bought it, no matter the cost. But I soon realized there was no quick fix for what plagued the Chargers. It became obvious that some hard choices and decisions had to be made. Johnny Sanders was general manager when I acquired the team. He was responsible for football operations, including coaching, players, scouting, training camp, equipment, and other administrative issues. We worked well together. But in 1986, I reassigned Johnny, making him assistant to the president and reducing his responsibilities to the signing of players. I opted not to renew assistant general manager Tank Younger's contract. I also began making sweeping changes in executive staff and player personnel. Midway through the 1986 season, with the team 1–7, I released Don Coryell as head coach.

I hired Al Saunders to step into Coryell's place as head coach. At thirty-nine, he was the youngest coach in the NFL, and I thought he showed promise. At the end of the 1986 season, I brought in Steve Ortmeyer as general manager. A longtime NFL veteran, Ortmeyer had done a good job for the Raiders as head of football operations. In retrospect, I should have let Ortmeyer hire Saunders so their relationship would have gotten off on a proper footing. But Saunders rejected Ortmeyer, and even more problems began.

At every turn, I was hammered with criticism. Newspaper reporters and fans didn't blame the coaches or the players for the losses. They blamed *me*. The irony of it is that when we won, which was rarely, the coaches and the players got the credit. But when we lost, it was all my fault. Some reporters suggested in print that I return to Stockton where I belonged and take the team with me.

Finally, at the beginning of the 1987 season, the first full year under Al Saunders and a rebuilding year, we got off to a 8–1 start. I believed something good was finally going to happen. I never dreamed we wouldn't make the playoffs—we were almost there, just a win or two away. But we lost six straight games to finish 8–7. Still, we finished in third place in the AFC West, our best showing since 1984.

The next year, we once again finished 6–10. At the end of the season, I fired Al Saunders. We had two priorities: hiring a strong-minded coach in the Mike Ditka vein and finding a quality quarterback. First, I hired Dan Henning, who had been the Chargers' backup quarterback in the sixties, as coach. (He had spent four years as head coach in Atlanta, and after that he had coached in Washington.) Henning had lulled me into believing that he could make us win. But he'd never had a winning season as an NFL head coach. In 1988, we signed Mark Malone as quarterback. He had been Pittsburgh's first-round draft choice in 1980 and Terry Bradshaw's apprentice. Malone was the Steelers' starting quarterback during the 1984 season, guiding the team to the AFC Championship Game.

The changes didn't help. In 1988, I attended the Super Bowl in San Diego, which Gene Klein had been successful in bringing to the city. Of course, I attended as "host" instead of contender. For four days, I entertained the owners of the contending teams.

At a bash I threw for all the NFL owners and executives, Bob Hope made an appearance. "The Chargers started off 8–1 and didn't win another game," he told the crowd. "You may think this is a party, but Alex thinks it's a wake."

Despite the jokes, Bob was supportive, as were all of my friends, especially Telly. No matter how dismal the score, he would smother me in a big bear hug, extol the positives, and give me a thumbs-up for the next game. My involvement in Telly's horses had been a leap of faith, and he put the same type of faith into my football team. Telly's enthusiasm and support never wavered. Friends like President Gerald Ford, whom I had met at Republican fund-raisers when he was still a congressman, would pat me on the back and try to boost my spirits. "Alex, stick it out, pal," the former president would say. "Things will get better."

But my dark mood deepened.

"If the team is making you so miserable, maybe you should consider selling it," said my son Dean.

"No, son, not until we achieve our goal," I'd reply. "I won't sell a losing ball club." When rumors arose in the press that I was seeking a buyer, I would set them straight. "The Chargers are not for sale," I would say. "I'm committed to bringing the Chargers to the playoffs and beyond. My disenchantment does not include giving up. I promised a Super Bowl in five years. It wasn't an empty promise, even if it now seems so."

By 1991, we were dead last in the AFC West, with an overall record of 49–78 in my eight years as owner.

I've always believed that running a business, whether a retail store, a corporation, or a sports team, is basically a simple proposition. "Keep it simple!" I've always admonished my staff. I don't believe in bureaucracy. When I became the number one builder of apartments in America, I had a staff of twenty people in my office. My closest competitor in Stockton, who was about number thirty on the list, had a staff of two hundred. In running my construction business, I would ask myself three basic questions: (1) What are your accounts receivable? (2) What are your accounts payable? (3) What is your cash in the bank? After fifty years in business, I still get my Monday morning reports. I always know what's on the books down to the dollar. It took me ten years of losing to learn that you can't run a successful sports franchise worrying about the bottom line. I was wrong to think I could, and it wasn't easy for me to admit it.

After the departure of Steve Ortmeyer as general manager at the end of the 1989 season, I knew the team was ready for a monumental change. We desperately needed a leader, someone with knowledge, expertise, and a sterling reputation in the football world. I needed someone who could take control of the Chargers. One name towered above the others: Bobby Beathard. He had helped rebuild the Miami Dolphins and then led the Washington Redskins to the Super Bowl in the eighties. He had resigned as the Redskins' general manager the previous year to begin a one-year contract with NBC Sports. Dean and I went to see Beathard and offered him the general manager's job. When I asked him to move to California, Beathard agreed. His parents, who lived on the West Coast, were in their early eighties, and he wanted to be near them.

When Beathard took the job, I breathed a big sigh of relief. I was suddenly filled with hope and optimism. Bobby began working miracles. He built up the team almost from scratch. It wasn't an easy reconstruction project. At the end of the 1991 season, Bobby and I fired head coach Dan Henning. The headlines screamed, "FIRING ENDS REIGN OF ERROR," referring to Henning's four-year, 16–32 record. Henning told the press that he hadn't spoken to the Chargers' "impatient owner," meaning me, for three months.

Bobby Beathard and I began interviewing candidates for what would be the ninth head coach in the Chargers' turbulent history. Beathard wanted to interview Bobby Ross, head coach at Georgia Tech. Ross had a good coaching record, solid values, and a dedication to doing the job right. During our first meeting, he spoke of his family more than anything else, which, being a devoted family man myself, I thought was a good sign. We hired him on the spot but kept the news secret until after Georgia Tech's last game, the Hula Bowl in Hawaii. At the last minute, Georgia Tech won. We announced the hire the following day, and both the press and the fans seemed to be happy.

Bobby Beathard and Bobby Ross were the shot in the arm that the Chargers so desperately needed. Their sense of direction and purpose and overriding determination for victory bolstered the team. Too bad the team's uplifted spirits didn't show on the scoreboard. In 1992, Bobby Ross's first year as head coach of the Chargers, we started the season 0–4. We should have been written off. I dreaded going through the same kind of disaster we had the year before, when we started out 0–5 and ended at 4–12. But Beathard and Ross never gave up, and, unbelievably, we bounced back and managed to win the 1992 AFC West title by winning eleven out of our last twelve games, including two wins against our archrival, the Raiders.

Never in the history of the NFL had a team rebounded from an 0–4 start to win a divisional title. As much as victory reflects talent and ability, it is also due to the attitude and mental toughness of the team and its leaders. Under Ross's coaching, the team began to *believe* it could win, and it did exactly that. After beating the Seattle Seahawks to clinch the division title, we hosted a first-round playoff game and shut out the Kansas City Chiefs, 17–0. The following week, we faced the Dolphins in Miami for the AFC Divisional Playoff Game. I had never anticipated a game so intensely. I was unprepared for the level of intensity, the emotional demands, and the tremendous stress. The fact that we got clobbered 31–0 was humiliating.

After 1992's impressive showing, everything fell apart.

In the summer of 1993, before the season began, general manager Bobby Beathard told Dean that he was going to resign. Dean asked Bobby not to say anything publicly and gave him a few weeks to figure out what to do about the rest of the season. Even though the news was quietly spreading within the Charger organization, it didn't become common knowledge until early January 1994. A year later, the January 27, 1995, edition of the *Los Angeles Times* reported, "Bobby Beathard quit. It was never reported, and is discussed now only reluctantly, but San Diego Charger General Manager Bobby Beathard quit. . . . It was the summer of '93, the Chargers were coming off their first playoff appearance in a decade, and Spanos' vice president of finances, Jerry Murphy, repeatedly insisted on Beathard justifying his genius. Instead, Beathard walked. . . . 'I told Mr. Spanos verbally that I was out of there,' Beathard said. 'I had a letter of resignation, and although I never got around to giving it to him, I didn't think I'd be there any longer.' "

"It wasn't a power play," Beathard was quoted as saying in the *Times* story. "I wasn't happy. Maybe he [Spanos] had the wrong guy, because I wasn't smart enough to hang around and try and do it a different way. It had a lot to do with the attitude toward people in the office. The morale was horrible. Mr. Spanos could not see the difference between [the construction] business up in Stockton and the football business."

The real source of Beathard's disenchantment was my refusal to approve the additional $8 million he had requested in order to sign both existing and new players after the 1992 season. Beathard felt he had an opportunity to sign top-quality players because of the NFL's collective bargaining agreement that had been ratified in the early part of 1993. With this new agreement came the salary cap and free agency. However, the new contract called for the 1993 season to be an "uncapped year," meaning there would be no salary cap in effect. Many teams took advantage of this by signing existing players and free agents to long-term contracts, paying them huge up-front bonuses and small salary amounts going forward, as the bonuses would not be counted against the future salary cap. Also, the lower salary for subsequent "capped" years would enable the teams to spend their money on other players. All of this made quality players very expensive in 1993.

Bobby wanted to sign new players and re-sign our marquee players...to the tune of $8 million. He wanted to sign them to long-term contracts and give them sizable bonuses the first year and smaller salaries for the years going forward. In the past, I had told Bobby to get us certain players, no matter the cost. But his request for an additional $8 million was incomprehensible to me. Having always been a bottom-line businessman, I felt Beathard was out of line this time. Beathard contended that the extra investment in players would pay off by getting us to the playoffs and, hopefully, the Super Bowl. Once that happened, he argued, we'd make our money back three or four times over. But it was a tough sell for me. My basic principles of business have always been just the opposite of what Beathard was proposing: in conventional business, a person or a project proves his or its worth and then is rewarded. I would soon learn that in football you pay up front and then hope you succeed. I argued that the Chargers had not generated revenues to justify such an expenditure. Besides, we had already exhausted the Chargers' signing bonus funds, which meant that the additional money would have to come out of my pocket. My business sense told me that to approve Bobby's request would be sheer madness.

Dean took Beathard to lunch and Beathard reiterated his intentions to resign. Dean tried to talk him out of it, but Bobby was adamant. When Dean told me of Beathard's mind-set, I brushed it off, thinking that he wouldn't follow through on his resignation.

I just couldn't believe that he would quit in the middle of the season and that he would walk away from what was quite an impressive salary. But Dean told me it wasn't just about money and that Beathard could get any job in the NFL. Still, I wouldn't allow myself to believe it. Whatever the reason, I refused to budge—and the pressure mounted.

It was an impasse. I did a great deal of soul searching. Questions raced through my mind. I went from one extreme to the other. Could Bobby Beathard be right? Could I risk losing one of the best general managers—if not the best—in the NFL? Did I have that much confidence in Beathard's abilities to ignore my own common sense? Could I rebuild the Chargers if he quit? I knew that if Bobby left, other personnel that he had brought with him would probably follow.

More than anything, I wanted to get the Chargers to the Super Bowl. Anyone who had made as big an investment in time, devotion, and money as I had could not afford to see that investment go down the tubes. But it wasn't only economics. Beathard's ultimatum wounded my pride, threatened my confidence, and unnerved my ego. The few attempts I made to ascertain the extent of his resolve confirmed my worst fears. Bobby would not budge an inch, and the standoff lasted several weeks.

The Beathard disagreement coincided with a period of tremendous emotional upheaval for me. That summer, everything came to a head. I was turning seventy, a milestone that I felt marked the beginning of the race toward the homestretch of my life, which left me with a tremendous sense of sadness. I knew I had to deal with the present and look to the future, but instead I began fixating on the past, specifically my childhood and the hardships my parents and our family had endured. As time passed, my melancholia deepened, mostly because of the pressures I was encountering, for which I could not find an acceptable resolution.

The pressure of everything—the team's failures, the nonstop negative press, fan criticism, my humiliation over not being able to turn the team around—all culminated in a sinking feeling of helplessness. For the first time in my life I didn't know how to fix my problems. One day, I broke down in front of a startled member of my staff. That day marked the beginning of an emotional and mental descent into a deep and dark depression. I felt helpless and hopeless. I had no energy to face anything or anyone. Each morning, I would force myself to get up, simply out of a lifetime's habit of waking up early no matter what. But throughout the day, I couldn't shake the feeling of despair that hung over me like a shroud. My work, always my all-consuming passion, could not hold my interest, although I tried to go through the motions of doing what had to be done. *What's happening to me?* I kept asking myself. For the first in my life I had no answers. My despair and sadness deepened. This was turning out to be one of the lowest points in my life.

During those days of overwhelming anguish, desperate thoughts crept into my consciousness, something that was entirely foreign to my character. I'd never been a man who dwelled on the negative; I'd always left the past behind to move on to the next day, the next opportunity. But now I was fast floundering in a darkness I had never previously fathomed.

Recently, a friend of mine, a very wealthy man, committed suicide with a shotgun blast to the brain. When I read in the paper that he suffered from chronic depression, I knew how he must have felt.

Those who knew of my depression felt helpless and concerned. Faye and my children insisted that I get some help from a psychologist. Unable to bounce back on my own, I agreed and began attending counseling sessions twice a week. We discussed everything: my frustrations, my sense of loss, my parents, and my feelings about entering the final period of my life. During these sessions, I was as vulnerable as a child. Having always been a strong person, I found this new vulnerability quite unsettling.

In the beginning, I couldn't understand how analysis could have helped. I've always been a man of action, not words. But as the sessions stretched on, I lost my initial reticence and began to open up to the psychologist. I experienced the value of analysis. My mood began to improve a little, and I saw a glimmer of light at the end of a very long and dark tunnel.

Bobby Beathard's resignation happened at the height of this personal crisis and created tremendous conflict between the principles that had guided my business career and the realities of running an NFL team. Giving him the additional funds would betray every business principle I ever had.

I clung to the standard definition of an entrepreneur: a person who organizes, manages, and assumes the risks of a business or enterprise. *Risk*. That's the key ingredient of entrepreneurship. Those who inherit wealth are not considered entrepreneurs, even if they increase or double that wealth. Even those in esteemed professions—doctors, lawyers, architects, teachers—are not considered entrepreneurs, no matter how great their economic success. Only a businessperson who assumes risk can be called an entrepreneur.

Up until this crisis, I had always believed that a risk worth considering must first be carefully calculated. Business is not a gamble, and no business deal should ever be a do-or-die proposition. But, as I painfully discovered, these beliefs are antithetical to owning a sports franchise, where maintaining a profitable bottom line does not mean success on the scoreboard. Had I lost my vision, my clarity of thought? In the midst of the pressures of pro football team ownership, had I lost the plan, the strategy, for getting the Chargers to the Super Bowl?

I knew that the sense of purpose that gives a person the drive to venture into unknown territories is indeed like the proverbial sound of a different drummer. At times it appears you may be out of step with your family, friends, associates, even the rest of the world. But it's the music to which you are attuned, and you must follow it. Was this an instance when I should heed the advice of those closest to me—or persevere on my own?

Thinking about all of this left me more lost than ever.

I knew I wasn't emotionally strong enough to handle the conflict. Feeling that the situation required consultation with my family instead of my board, I called a family meeting in Stockton to discuss the Beathard situation. My two sons sit on my company board and are instrumental in all business decisions. But in this specific situation and because of my mental condition, I wanted the counsel of my entire family. I made up my mind to follow whatever advice they gave me.

At the dinner table, I sought their advice.

Their reaction surprised the businessman in me. All four of my children sided with Bobby Beathard. They urged me to give him the additional $8 million. They were well aware of my concerns, but they didn't want even to contemplate the Chargers without him. They knew that Bobby's presence as general manager gave me a level of comfort: as long as he was there I could cling to some hope for the team. Each member of my family made his or her point, all of which hit home painfully. I conceded that their argument about Bobby was right, but I was still reluctant to give him the additional $8 million. My heart just wasn't in it yet. I still foolishly clung to the belief that there may have been other reasons why Bobby wanted to resign. I even thought that maybe the real cause of our disagreement was that I had offended him in some way. I asked Bobby's circle of friends and the team coaches about it but came up essentially with nothing.

Although I was finally seeing myself in a little clearer light, I was still making absolutely wrong assumptions. Sitting at the dinner table with Faye and my children, all of them urging me to give Bobby the additional $8 million, I once again felt a sense of unresolved frustration.

Finally, after all the kids had their say, Faye spoke up. In all the years we have been married, she has never once questioned my decisions and has rarely volunteered a suggestion on what I should or shouldn't do. She always has the kind of faith that she sums up in three simple yet extraordinarily powerful words: "I trust you." So whenever Faye voices any reservation to me or our children, we all know immediately that it's time to reconsider our ideas. "I think the kids are right," she said at last. "It's time to just simply enjoy the games. Leave the running of the team to others."

That's all I needed to hear. Once again, Faye gave me the strength to change the course of my life. She was absolutely right, as she has always been, and I immediately gave in. Perhaps I had already made up my mind to give Bobby what he wanted but couldn't bring myself to abandon my lifelong business principles without a struggle. Whatever the case, my trust in Faye opened a new door for me—a door leading out of the day-to-day management of the Chargers. Once I heard Faye's suggestion, I clung to it like a drowning man clings to a life raft. I made up my mind to go with her recommendation immediately, and a tremendous sense of relief flooded my heart and mind.

I acted quickly. I directed Dean to give Bobby the $8 million he'd asked for and went one step further. I told Dean that he would take over the Chargers. As the family's point man for the team, he had done his job beautifully, developing great administrative and people skills. He had also developed a close personal relationship with Bobby Beathard and other members of the staff. In comparison to me, Dean is as calm as can be. He works through problems without emotional outbursts. I trusted him both as a son and as an employee. I had watched him grow into an extraordinary administrator, and it was time to see him in action as his own man. "I'm stepping aside," I told Dean. "You're running the ball club from here on out. I'm giving you and Bobby the money he asked for. All I ask is that you get us to the playoffs."

I not only gave Bobby Beathard the $8 million he demanded; I pulled out of the daily management of the team. "An old dog can learn new tricks," I promised Bobby, who, after my decision and the intervention of his agent, decided to stay with the team. I vowed to myself that I would stick by that decision to step aside no matter what. This turned out to be the best decision I could have made. Dean and Bobby's good working relationship spilled over to the rest of the staff.

"SHARING WEALTH," read one headline, announcing that I'd turned the team over to Dean. "Things are changing as Spanos begins his eleventh year as the owner of the Chargers," the story read. The change in the team's morale was dramatic. Dean's sure hand and steady disposition had a calming effect on the entire Charger organization. Bobby could now go on to acquire draft picks and free agents and re-sign the existing players he needed to accomplish his goal of victory. The additional money showed on the field. "You know what my expectations are?" I told the press during one practice session. "I can't stand to lose one game. I want to win all the games. I'm always predicting the playoffs. Always. We'll make the playoffs."

My initial $8 million commitment grew by $3 million more. But I stuck by my decision. No recriminations, no criticism, and no interference. During the 1994 season, Faye and I went to every game, whether at home or away. That season turned out to be a milestone, and not only for the Chargers; it was also a turning point for me. Faye and I never had so much fun as we did during that season, watching the team move toward the ultimate goal, the Super Bowl. The season began typically, with sports pundits predicting that we'd end up in the bottom of our division. But the new me who emerged after turning over the team to Dean was a calmer, gentler man. Gone were the days of incensed Monday morning tirades or telephone calls to San Diego demanding explanations of why we had lost, why we had not used this-or-that game plan, or why we had adopted such-and-such a strategy. My relationship with everyone at the Charger organization vastly improved. I learned to control my anger and anxiety, no matter how edgy and nervous I felt about the games. I was

bound and determined to remain calm and detached from management, win or lose. The wins thrilled me, and when we lost I learned
to accept defeat without recriminations.

Then I was blessed with two miracles. Thanks to my new attitude,
my depression began to subside and I began to feel like my old self
again. The clouds parted both in my mind and on the playing field.
My $8 million gamble paid off big-time. Bobby, Dean, and the team
managed to make my Super Bowl dream come true.

It was a perpetual come-from-behind season. These were nail-
biting, heart-wrenching contests, in which the players fought until
the last second on the clock, repeatedly snatching victory from constantly predicted defeat. It was a wild, wooly, and eventually winning
year, culminating in the challenge that every owner, player, coach,
and fan dreams about: getting a shot at going to the Super Bowl.

On January 15, 1995, we faced the Pittsburgh Steelers in the AFC
Championship Game at Three Rivers Stadium in Pittsburgh. Before
we even got to town, doomsayers were rattling their sabers, predicting a slaughter. A week before the game, Rush Limbaugh predicted a
win for the "men of steel" on his radio program. Apparently almost
all of San Diego listened to Rush; his prediction didn't sit well with
his San Diego listeners, especially Bobby Beathard, who was such a
huge Rush fan that he kept a picture of him in his office.

The naysayers had every right to their doubts. After a great 11–5
season, the Pittsburgh Steelers were the confident, cocky darlings of
the AFC. Their offense and defense were phenomenal. They were
one of three teams, including the Dallas Cowboys and the San
Francisco 49ers, on which football experts lavished unilateral praise.
Everyone had been predicting that the Steelers would represent the
AFC at the Super Bowl. Only Chris Berman of ESPN gave us even
a slight chance of winning.

I flew into Pittsburgh with Faye and our entourage—my children
and grandchildren, my brothers and sister and their families, my

friends and their families, and my gin-playing buddies, who always fly with me for cross-country (and sometimes intercontinental) gin games. Pittsburgh was in full-tilt Steeler frenzy. "A Matterhorn of arrogance," is how one reporter described the Steeler town's mood. They had every right to be confident. We were the perpetual underdogs. The Steelers were eight-point favorites; many people predicted that we wouldn't even score.

There were Steeler banners, Steeler slogans, Steeler buttons, and Steeler T-shirts. It seemed that no one was immune to Steeler Fever. The local TV stations aired nonstop Steeler news. From sportscasters to station anchors to fans, everyone predicted a blowout Steeler victory. Even the weather girl at one of the TV stations predicted the winning Steeler point spread right after she rattled off the weather forecast. In sports bars, restaurants, stores, and on street corners, fans were already savoring a win. The Steeler players were equally arrogant. They had taped a "Blitzburg" Super Bowl song video, which played on TV on game day, early Sunday morning. The Steeler enthusiasm was vibrant, strong, and contagious.

Thank God, I was there for only three days. Everywhere we went, I could sense the sneers. We had a police escort throughout our stay. During the game, we were warned not to venture from our box without a security escort. The town was hostile territory.

I still thought that we had a fighting chance. Bobby Beathard assured me that we could win, and I had learned at last to trust him. He said our players were focused on the game and that Coach Ross felt good about their mental state and recent practice sessions. We would finally have a chance to prove everyone wrong and maybe even gain the respect we had been so long denied.

Game day at Three Rivers Stadium in Pittsburgh: the forecast was rain. But by midmorning, the sun came out and this event became a cause of jubilation in our camp. Sunshine in Pittsburgh on January could only be the harbinger of good things for us; California weather had beat out the threat of Pennsylvania rain and cold. Increasingly superstitious, we clung to whatever good tidings we could. I had always prided myself in being a practical and rational man, believing that good things come only through preparation and hard work. Yet throughout the 1994 season, I wore the same outfit on game days: blue slacks, turtleneck, and cream sweater, afraid that I might jinx the team if I dared to wear anything else.

During the game, the clouds beat back the sun and it began raining heavily. Steeler fans were gleeful, a sea of sixty thousand screaming and waving "Terrible Towels." Throughout the game, the fans never sat down and never stopped stomping their feet with a deafening roar.

The first half was as dismal as everyone had predicted, with only one Charger pass completion. After blowing a goal line series at the Steelers' 20, we had to settle for a field goal, leaving us down 10–3 at the half. I settled in for the usual long tough fight ahead.

Early in the second half, the Steelers tacked on a field goal to extend their lead to 13–3. But midway through the third quarter, Charger quarterback Stan Humphries, who had emerged as a desperately needed team leader after Beathard imported him from the Redskins, dropped back and faked a handoff to running back Natrone Means. The Steelers' defense went for the fake, which allowed Humphries to throw the ball to a wide-open Alfred Pupunu, who rumbled for forty-two yards. *Touchdown!* I was on my feet and screaming along with everyone else in our box, one small square of celebration in a stadium that had suddenly turned absolutely silent with shock.

Steelers 13, Chargers 10.

We got the ball again on our own 20. On the second play of the drive, quarterback Humphries completed a twenty-three-yard pass to Pupunu, and I was up on my feet and screaming again. We came to third down and one at the Steelers' 47. Our third-down conversions had been an abysmal one of eight so far that game, but Natrone Means broke free for eight yards, giving us a desperately needed first down. Three plays later, we had a third down again on the Steelers' 43, this time with fourteen yards to go for a first down. Offensive coordinator Ralph Friedgen decided it was now or never.

I frequently flash back to everything that happened from that marvelous moment forward: Humphries dropping back, Tony Martin racing forty-three yards down the field, and the ball dropping right into Martin's hands for another touchdown. I could hear my heartbeat and feel a lump growing in my throat.

We snatched a 17–13 lead!

When the Steelers got the ball again, they marched systematically down the field. With one minute and three seconds to go in the game, Pittsburgh had first-and-goal at the 3, with four chances left to score and send us back to San Diego. The NFL officials kept urging me to go down to the field in case the Steelers didn't score and we won. But I refused to go until the third down. Finally, on fourth down, Steeler QB Neil O'Donnell threw a short pass, and, in one of the most majestic moments I've ever witnessed, our linebacker Dennis Gibson, an eight-year NFL vet, dove and blocked the pass with one hand.

The stadium turned deathly quiet, but all hell broke loose in our box. I was like a champagne bottle that exploded: screaming and dancing and crying with joy. I couldn't have been more proud of our team and our coaches. "In the 35th year of its existence, the team most of America had dismissed as an impertinent wallflower is going dancing in the main ballroom," wrote Tom Cushman of the *San Diego Union-Tribune*.

Against all odds, we had won, beating a team that was considered a sure bet to represent the AFC in Miami. For the first time, the San Diego Chargers were going to the Super Bowl! I had finally made good on my promise, but it didn't happen in the time frame or in the fashion that I'd envisioned. This wasn't my victory; it was the team's. Only by relinquishing control had I learned how to win.

Bobby Beathard took us to the Super Bowl. It cost me an additional $11 million, but it was worth every penny—and in my enthusiasm I admitted as much to the press. "I have been a businessman all my life," I told the reporters. "I am a bottom-line man. Good business sense tells you, don't put your hand in your pocket. If you have to spend, spend from the profits. But owning a football team is not like running your ordinary business establishment. If you want to win, you have to put your hand in your pocket. You have to risk operating in the red, if you care at all about winning football games. It has taken me eleven years to learn that. It's not easy for a man like me to admit I was wrong, but the truth is I was wrong, and look where we are now! The Super Bowl!"

When the game ended, I was swept up by a wave of media and team members and carried along in a sea of enthusiasm toward the Chargers' locker room, where the AFC trophy was presented to me by NFL representative Neil Austrian. "Super Bowl San Diego!" I kept yelling, in a voice that had become hoarse and raw from screaming. I remember thanking everyone and seeing Bobby Beathard and Bobby Ross in the crowd making their way toward me. I handed the trophy over to Bobby Ross. If there had been another trophy, I would have given it to Bobby Beathard. He had indeed proven himself a miracle worker.

We left Pittsburgh not entirely comprehending how much this win would alter our lives. I flew home to Stockton, where the rest of my children and their families and my friends and staff greeted us at the A. G. Spanos Jet Center with screams, signs, and balloons. The local press was also there. Becoming AFC champions had even energized my hometown, which is predominantly 49er country.

As soon as we landed in Stockton, I was told that San Francisco had beaten Dallas. The Chargers would face the 49ers in Miami in Super Bowl XXIX.

The Charger jet with players and staff on board flew directly to San Diego, where close to 100,000 ecstatic fans greeted the team in and around Jack Murphy Stadium. This was a day San Diego would never forget. The Charger lightning bolt became a symbol of unity. People told me that it was a first for the city: everyone basked in the victory and set aside anything that had divided them. The euphoria left no one unaffected. For the next two weeks, San Diegans posted the lightning bolt on every available surface. After thirty-five years of highs and lows, the fans finally had a big reason to celebrate.

On the Monday after the Pittsburgh game, congratulatory telephone calls, telegrams, and faxes poured into my office from all over the country—from friends, relatives, business associates, and college buddies with whom I had lost contact for years. That same Monday, I received a congratulatory call from Dan Rooney, owner of the Steelers. *What class*, I thought to myself after completing the call. As peers, NFL team owners observe the usual courtesies toward each other and abide by certain unspoken rules. However, it's not customary to call and congratulate the owner of the team to whom you have just lost, especially in a critical playoff game. Such losses are taken far more personally than others. Dan Rooney's telephone call was a gesture full of dignity and style.

For the next two weeks, my construction offices came to a standstill. Preparations for Super Bowl Sunday took over everything and everybody. I couldn't wait for the game and nothing could keep me at home for the two weeks before the Super Bowl. I made plans to leave for Miami one week early. The following week, my children and grandchildren, relatives and friends began to arrive. By Thursday of Super Bowl week, the entire Spanos clan was ready to rumble in Miami.

The week prior to Super Bowl Sunday is about public relations as much as sport. I never gave so many interviews in such a short time. Most of them were enjoyable, but many of the interviewers were condescending to the Chargers. They didn't think we had a snowball's chance in hell, and although the media tried to be polite, their attitude stung. The big question remained: How good were we? We had proven ourselves to be better than any other team in our conference, but were we good enough to beat the fabled 49ers? The general feeling was that the Chargers were doomed. The San Francisco 49ers had been the best team in the NFL for years. They were unstoppable. Still, I was on a Super Bowl high and not much could dull my excitement.

Then came the game.

What can I say? I'm not going to give any excuses. It was, as predicted, a rout, the bloodletting ending at 49–26. "Confirming predictions of a mismatch that were offered in virtually every corner of the land save one, the Super Bolts last night were victims of a super blowout," began one typical newspaper account. In my heart, I knew that our main goal had been to reach the Super Bowl. Still, the loss stung. I will never forget the faces of Bobby Beathard and coach Bobby Ross in the locker room. They were both devastated, speechless, and withdrawn. A loss is a loss and nobody likes to lose, least of all me. But football had taught me to rein in my impatience and realize that ultimate victory is achieved incrementally, sometimes in large strides, sometimes in small ones. I chose to look at the Super Bowl loss as an incremental victory. There are teams that have never reached the Super Bowl. In the 1994 season, the Chargers had gone to the Super Bowl, while twenty-six other teams sat at home watching the game on television. We were the AFC champions. No one could take that away from us.

Throughout the drama of that victorious season, San Diegans stood by the Chargers steadfastly. I was proud of how they cheered the team when we came back from Pittsburgh, AFC champions for the first time ever. But nothing touched my heart more than the welcoming parade the city gave us after our Super Bowl loss. The newspapers estimated that a crowd of close to 200,000 cheered the team's return.

Where do we go from here? I hope for a Super Bowl return—this time with a victory. As of this writing, the Chargers have not made the playoffs since 1995. Bobby Ross remained head coach until the end of the 1996 season, when Kevin Gilbride took over. In 1997 Gilbride coached the Chargers to a 4–12 record, earning last place in the AFC West. After Gilbride's departure in October of 1998, quarterbacks coach June Jones took over the helm. Jones didn't do much better, and we finished the season at 5–11—still last place.

Losing season after losing season led to more staffing changes. We hired John Butler, formerly with the Buffalo Bills, as the new general manager. He made four trips to the Super Bowl with the Bills and I am hopeful that his experience will help the Chargers. I feel we've put together a team capable of victory. I remain an integral part of that team, although still taking a backseat to my son Dean.

Today, the Chargers are worth many times my original investment. The latest expansion team was acquired for more than $700 million and the expectation is that in a few years NFL teams will be worth around $1 billion. Prices have exploded because of the $18 billion, eight-year TV contract NFL commissioner Paul Tagliabue negotiated for the teams and the anticipation of the Internet's effect on professional football. Of course, football is the number one sport on television and there are only thirty-two teams in America. That alone puts a huge value on each team. But the Chargers aren't for sale.

My stormy experience with the San Diego Chargers taught me a valuable lesson about my limitations.

The Chargers' 1994 season was simultaneously triumphant and tragic. In January of that year, we lost one of the team's biggest fans and one of my best friends. Telly Savalas died, at seventy-two, of bladder cancer.

"No One Can Enter Without Permission from the King," read the sign on Telly's suite at the University City Sheraton in L.A. where he lived for the thirty years I knew him. Even though he and his wife, Julie, had two homes in California and another in London, Telly felt most at home at the hotel. I was one of the few people that knew proud Telly had been battling cancer for seven years. But he wouldn't take care of what was, even back then, a curable disease.

Too proud for his own good, Telly refused to go to the doctors and wouldn't see any of his friends. He was truly larger than life and was embarrassed to let anyone see him in his weakened state. I spoke to him regularly by phone. When he died, Julie called us and said that Telly had asked to be buried in a Chargers jacket—and he was.

His funeral at St. Sophia Greek Orthodox Church in Los Angeles was extremely emotional. All of Telly's family, including wives and children, Hollywood colleagues, and admirers from the Greek-American community, were there to say good-bye. He was from old-school Greeks in every way. When he was gone, I felt as if an era had passed.

I kept thinking about the love Telly had for Greece. A proud son of Greece, his mother a former Miss Greece, he never forgot where he came from: not with his Oscar nomination for *Bird Man of Alcatraz*, not with the international success of his multitude of films like *The Dirty Dozen*, and especially not with the multiple Emmy Awards and superstardom of *Kojak*. The hit TV series introduced much of America to Greek-American culture. Telly made sure of that. He insisted that his character show his Greek-American heritage in name, attitude, and actions. He hired fellow Greek-Americans to work on the series. And he insisted that his supporting characters have Greek-American names. Telly made absolutely no concessions to gentrification.

"My name is Aristoteli Savalas!" he once proclaimed to *Greek American* magazine. "I say it with pride and pleasure." He went on to say, "For a long time, I thought the only Greek we could be proud of was Jim Londos, the wrestler, the famous Golden Greek. By the midfifties, I learned better. At that time Dimitri Mitropoulos was one of America's premier conductors, Alexander Scourby was reaching new heights as a narrative actor, Elia Kazan was the foremost stage and screen director, Katina Paxinou had won an Academy Award, George Christopher was mayor of San Francisco, George Papanicolaou had devised the Pap smear for detecting cancer—and a Greek jockey had even brought in more winners than Eddie Arcaro. I could go on an on, but you get the point."

Once when he was interviewed by a Greek-American woman reporter who apologized for not being more attractive, Telly cut her short by reminding her of her roots. "You've been beautiful for two thousand years!" he roared. "And don't you ever forget it!" Back at you, Telly.

CHAPTER 12

Giving Back to Greece

"Be proud of your heritage," my father repeatedly said for as long as I can remember. As children, these words sent us hurtling into the worn-out books at St. Basil's Greek Orthodox Church, where we learned the language, history, and customs of ancient Greece. As young adults, we were continually regaled by Dad with stories of the "Old Country," the cradle of democracy, the homeland of Socrates, Plato, and Alexander the Great, the land where mythical gods once resided, and where Dad regularly sent money and salutations to relatives who lived and worked there.

By the summer of 1984, Dad had been dead for a decade. But I still carried his admonishment in my soul.

That year, I got a call from Greece—not from my Greek relatives but from a representative of the prime minister of Greece, Andreas Papandreou.

At first, I didn't know why I had received the call. Although I cherished my Greek-American heritage, I didn't have a close association with Greece. However, my profile as a prominent Greek-American had grown. In reporting my rags-to-riches story, newspapers always mentioned my deep devotion to my Greek roots. I had received several awards from Greek-American business and civic organizations because of my financial contributions and overall business success. In 1984, my purchase of the Chargers directed further attention to me, and by 1986 I was regarded as one of a handful of Greek-Americans who had reached the pinnacle of financial success. Even so, none of these things merited a call from a representative of Prime Minister Papandreou.

I would later discover that there were two main reasons for the call: my relationship with President Reagan's administration and my well-known commitment to helping my fellow Greek-Americans. That commitment mainly involved helping Greek-American communities construct churches and community facilities wherever we built apartment projects. From time to time, I would give to other causes that supported Greek-American efforts to strengthen our national community and spirit. But it was my Republican affiliation, I would soon discover, that made the Greek government seek me out.

I would estimate that 90 percent of the Greek immigrants who came to America are Democrats. The word "democracy" comes from the Greek word *demokratia*, and the name of the Democratic Party was a familiar sound to Greeks in an unfamiliar country. My father, like his contemporaries, registered as a Democrat and when we reached voting age we did the same. But in my thirties, I changed my party registration to Republican.

In recent years, Greek-Americans have come to the forefront of political participation and involvement. One of the first prominent politicians of Greek-American descent was Maryland governor Spiro Agnew, who was selected by President Richard Nixon to be his vice president. Although there was no great wave of support behind Agnew among the mostly Democratic Greek-Americans, his position was a source of pride. Massachusetts governor Michael Dukakis, who ran for the presidency in 1988 against George Bush, stirred genuine exuberance among Greek-Americans, and the community at large raised millions in support of his candidacy. Although Dukakis lost the election, Greek-Americans gained renown in national political circles for the tremendous amount of funds they had raised for him and came to be regarded as a new and potent revenue source for political races, which had not been tapped to its full potential in the past.

I was one of the few Greek-Americans who were on the other side, throwing my support behind George Bush. When I met with Dukakis during his California primary campaign, I was explicit about my support for Bush, and the governor responded like a true gentleman. I've always had a policy of contributing to candidates of Greek-American descent, regardless of party, because my Greek-American pride transcends political affiliations. But if they run as Democrats, I support them only during the primary race and not during the general elections, if they're running against Republican candidates.

My deeper interest in politics was sparked by Ronald Reagan's election as governor of California. Californians had just survived Jerry Brown's years as governor, and I was encouraged about the prospect of having a Republican in control of the state. I had met many of Reagan's close supporters on my trips to Palm Springs, and I felt I knew what he represented. Ronald Reagan exuded warmth, charisma, and a rare gift of expressing himself in a manner that struck deep in the heart. After Ronald Reagan had moved to the White House, another Republican, George Deukmejian, was elected governor. George was of Armenian descent, and I felt a real kinship with him. He was a marvelous man of impeccable integrity, and whether one agreed or disagreed with him on principle, no one could deny his sterling character and honesty. These two Californians really inspired me to become more active in politics.

The next political events to energize my interest in politics were Pete Wilson's race for a seat in the United States Senate and George Bush's campaign for the presidency. Both were personal friends. Pete's subsequent election as governor of California was a cause for celebration. We could not ask for a more dedicated and skilled man in that job. As for my friend former president George Bush, I've never known anyone with more heart or conscience.

Andreas Papandreou was elected prime minister of Greece on October 18, 1981. He governed Greece throughout the eighties and into the nineties. An expert charmer, he was, as Greeks like to say, the charismatic equivalent of a thousand Bill Clintons. He had won election on a defiantly independent platform, basically saying, I'm not going to be anybody's yes man. His every speech ended with the line, "Greece belongs to the Greeks!" He saw Greece as the leader of a third force, a third road, between the capitalistic West and the communist East, a stance that rallied support at home but wasn't viewed well by the United States. Vocally anti-American and anti-European, Papandreou had vowed to pull Greece out of NATO and the European Union, without proposing any specifics. Although he never actually pulled Greece out of NATO, many Greeks applauded the idea.

Papandreou was a puzzle I could not quite figure out. Here was a man who had lived in the United States for more than twenty years as a naturalized American. Educated in American schools, including Harvard, he taught for many years as a professor of economics at the University of California at Berkeley. He married an American woman and had children who were born in the United States. But when he returned to Greece to claim his political inheritance from his father, who served as prime minister before him, Papandreou seemed to turn against the country that had given him his education, his family, and his career.

Ronald Reagan had just been elected president, and with his election the world turned bipolar: you were either for America or against America. Papandreou was perceived to be against America. His major foreign policy issue was the status of American military bases in Greece. After a lengthy and difficult series of negotiations, the two governments basically agreed to use different languages in two different agreements, one in Greek, and the other in English. The Greek document was written so the Greeks could say it terminated the base agreements; the American version was written so Americans could say it renewed those agreements. Papandreou may or may not have wanted to boot the American bases out of Greece, but he wanted to sell the notion of a Greece that made its own decisions. Later, however, Papandreou went overboard with his aggressive rhetoric and actions. He irritated the Reagan administration and Americans in general, and they could no longer tolerate him. This brought negative effects on tourism, on investments, and on the already precarious Greek-Turkish relations regarding the Cyprus issue.

By 1986, the prime minister wanted to mend fences. That's where I came in.

Later, I discovered that my invitation to Greece had been instigated by John Liveris, who was at that time the bureau chief for Greek television in Washington, D.C. A strong supporter of Papandreou, Liveris felt that Papandreou should officially visit Washington. Liveris called his childhood friend, Papandreou's economic advisor, Yiannis Papanicolaou, and said, basically, "Forget grassroots, Congress, and the Greek-American lobby—let's go directly to the president. Let's find a Greek-American who has access to the top levels of the American government and persuade him to intervene with the Reagan administration to get the invitation. Then Papandreou can explain his case to the Americans."

But what Greek-American could get Papandreou an official invitation from the White House? Canvassing America, they came up with a list of prominent Greek-Americans that they eventually narrowed down to two: the oilman George Mitchell of Galveston, Texas, and me. The more John Liveris read about me, the more he believed that I was the one who should be approached. He was impressed with my reverence for my roots, which I'd exhibited by bringing "The Search for Alexander" exhibit to San Francisco and by supporting the restoration of the Temple of Zeus at Nemea. Liveris later told me that he felt I was the epitome of the Greek-American: extremely individualistic, not an organization man or a corporate leader; a family man; and, most importantly, a doer. "This Spanos in California should be invited," Liveris told Papanicolaou. "He will be able to understand what we're talking about."

So Papanicolaou called me. He said he was visiting Washington, D.C., on government business. Would I receive him for a visit? Of course, I said yes. From Washington, he flew to Stockton in July 1986. He stayed for two days, discussing Greece and the American misconceptions about the prime minister with me. I had never met Prime Minister Papandreou and knew him only by reputation. I had, however, met his first wife, Margaret Papandreou, in 1984 when she and Melina Mercuri, the famous Greek star of the popular movie *Never on Sunday*, had visited California. They were trying to raise funds for the Greek cultural delegation to the 1984 Olympics, which was to be held in Los Angeles that same summer. Margaret Papandreou was extremely charming and impressive. I agreed to make a donation to her cause and give her the use of my personal jet while she was in California.

My impressions of Prime Minister Papandreou were not at all favorable. His anti-American stance was incomprehensible, if not downright indefensible. Regardless of any political motives he had for adopting such an attitude, I couldn't support anyone who pursued policies detrimental to my country. But Papanicolaou argued that the prime minister's anti-American expressions were for "internal consumption only." In reality, the prime minister was a realist, Papanicolaou said. His anti-American stance and statements were what the prime minister had to say and do to get elected, Papanicolaou insisted. Once in office, the prime minister believed that he could steer the country on the third road, not with the communists, not with the Americans, but in the middle.

Yiannis Papanicolaou was an extremely eloquent spokesman for the prime minister. He spoke of Papandreou's policies within the realities of what had taken place in Greece after the fall of the military junta that had governed the country from 1967 to 1974, when Middle Eastern and Arab international terrorist groups imported their activities into Greece. He tried to convince me that Papandreou had no choice but to adopt anti-American language. The Greek people blamed the U.S. for being deprived of representative government during the years of the junta and for the Turkish invasion and subsequent occupation of half of the island of Cyprus in 1974, which was accomplished with U.S.- and NATO-supplied arms. He told me that Papandreou could not survive politically unless he voiced the people's frustrations at what had taken place in Greece and Cyprus. "If he were truly anti-American, wouldn't he boot all American military bases from Greece?" Papanicolaou asked me. "Yes, he is a socialist, but in spite of it, he does not pursue hard-line policies. And yes, we have socialized utility and service industries, but this was done by the conservative governments that came before us. And don't forget, the private sector in Greece still flourishes."

For the duration of Yiannis Papanicolaou's visit to Stockton, I put aside all business matters. Although Papandreou's policies still alienated me, I kept an open mind and listened intently. I was fascinated and intrigued by the subject matter. Never before had I spent so much time discussing the political affairs of Greece.

Throughout our meeting one question remained squarely in my mind. *What did Papandreou want of me?* When I finally asked the prime minister's representative, he gave me his answer without hesitation: Prime Minister Papandreou was not only painfully aware of his anti-American image, he wanted to take active measures to repair it—and he wanted my counsel. "The prime minister would like you to visit Athens as his guest," Papanicolaou told me.

Similar visits by other prominent Greek-Americans would take place at later dates, he added. It was their hope that through such visits they could move beyond the misconceptions of the past and toward a better understanding between Greece and the United States. However, the prime minister's representative didn't tell me that I was the main focus and would be the only Greek-American invited.

My inclination was to disregard all the explanations and politely refuse the invitation. I've never liked socialist governments. I don't trust their leaders. But Papanicolaou's eloquent appeal and the fact that he had come all the way to California to deliver the invitation personally had impressed me. Maybe the Greek prime minister was like my dad and like so many other Greeks I've known: fiery, stubborn, and much too hotheaded for their own good. Maybe he really was being misunderstood.

Perhaps I was naive, but I accepted the trip in homage to my ancestry. Papanicolaou appeared delighted. I found out later that it would have been a great embarrassment to him had I declined.

During August, I received an official invitation and itinerary from the prime minister's office. "May I assure you that your well-known personality and reputation in so many achievements are highly appreciated here in your mother country," the prime minister wrote. On September 5, 1986, I boarded my plane in Stockton and flew to Greece. Faye could not come with me, so I took my youngest son, Michael, and several members of my staff, including George Filios. I could tell that everyone on the plane was excited, while I just kept hoping that taking the trip had been the right decision. We were expected to stay in Greece for five days, during which we would have meetings with Prime Minister Papandreou and members of his cabinet.

We touched down to find a jubilant crowd awaiting our arrival. At the airport, I met John Liveris for the first time, and we've stayed close ever since. Liveris organized the trip as if I were a head of state. A police escort traveled with us everywhere and policemen with machine guns were posted outside our hotel room. The media followed our every move as well, constantly asking if I was going to take over a major business, buy a Greek airline or shipyard, or build a major real estate development.

Despite all the questions, I remained focused on Greek-American relations. "I am a first-generation American, and I consider myself a patriotic American in every sense of the word," I said in a speech before the media and our governmental hosts. "But there is one thing I could never forget or deny, for to deny it would be to renounce part of myself. And that is my Greek heritage. It's a special blessing to have such an honored history, to descend from men and women who were great of heart and soul, men and women who carved a place in history as few can boast of.

"There is a great deal to be said about pride in oneself. It's a force that propels and motivates to special deeds and accomplishments, even to greatness. I am proud of who I am and where I came from. As an American of Greek descent, I can tell you, without a doubt in my mind, that if it were not for the teachings of my heritage I wouldn't be where I am today."

Then I met the prime minister. I was driven to Maximou, the beautiful classical white marble building where the prime minister's office is housed, and I was ushered into his office. I had heard so many negative comments about Papandreou that I was extremely curious to finally meet the man who had managed to create such animosity in the United States. The role of prime minister fit him well. In his late sixties, he was tall, robust, and immaculately dressed. He spoke perfect English and, I would soon learn, was a master at communicating his message. But our first meeting was purely social, exchanging pleasantries, nothing substantive.

Papandreou turned out to be an exceptional host. He showed us an insider view of Greece, which I enjoyed immensely. During our five-day visit, I met government officials and foreign affairs, economic, and cultural ministers, as well as the mayor of Athens, banking executives, and Greek businessmen. They were all very eager to put their best foot forward. They all seemed to know about me and my interests, including American football.

I visited the Department of Defense and got a briefing from legendary defense minister Yannis Haralambopoulos, vice president of the government. He was a romantic figure like someone straight out of the Greek revolution of 1821. Tall, lean, with an impressive curly moustache and wavy long hair, Haralambopoulos stood as defiant as a knight. Meeting with him, I felt as if the heroic Greece of the past, which I'd read about as a child in Greek language school, had dramatically returned to life. I also met the extremely popular minister of health, George Yenimatas, who showed me the government's efforts to renovate and modernize health systems.

I didn't really care about Greek politics. All I cared about was that these people sounded sincere. I began to see the prime minister's government as progressive and extremely active. But no one impressed me as much as Prime Minister Papandreou. As I got to know him through several private conversations, I found him to be frank, open, and receptive to my comments about the strained relations between our two countries. He displayed a genuine willingness to make every effort toward improving these relations, to mend fences, and to overcome the existing ill will. He answered all of my questions. He never hedged, never evaded.

Throughout my five-day stay, I had a strong sense that there was something specific the prime minister wanted to ask me. Each night, when my staff and I would return to our hotel, I'd tell them that I felt there was something to this invitation that remained unspoken. It wasn't until the very last day of my visit that Papandreou finally mentioned what was really on his mind.

We were out on a cruise on the famous Greek liquor magnate Spiros Metaxa's yacht when we got a message that the prime minister wanted to see me. We met at the Astir Hotel in Vouliagmeni, a resort suburb outside of Athens. I thanked him for his hospitality, which was beyond anything I had ever expected. I also assured him that I would always help Greece in any way I could. I meant this from my heart. I told him I was deeply moved by the many economic and political problems the country faced and by how these problems made life so difficult for the average Greek citizen.

I honestly felt that many of Greece's problems were solvable. But the current government, like previous administrations, was held captive by a bureaucratic system entrenched in waste and complacency. I felt that the simplest way to reform the country was to make a clean sweep of the bureaucracy. Incremental changes, like those of the past, had not helped. But any radical reform of the system would have encountered stiff opposition; about 25 percent of the Greek population was employed either by the government or by government-operated businesses such as Olympic Airlines. Radical reforms would have cost them their jobs, in a job market already crippled by a high unemployment rate, and would mean political suicide for any Greek politician considering such solutions.

During our final meeting, as I was preparing to say good-bye, the prime minister mentioned his desire to visit the United States. Not knowing that his interest in visiting the U.S. had been the ulterior motive for my trip, I simply said, "That would be great. You must visit the United States."

"I won't come unless an official invitation is issued by the president," he told me.

Then the prime minister asked if I would help him get an official invitation from President Reagan. No Greek prime minister had been officially invited to Washington since 1963, when Prime Minister Constantine Karamanlis visited President John F. Kennedy. Would I be willing to lend my influence toward this end? He had cast the hook, and I bit on it. At that time, I couldn't see any problems or obstacles. Papandreou sounded sincere in his desire to mend fences. Why wouldn't the president invite him to Washington to give him at least a chance to improve the relationship between the two countries? I told the prime minister that I would do everything in my power to see that the invitation would be issued. "All I ask of you is that nothing takes place in the next few months that would cast a negative light on my efforts," I told the prime minister.

"If you hear of anything detrimental attributed to me, call me immediately and I will set the matter straight," he said. I assured him that I would do exactly that.

As soon as I got back to Stockton, I went to work. I was close to President Reagan and called him first. The president told me that he didn't think the invitation would be a problem. I lined up meetings at the White House and the State Department. I retained two consultants: Sig Rogich, a longtime friend with strong Republican contacts, and Ed Allison, who came highly recommended for his knowledge of Washington. But I soon discovered how tough getting the official invitation would be.

Meanwhile, other events intervened.

A week after I returned from Greece, southern Greece suffered a devastating earthquake near the city of Kalamata, only a few miles from my father's village of Naziri. There was tremendous damage and many casualties. Entire residential areas had been flattened and hundreds of people were left homeless. Greece was ill equipped to face this disaster. Greek-Americans responded immediately with donations to the earthquake victims. My immediate reaction was to send $100,000.

"Don't you think we can do better?" asked my son Michael. Having accompanied me on the trip to Greece, Michael had developed a strong allegiance to his ancestral homeland.

"All right, I'll double it then," I told him.

"What if I send some money of my own?" Michael asked.

Michael had never shown such interest before, even though he was wealthy in his own right. I realized what a profound effect the trip to Greece had had on him. The hospitality that was afforded us, the people we had met, and the problems we had witnessed had left an indelible impression on my son. Before Michael left for his weekly trip to our division offices in Atlanta, we called Yiannis Papanicolaou in Greece and informed him that we would contribute 100 million Greek drachmas, which in 1986 translated to $750,000, for the relief effort for Kalamata. Papanicolaou was thrilled. I also informed him that I had begun my initial contacts with Washington to see what could be done in obtaining an official invitation for Prime Minister Papandreou.

My efforts on behalf of Papandreou surprised several of my Greek-American friends. To them, he did not deserve my support. As for my Republican friends, they were even more puzzled by my efforts. They could not understand why I would go to such lengths. After all, I was a conservative Republican trying to help a socialist. But my involvement was *cultural*, not political. It had everything to do with the love I felt for my heritage and what I thought was best for Greece, regardless of who the prime minister might be or what his politics were.

My friends' reaction was mild compared to what I encountered in Washington. The State Department officials with whom I met harbored deep hostility for the Greek prime minister. The officials tried to convince me of Papandreou's insincerity, even suggesting that I had been naive in trusting his goodwill. Was I being naive? Perhaps in Washington terms. But not as a Greek-American. I've never regretted the work I did on the prime minister's behalf. But friends at the

Pentagon and the State Department told me that there was a pro-Turkish stronghold in the Reagan administration and that any friendly maneuvers toward Greece would be squelched. "Don't waste your time," they all told me. But I was determined. There were other avenues in the administration, and I scheduled many appointments to discuss my request.

Papandreou kept his word. No major controversies occurred in Greece. For the next two years, Washington consultants Sig Rogich, Ed Allison, my staff, and I continued our efforts to achieve our goal of promoting friendlier relations between Greece and the United States. I met with President Reagan, Howard Baker (then the White House chief of staff), Frank Carlucci (head of the National Security Council), Colin Powell (who was also with the NSC), Vice President Bush and his chief of staff, Lee Atwater, Senator Paul Laxalt, and many others. We left no stone unturned. But although we were treated cordially, I failed to make any inroads. Papandreou had been pegged as anti-American, and the label stuck. Still, I was not ready to give up—until I hit an impenetrable roadblock: Secretary of State George Schultz. Everyone had deferred to Schultz, and the secretary was adamant about his feelings for Papandreou. He just did not trust him and tried to convince me of Papandreou's insincerity. I had never realized how hard-nosed George Schultz would be or how much Papandreou was disliked in certain quarters of our government.

The two years I worked on the official invitation cost me considerable time, money, and disappointment. By 1988, two events slowed our efforts considerably. First, Prime Minister Papandreou separated from his wife, Margaret, because of a very public affair with a young woman whom he eventually married. The worldwide scandal surrounding his affair sounded the death knell for our advocacy. Simultaneously, the prime minister underwent an operation in London, which, although successful, seriously affected his physical condition and stamina. Those two events diminished any small hope I still harbored for my goal. My hope had been that the new administration of George Bush would take a fresh look at my request. But with the scandal over Papandreou's personal life, I knew that there was no chance. Any momentum we could have had was lost amid the lines of the international gossip columns.

In April 1990, Papandreou was defeated at the polls. The party of New Democracy won the election. The new prime minister of Greece was Konstantinos Mitsotakis, who was regarded favorably by our government.

In spite of the obstacles I encountered in my efforts on behalf of the Papandreou government, I continued to remain involved in issues important to Greece. My next project arose sometime in February 1990, when I received a telephone call from George P. Livanos, a prominent Greek ship owner. He said that he and Alexandros Samaras, brother of Antonis Samaras, one of Greece's most promising, charismatic young politicians, wanted to come to California to meet with me on an important matter. During our meeting, George and Alexandros informed me that they were part of a task force appointed by Greece to lobby the International Olympic Committee (IOC) to select Athens as the site for the 1996 Olympics. This was an especially significant date for Greece because 1996 would mark the centennial anniversary of the modern Olympics. The Greek government believed that holding the 1996 Olympics in Athens would be a fitting tribute to the land where they had originated centuries ago. Once again, for sentimental reasons, I wholeheartedly threw in my support.

The IOC was scheduled to meet in September 1990, in Tokyo, where the city chosen to host the 1996 Olympics would be decided and announced. Samaras and Livanos asked if I would assume the chairmanship of the effort in the United States to bring the Olympics back to Greece. I agreed. I felt the project had a tremendous visionary appeal. What could be a more perfect homage to the spirit of the

Olympics than to celebrate this special anniversary in the country where the Olympics were born?

One of my first tasks was to recruit individuals around the U.S. to form a core group of supporters. In May of 1990, Prime Minister Mitsotakis came to New York. I hosted a dinner of about thirty prominent individuals who agreed to help in the Olympics effort. At this dinner, I met Prime Minister Mitsotakis for the first time. For the next few months, we worked hard to gain the support of IOC members. I personally lobbied Alejandro Orfilla, who had just retired as secretary general of the Organization of American States and was living in San Diego. We traveled together to Mexico in an effort to secure the Latin American vote on behalf of Greece. We hoped that all countries, including Mexico, would recognize the sentimental and historic significance of bringing the Olympics back to Greece in 1996. Our trip won many votes.

In September 1990, my staff and I traveled to the official IOC meeting in Tokyo to fight for the Olympics. The Greek delegation, headed by Prime Minister Mitsotakis, had already arrived and everyone was almost euphoric with anticipation. Each bidding country displayed its presentation for public viewing. When I saw Atlanta's presentation, I was impressed. It was sleek, progressive, and attractive. Greece's presentation was beautiful, too, but the Atlanta presentation was definitely a notch above. I was not surprised when, during the last day of the meetings, the games were awarded to Atlanta.

When I left Tokyo, I was disappointed with the decision. I still felt that the proper venue for the centennial Olympics should have been Greece. Had Greece won and the games held in the land of their birthplace, perhaps some of the commercialism that has come to dominate the Olympics would have taken a backseat to the true spirit of the games. But it was another lost cause.

All my life, I had devoted my time to building my business and making my fortune. Once I began helping Greece, I was pursuing goals that were intangible and, frequently, unsuccessful. Still, I found this kind of work to be rewarding in its own way; it brought me closer to my heritage. From 1986 to 1992, I worked on behalf of practically every issue that arose affecting Greece and Cyprus. Several others like me put their hearts and souls in those projects, but none worked harder than John Liveris, the Greek government television bureau chief who first suggested that the prime minister invite me to Greece. Liveris's brilliant insights and intimate knowledge of these issues was invaluable. What amazed me most about him was his heartfelt commitment to assist on these issues without any compensation. The satisfaction of knowing that he was helping his country was apparently enough.

In July of 1991, President George Bush decided to make an official visit to Greece and Turkey—the first trip by a U.S. president to Greece since Dwight Eisenhower had visited for only six hours in the fifties. President Bush was going to spend two-and-a-half days in Greece and an equal amount of time in Turkey. It was obvious that the administration was engaged in a balancing act and was being careful not to treat either one preferentially during the presidential tour.

While Bush was vice president, I had discussed U.S.-Greece relations with him and we seemed to be on the same page. Three weeks before his scheduled visit, President Bush, knowing of my love for my heritage and my efforts to help Greece, invited me and Alec Courtelis, another of his strong Greek-American supporters, to fly with him to Greece on Air Force One. The plan was that Alec and I would meet up with the presidential party in London, where Bush was scheduled to hold economic talks with other European leaders, and then fly with him to Athens.

Faye, my daughter Dea, and her two sons accompanied me. We flew to London, where we were to rendezvous with Alec and Louise Courtelis on their way from Florida. Alec and I stayed in London to fly with the president on Air Force One while the rest of our group continued separately to Greece. They would meet us at the Athens airport when we arrived with the president the following day.

For once, the world's attention was drawn to Greece for something other than a political crisis. President Bush received an enthusiastic welcome in Athens, and I was proud to see it. One of my most unforgettable moments came when President Bush recognized both Alec and me in his speech before the Greek parliament, praising our contributions and success as Americans of Greek heritage.

After the president's speech, I visited former prime minister Papandreou, who was still a member of the Greek parliament and leader of the opposition party. In the rush and excitement of Bush's visit to Greece, I wanted Papandreou to know that he was not forgotten, even though he was out of the limelight. My gesture was not without controversy. Although Athens is a city of four million people, everything is in close proximity, and everyone seems to be within earshot. When I expressed a desire to visit Papandreou, some of my Greek acquaintances suggested that it would not be a good idea. I was considering a future business enterprise in Greece. My friends felt I risked alienating the new government at a time when I needed all the friends I could find to promote my project (more on which later). But that's not the way I did business then or now, and no business deal would make me ignore common courtesy.

Papandreou was as pleased to see me as I was to see him. He looked weaker after his operation, and I felt a slight regret that President Bush's visit had not taken place when he had still been prime minister. Among the many old faces I saw at his office was his new wife, and it was quite apparent how much he doted on her.

The next time I saw Papandreou was the following year. This time we met at his residence, and it shocked me to see how fragile he had become. He joked that I had become a regular visitor to Greece, and I told him that it was all due to him. I informed him that I was considering making a business investment in Greece and he seemed genuinely pleased to hear of it. When I left his home that day, I realized that I felt a kind of friendship for this man, even though we were diametrically opposed in our politics. I had grown to respect and like him.

The business project that had sparked my interest was an old obsession: a casino. Trying to raise desperately needed revenues, the Greek government had proposed an increase in the number of casinos in the country. But the government wanted to remove itself from the gaming business and bring in experienced owners/operators from all over the world who would make sizable investments and infuse the country with new capital. Under the proposal, the three existing government-run casinos would close, and new casino licenses would be awarded to private operators selected through an international competition. The idea was to have the best bids win the right to establish and operate Las Vegas–style casinos in several proposed locations spread around Greece.

I first heard of the proposal in the fall of 1991 through my participation in the United States trade mission to Greece, headed by then–U.S. secretary of commerce Bob Mosbacher. It was part of a new joint effort between the two countries to improve trade relations. It seemed like the perfect opportunity, with threefold benefits: not only could I honor my heritage, I could grow my business internationally and reconnect with my lifelong dream of owning a casino/hotel. When I told Barron Hilton of the Greek government's casino proposal, he was also intrigued. The Hilton Corporation, besides its gaming interests in the U.S., operated several casino establishments overseas under the Conrad name. While in Greece, Barron, his top advisor, Greg Dillon, and I met with Prime Minister Mitsotakis and his staff to discuss our interest in opening a casino in Greece. Our interest was well received. We were told that as soon as the Greek parliament enacted the casino legislation, it would allow casino operators to put in their bids.

Arthur Andersen & Co., the internationally recognized accounting and auditing firm, was hired to evaluate the bid proposals and award the licenses. The Greek government had hired the firm, but it would be independent of governmental influence. The government wanted to assure the major casino operators that everything would be above-board and that no external influences would affect the outcome.

I believed that with Barron Hilton's expertise and my personal interest in and ties to Greece, our casino would be the perfect vehicle for my first business investment in Greece. Barron and I went to work, and our proposal, prepared by the best consultants and architects, all with exhaustive casino expertise, was a wonderful thing. It was designated for a neighborhood outside central Athens. We called our joint project "The Alexander Conrad," a name reminiscent of my ill-fated attempt to open Alexander's casino in Reno in the seventies. We envisioned the hotel/casino as one of the finest destination resorts in all of Europe.

Several other prominent U.S. casino operators, as well as operators from Europe, South Africa, and Asia, bid for each of the licenses assigned to the different areas of Greece. The announcement of the winning bids for each location was to have been made at staggered intervals during the months of November and early December 1993. But in September 1993, almost thirty days before the first successful bid was to be announced, Prime Minister Mitsotakis's government of New Democracy toppled. New elections were scheduled for October 1993, and the competition for the casino licenses was abruptly put on hold. All the bidders who had spent millions and worked for almost two years on their proposals were left high and dry.

In the 1993 elections, Andreas Papandreou was returned to power as prime minister. But by then he was in his seventies, and the old firebrand was no longer the passionate leader he once had been. His deteriorating health required long periods of rest, and many issues were left to others within his new administration. One of those issues was the competition for the casino licenses in the Athens area.

Those in charge of the casino licenses showed total disregard for the foreign investors and a monumental lack of professionalism. Ignoring the time and costs spent in preparing the proposals, the new administration repealed the existing law and enacted a new one with unreasonable provisions that drove away almost all of the internationally known operators. The new Papandreou government became captive of the special interests lobbying for the existing government-run casinos and missed a tremendous opportunity to benefit Greece. The few bidders who chose to enter the new competition were for the most part little-known operators who wanted to build their experience in the gaming business by opening a casino in Greece. Barron and I withdrew our own proposal and shelved our project. Disappointed? You bet. Discouraged? No way. I don't consider my unsuccessful experiences in Greece to be failures. I learned a great deal about the business environment in Greece.

Shortly after finding out that there would be no new casino licenses awarded for the Athens area, Dean and I met with Michael Vranopoulos, the former governor of National Bank of Greece, the state-run largest bank in Greece. Vranopoulos was a member of the Mitsotakis regime, which had just been ousted when Papandreou returned to power. He had come to the U.S. for a series of meetings. We arranged a breakfast meeting at the Fairmont Hotel. He was very nice and gracious, but his insights into the political situation in Greece were vague at best. Two weeks later, in January 1994, the notorious terrorist group called November 17 assassinated Vranopoulos as he walked to work.

I have always marveled at the immigrants who came to America from Greece. They flourished and thrived because of their entrepreneurial zeal and indomitable spirit. Yet in Greece, people from this same determined stock are content to live off the government, resisting any modernization or change in the status quo. I had been courted for years by the Greek government to invest in the country. But when I finally took the step, I found that the rules of the game made progress difficult, almost impossible. The absence of continuity of government policy between succeeding administrations, magnified by the basic distrust between different political parties, made business planning almost impossible. Greece's vast bureaucracy compounded its problems. No one can reform it or reduce its size without risking tremendous social upheaval.

As disappointed as I was over the casino experience, my commitment to Greece remained steadfast. In May 1993, Prime Minister Papandreou finally received an official invitation to visit the United States from President Clinton. I attended the welcoming events in both Washington and New York, where I had a brief meeting with Papandreou. He appeared quite ill and exhausted, and I didn't have the heart to advise him of my frustration over the handling of the casino issue.

While Papandreou was in Washington, a joint announcement was made at the White House creating the United States–Greece Business Council. Its membership would include major U.S. corporations and Greek companies; its purpose would be to foster and promote trade and investment opportunities between the two countries. I was asked to take a leading role in the new effort. Putting aside my reservations, I accepted the chairmanship of the newly formed council, secretly hoping that maybe we could effect some needed changes, which would eventually result in sorely needed investments and business opportunities in Greece.

Many friends and other Greek-Americans have asked me why I spend so much effort on Greece. I don't have a quick answer. I'm frequently so frustrated by the difficulty in getting Greece to move forward and try new things that I wish I could just walk away. But I will never turn my back on the land of my ancestors. I will forever have a deep and sentimental attachment to my heritage, which has graced me with the values that have guided my life and made me who I am today. The vast majority of Greek-Americans, first, second, or third generation, share this deep and abiding attachment to their ancestral homeland. It is this connection that mobilizes the Greek-American population to rally repeatedly on major issues that affect the future of both Greece and the island republic of Cyprus.

Greek-Americans could become a powerful lobby in Washington, much like the Jewish lobby for Israel. But they have neither the effective organization nor the capable representation by top-notch professionals, and they lack people who know how to build bridges, keep the channels of communication open, and create an ongoing dialogue for progress. The Greek-American lobby remains a fragmented effort whose sole strengths are its drive and zeal, and its ability to mobilize large numbers of people, but only in times of crisis. But not every problem that arises is a crisis, nor every dispute a major conflict. There are daily issues that need to be followed with diligence but that are instead ignored and mishandled because there is no one within the Greek-American lobby who really knows how to work effectively within Washington's maze.

Just as Greece needs a new breed of young politicians whose inspired leadership will move the country into the next century, the Greek-American lobby also needs to reinvent itself. Individualism, a character trait of most Greeks, has hindered the effectiveness of the lobby, breeding turf wars and fragmentation in the ranks.

I believe in people, not politics, in community service, not lip service. I believe that we are all members of one family, whose common good depends on everyone's personal involvement. Each individual's welfare depends upon the world's welfare. My life has been extraordinarily enriched by my involvement not only in Greece but in whatever causes and projects presented themselves to me, whether political, philanthropic, or involving private individuals. I believe it's essential to get personally involved in my community, my nation, and my world, whether or not the outcome is always 100 percent successful. Action always counts.

CHAPTER 13

The Fundamentals of Success

Sometimes it takes a crisis to put everything in perspective. Mine came in August 2000. I went in for my annual physical. I felt great and had never had any major health problems. So I had no reason to believe that the stress test or the thallium test that my doctor ordered would be anything but routine.

Faye had gone to church for the Feast of the Dormition, an annual day of worship in the Orthodox Church commemorating the anniversary of the death of St. Mary. The second she got into the car after church, her cell phone rang. It was our daughter Dea. "Quick, get to the office!" Dea told Faye. "Dad flunked both of his tests. The doctor wants him in the hospital immediately!"

Within a day or two, Dea, Faye, our son Michael, daughter Alexis, son-in-law Barry, and I were at a cardiologist's office in Mercy Hospital in Sacramento. The doctor asked me if I'd ever had chest pains. I told him that I hadn't. "Well, I've got good news and some not-so-good news," he said. "The good news is that you're healthy. You've got the heart of an eighteen-year-old. The bad news is you have 100 percent blockage in one artery and 95 percent blockage in another. You need immediate bypass surgery."

Surgery? The word hit me like a knockout punch. I had never felt healthier. I was exercising daily. My spirits were high. This was more than a shock; it was unacceptable. And the timing couldn't have been worse. I couldn't have surgery! It was the beginning of football season. I asked the doctor if it could wait until season's end. Anticipating my reaction, my wife and family members began shaking their heads. They were adamant that I undergo the bypass surgery immediately. By the time we left the doctor's office, I realized I had no choice in the matter, and the surgery was scheduled for the next morning.

Everyone assured me that I would be okay, but I kept thinking of the worst. *Who knows?* I thought. *There's always the chance of a complication. I might not make it through the operation.* I had written my will and planned my estate years ago. But the night before the operation, as I was lying in the hospital bed, I felt a rush of emotions. I kept thinking of all the people who had done so much for me, some of whom I'd almost forgotten: loyal employees, relatives, and personal friends. Before anything happened, I thought, I needed to do something for all of these people. That night in the hospital, I asked Faye to help me write out a list of the people I wanted to remember. "Just in case anything should happen," I said.

"Nothing's going to happen," Faye assured me.

"Just in case," I said.

While the operation was successful, it turned out to be much more serious than the doctors had anticipated. I required three major and four collateral bypasses, one short of what the human heart can take. I spent six days in the hospital, and Faye stayed by my side day and night.

When I was finally allowed to go home, the doctor told me that it would take five weeks for my sternum to heal. By the third day in bed, I got restless. I put on a jogging suit, carefully crept downstairs, and asked Faye to take me to the office. She was reluctant at first, but eventually agreed. "With one condition," she said. "You're going in for only five minutes, just to say hello." The next day, I asked her to take me to the office again, and, with the concurrence of my doctor, who told her it would be good therapy, she agreed.

Within a week, I was back at the office daily. But while I could go to the office, I couldn't fly. I ended up missing all of the out-of-town Charger games that season. Thankfully, my heart surgery spared me the agony of witnessing the worst season ever, when we finished 1–15.

Looking back on those tough times today, I realize that I forgot a few things in that list of notes that Faye and I hastily compiled before my surgery. I'd like to pass them on to you now.

The world is full of smart, intelligent, well-educated individuals who never achieve the success they dream of. They may end up with well-paying jobs that satisfy their basic needs, but their ultimate goals remain elusive. The world is equally full of nondegreed and basically unskilled people like me, men and women who start with nothing but dreams, hoping for the big break that will bring success. But the big break never comes to many of them, either.

Why do some people become successful while others don't? No one really knows. But I do know from personal experience that successful people are generally equipped with certain basic tools, which I call the Fundamentals of Success. Without these tools there can be little or no chance for success. At every turning point in my life, I've relied on these fundamentals to move from one point to the next, or to see more clearly what lay ahead and which path to take. These fundamentals are seemingly simple values and principles, but properly applied they can yield extraordinary results.

Here is my list:

A Solid Family Foundation: This is the basis of everything. Without family, you're destined to drift through life without a source of love and support and the security of home. Without family, you will be left emotionally empty, no matter how fabulous your accomplishments. As I wrote earlier, I didn't start out to fulfill a get-rich fantasy. All I sought was to provide financial security and peace of mind for my family. With this seemingly simple goal, as opposed to anything more ambitious, I built a fortune. The rock-solid stability of my wife and our family became my most valued tool in my arsenal. The knowledge that they were always there for me meant everything. And while the most widely accepted notion of success involves fame and fortune, that's not a success that's lasting. Financial wealth pales in comparison to the love, security, and peace of mind I get from Faye, my children, and grandchildren. Your family is your rock, your base, your rudder. Keep those you love close and always in the forefront of your attention and your plans. Without them, you'll have little of permanent value.

Discover Your Purpose: Some people find their direction early in life; others struggle to find it and eventually do so; still others never find direction and drift aimlessly from day to day, year to year, never finding fulfillment, never finding that incredible feeling of knowing they've discovered *exactly* what they're meant to do with their lives. Those who discover their purpose early on are fortunate. However, most people, like me, start out without any direction and, somehow, accidentally find it along the way. Whatever your case, discovering and defining your sense of purpose will set you on your course. Otherwise, you will be destined to become stranded on the shoals of uncertainty and self-doubt.

How will you know when you've found your purpose in life? Simply look to your heart. Do you love your work? If the answer is no, then you haven't found your purpose, no matter the size of your paycheck. When work doesn't seem like work, when you do it purely because you derive pleasure from it, that's when you've found your purpose in life. Once I started my own business, I knew that I'd found my place, my purpose, in the world. From that moment forward, I have derived tremendous love and excitement from working. My reason for being such a hands-on manager is not because I don't trust others to do a good job; it's because I just can't help myself. I love the excitement and activity a business deal generates and the feeling of satisfaction I receive from accomplishing my goals.

Believe in Yourself: You must believe that you are capable of achieving what you set out to do. It's as simple as that. Without conviction, there can be no progress. Knowing your purpose and believing in yourself will not only push you forward but also soften the impact of temporary setbacks and disappointments. Ups and downs are what make life and business exciting, challenging, and, in the end, worthwhile. If you don't believe in yourself, you're going to lose conviction when disappointments knock you off-course. Build yourself up psychologically and physically, believe in yourself and your purpose, and don't let anything break you down.

Vision: The dictionary describes vision as "the act or power of anticipating that which may or may not come." It is often at odds with conventional wisdom, sometimes seemingly impractical and unfeasible in the context of every day's realities. But the successful entrepreneur sees the opportunities and the obstacles and develops plans for dealing with both. Scratch the surface of any entrepreneur and you'll find a visionary. Henry Ford envisioned the revolutionary impact of a cheap, reliable automobile on the American landscape. Ray Kroc envisioned a world in which thousands of McDonald's restaurants provided quick, consistently tasty meals at an affordable price. Steven Jobs envisioned putting personal computers on millions of desktops around the world. Each of these visions seemed absurd at the time; thanks to the determination of the entrepreneur, each came through. You have to have the clarity of thought to see where you want to go and what you want to do—and then to follow that vision relentlessly.

Loyalty: Knowing your purpose, believing in yourself, and having a vision for your future will send you on your way, but after that comes another vital ingredient: loyalty. Next to attitude, I value loyalty, a person's dedication to his or her cause and, in the case of my business, to my company. Maybe I put so much stock in loyalty because we're a family-owned company. I consider my employees part of my family, and I am just as loyal to my people as they have been to me. In 1990, when the effects of the recession hit the building industry especially hard, unemployment in the real estate and building sector soared to new records, but my employees kept their jobs. In order to be able to accomplish this, I called each member of my executive, construction, and maintenance staff into my office and explained our economic situation to them. For a year or more, I said, I would be receiving little or no income from the business. I would survive personally, but maintaining payroll at its current standards would be impossible. I asked each of them to take a pay cut and ride the bad times along with me. If they couldn't remain with me under these circumstances, I added, I would completely understand. And I promised that once the financial picture brightened, their salaries would be restored to their original levels. All of them agreed. From 1990 until 1993, we didn't build a single project, not one apartment unit—and didn't lay off a single person. But when activity in the industry picked up, the salaries were reinstated, and many of these employees still work for me today.

The Steady Achievement of Reasonable Goals: Every success is comprised of a myriad of small, incremental, step-by-step goals. The slow and steady achievement of these goals will advance your cause and provide the emotional satisfaction of knowing that you're getting somewhere.

I have always pursued both short-term and long-term goals. When I went in business for myself, my goals were clear, and I achieved each of them in five-year increments: becoming a successful caterer, expanding my construction business across California, expanding to many states, and so forth. But these long-term goals were achieved not in one fell swoop but by a series of small, definable, and easily achievable smaller goals. So set small, reasonable goals through which you can experience small but vital victories.

Remember, nobody hits a home run every time at bat. Baseball greats know that singles win ball games, too. If all you try to do is hit homers, you're going to strike out more often than you will connect. If your goal is base hits, you'll eventually cross home plate, just as surely as if you'd hit the homer. Start with small, achievable goals and build your confidence.

Accept Risks and Trust Your Instincts: As I've said earlier, entrepreneurs have one overriding commonality: they're risk takers. If you look behind any entrepreneurial fortune, you'll see that it's comprised of a series of risks. Risk is imperative to entrepreneurial success. Some risks are small, others enormous; all are important, especially the first one, when you leave the security of everything you know to step into the larger, but frequently frightening, realm of all that you can become. The risk I took the day I walked out of the basement of my father's bakery, climbed the stairs, and told him I was quitting was far greater than any risk I took from that point forward in my businesses. My prospects of employment were grim. By quitting, I risked everything—most of all my security—to step into a void where I had absolutely no guarantee of anything. But staying on with my father was an option I felt I could no longer accept.

Most people are fearful of venturing into the unknown. But you can't experience the ocean if you cling to the shore. You must have the insight to recognize opportunity and the courage to take the risk. Any risk worth considering must first be carefully calculated.

Business is not a gamble, and no business deal should be a do-or-die proposition. Good instincts will guide you at critical moments. Do your research. Gather all the pertinent information you need. Consider the advice of others. Then trust your instincts on whether to move forward or to hold back.

I say "consider" the advice of others, but don't follow it blindly. Sometimes, a risk worth taking will go against what everyone says you should do. When I took the risk to begin building apartments, my family and most of my friends advised me against doing it, saying that I didn't need the extra headaches. I was doing well enough buying and selling property, they said, and I should stick with what I knew. But I plunged ahead against their advice, knowing in my heart that it was the right move for me. It was agonizing to proceed without the agreement of my family and associates, but the decision worked in the end.

Good instincts are comprised of basic common sense. In 1987, the DeBartolo family of Youngstown, Ohio, brought me a proposal to participate in the purchase of the Singer Corporation as a limited partner. I had become close to the DeBartolos through our NFL association after the family successfully outbid me for the San Francisco 49ers. The chief architect of the plan to take over Singer was Paul Bilzerian, a Wall Street wizard who had enjoyed a meteoric rise in the financial and investment worlds through company takeovers. Eddie DeBartolo Sr., who had amassed a fortune developing shopping malls around the country and was legendary for his business acumen, was one of several investors who had made a great deal of money from Bilzerian's deals.

But regardless of the high recommendations of Mr. Bilzerian and his proven track record, my instinct told me to stay out of the Singer buyout bid. At that time, Wall Street was in a frenzy of takeovers by corporate raiders, who bought companies through hostile bids—and I didn't want any part of that world. After reviewing the proposal, I had strong reservations about the deal's financial soundness. But on the morning that I finally decided to turn down the deal, my secretary said that Eddie DeBartolo Sr. was on the telephone. I took the call, ready to tell him of my decision, but he spoke first. "What's taking you so long, Alex?" he said. "Sign those papers. All of us will make money on this deal. I promise you. I know what I'm talking about. Sign those papers today."

I was swayed by my admiration for DeBartolo's intelligence and accomplishments and I changed my mind and signed the papers. Eventually, as I feared, we lost all the money we invested. The experience confirmed for me that no one has ever made money for Alex Spanos but Alex Spanos. (As for Mr. Bilzerian, he went to federal prison about three years later on charges unrelated to the Singer takeover.)

The Singer deal soured me on public companies. When another opportunity came along and my instincts told me to move forward, I temporarily lost my rudder and went against my better judgment. The deal involved purchasing a large block of Bank of America stock. But because I got so badly burned on the Singer deal, I decided against buying the Bank of America stock. While the Singer deal sank, the Bank of America stock skyrocketed.

Good Timing: Sometimes, when all of the ingredients are in place, success will still remain elusive because the timing is not right. Timing is when the forces of business and nature combine to create a need for your idea to succeed. Timing is the fantastic force that makes everything come together for a desired goal. When the timing is right for an idea, everything comes together perfectly. But it's easier said than done.

The annals of failure are filled with people whose great idea was either too early or too late. Is your product or service needed right now? Again, use common sense. A slump in the housing market is not a good time to build houses, while a housing boom would be a signal it's time to move forward, even in the face of increased competition. Between these two extremes is the art of reading an uncertain situation much like a skilled gambler reads the odds of a blackjack hand. Anticipating the housing boom before your competitors do is how fortunes are made.

How do you hone your sense of good timing? Some people seem to be guided by an internal compass. For the rest of us, good timing can be an acquired skill. I've learned to gauge a project's timing by asking a few key questions, including, *How realistic are our profit projections in the current and foreseeable economy?* The answer to this question will cause me to rethink the project's timing.

A system of continuous assessment gives me the ability to make an intelligent decision on whether our timing is right. Sometimes it will lead me to accelerate the project; in other cases, I'll delay it or cancel it altogether. Sure, periods of inactivity drive me crazy. But eventually, we are always able to move forward with even more power and purpose because we had the foresight and patience to wait until the timing was right.

Don't Be Defeated by Failure: Success demands perseverance in the face of repeated adversity and failure. A baby learning to walk falls down and gets up again and again, by sheer instinct. Babe Ruth not only held the home run record; he also held the record for strikeouts. Achieving success is like perfecting any skill: it's a process of trial and error. Most people get disheartened and give up when they fail. But failure is where success begins.

I learned valuable lessons from a major business failure in 1989, when, against my better judgment, I acceded to the recommendations of my executive staff to build two major projects in Atlanta. The projects had been in the works for some time, but my instincts told me not to move forward. The country was in a deep recession and I believed that proceeding would be sheer folly. But I couldn't get any of my staff to go along with me. I relented to staff pressure and gave the go-ahead on the projects, which turned out to be abysmal failures. For a while, I kicked myself for this mistake. Then I realized I could learn from it. During slow times, don't push the envelope. In my business, I have used periods of inactivity to explore ways of better management.

The lesson? Let go of your emotional involvement in projects. Go by the facts, not your fantasies. When your projects don't turn out the way you expected and failure is imminent, take your losses while they're still small. Learn from your failures and move on.

Don't Look to Loans for Salvation: Most people use banks in a financially ruinous way. They get loans to start business projects, a legitimate reason to borrow, but lack the necessary resources to service the loan adequately. They mortgage their homes or otherwise leverage personal property, hoping that their profit projections will come through. It is a precarious position, because if anything goes wrong, everything collapses like a house of cards. I have seen businesses fail, personal fortunes jeopardized by foreclosure, and people in unrecoverable financial calamities, all of which they could have avoided if only they had exercised more caution.

Although I built my business with financial assistance from banks, I've learned never to look to a bank for a make-or-break loan. I always make sure that I have enough cash to cover the majority of the capital for any new venture. So don't bet the farm on any single project. A successful entrepreneur must have the freedom to pursue and make creative choices, and that's possible only if you're not financially overextended.

Don't Make Enemies: Conflict is endemic to business. Many people walk away angry in the heat of a disagreement, slamming doors and burning bridges. I've had my share of disagreements with bankers, subcontractors, employees, and others. I'm an impatient, sometimes hot-tempered person, but in business I always strive to keep a cool head. Most people think that storming out of a disagreement at least leaves them with their pride intact. But that does no one any good. I could have huffed off angrily when Gene Klein reneged on his original deal to sell me controlling interest in the San Diego Chargers. That would have left me with my pride intact, but it could have prevented me from achieving my dream of owning the NFL franchise. Instead, I remained calm and got a second chance at buying the Chargers.

Lead, Don't Follow: As I tell my staff, if we can build the best apartment at the best price, we'll beat our competition every time. "Don't be so concerned about what anybody else is doing," I'll say. "Worry about what *we're* doing. Let the competition worry about us. If we stay on top of our game, they'll be worried plenty." If you spend your time focusing on your competition, you'll stifle your ability to create and grow. You'll always be chasing the "other guy," instead of fulfilling your own distinct mission. Remember: innovate, don't imitate; lead, don't follow.

Take Your Profits Whenever You Can: My success in the construction business has been based on selling my properties before they were completed. In many cases, I could have made considerably more money by holding onto the properties. But I always wanted to take my profits early and move on to the next project. I often left money on the table by following this strategy, but it kept my company financially strong. So I never knock profit, no matter how small. My point is clear: stay liquid, never be pressed for cash. Don't look at what you might have left on the table; look at what you put into your pocket. As they say on Wall Street, nobody goes broke taking profits.

Stay Alert and Plan Ahead: In my fifty-one years in business, I have lived through seven recessions. There's no formula for foreseeing bad times, but staying alert helps. In 1984, for example, I was able to save millions of dollars and avoid unrecoverable losses by foreseeing the recession, which eventually crippled the housing industry. I became so alarmed that I told my board to begin selling our real estate holdings, turn our assets into cash, complete the projects we already had under construction, and scrap all plans for any future construction. When the recession hit, we didn't build a single apartment unit for three years, but we managed to remain financially liquid.

Fortunately for me, I made the right decision at the right time and spared myself a great deal of trouble. While I was engaged in solidifying my company's financial position, most other builders either didn't see the signs or refused to acknowledge them. Many developers continued to build as if poised on the brink of a great economic revival. Many declared bankruptcy. These problems were not confined to small or regional builders; some of the national giants in the building industry were also stricken. Those who had cash reserves survived, but those who had leveraged their holdings went under. Stay alert to the obvious warning signs and plan ahead for both good times and bad.

Recognize Opportunities: Opportunities abound, but rarely in the form of earth-shattering miracles. They come in the form of chance encounters, unexpected events, and fortuitous circumstances. You have to look them in the face, recognize their value, and take action. I ran into opportunities by sheer luck and by showing up in the right place at the right time. I had no idea where these events would take me, but I accepted them as the gifts that they were.

Looking back on my life, I can see my success as a series of doors, each door representing an opportunity. One door led to another and then another in the sweep of my lifetime. Had I failed to recognize them, or hesitated in opening these doors and walking through them, I'm sure my life would have turned out very differently.

I can't tell you where your own doors of opportunity are located. But I can say with certainty that they exist. May you recognize them as the wondrous gifts that they are and walk through these doors into the success that awaits you.

❖ ❖ ❖

As I write these words, it's August 2001. I'm flying into my seventeenth year as owner of the San Diego Chargers, and into a new season, a new challenge, a new opportunity for success. As we always do, rain or shine, Faye and I fill the plane with family and friends and fly to each Chargers game. But since turning the management of the team over to my son Dean, I remain on the sidelines as owner, advisor, and, most of all, fan, still driven by the one goal that has thus far eluded me: winning the Super Bowl.

The Chargers finished the 2000 season at 1–15, our worst season ever. But we entered this new season with new management, renewed purpose, and our vision and goals firmly in place. Ushering in a new era of Charger football, with the slogan of "Winning Now," Dean and the team's management devised a four-step strategy: hiring the best general manager, bringing in an experienced offensive coordinator, revamping the team's roster, and, finally, taking advantage of the Chargers' top position in the NFL draft with some key player selections. Once again, there is hope and excitement among football fans in San Diego.

At this point, at seventy-eight, I am secure in my life but not completely satisfied. Challenges are what make life exciting. Will I finally achieve the one goal that has eluded me, winning a Super Bowl? There are no guarantees, no crystal balls. All I can say is that we'll either make it or go down charging. If I've learned anything, it's this: in football, as in business, and in life, it's not over until *you* say it's over.

You always have a chance to win.

ACKNOWLEDGMENTS

I would like to express my personal gratitude to my family and friends who helped me write my story by adding their recollections, anecdotes, and memories.

My thanks go to my children and their spouses, Dean & Susie, Dea & Ron, Alexis & Barry, Michael & Helen; my brother George; my sister Stella; cousins Pete, Fran, and Tony; and my friends Bobby Beathard, Herb Bowman, Chuck Brenner, President George H. W. Bush, J. P. Butorac, Nick Canepa, Bill Chapman, Andy Coffey, Irv Corren, David Coulter, Al Davis, Marvin Davis, President Gerald R. Ford, Max Freeman, Bill Fugazy, David Gerber, Connie Glafkides, Russell Glass, Ward Grant, Barron Hilton, Bob Hoffman, Bob and Dolores Hope, Monty Hundley, Irby Iness, Marian Jacobs, Hank Kalb, Bob Kaplan, Father Alex Karloutsos, Sherman Lewis, Rush Limbaugh, John Liveris, Barry Lorge, Pat McDowell, Mr. and Mrs. Nick Mahleres, Leo Michaelides, Art Modell, Sylvia Minnick, Jim Montgomery, Gregory Nicholas, Arnold Palmer, Lou Papan,

Carmen Policy, Ben Pores, Mort Poznak, Jerry Reinsdorf, Chuck Riach, Jim Robinson, Lou Souza, John Streicker, Paul Tagliabue, Bob White, and Governor Pete Wilson.

INDEX